STRATEGIC PUBLIC RELATIONS

Strategic Public Relations

Edited by
Norman A. Hart

Foreword by Mike Beard
President of the Institute of Public Relations

First published 1995 by
MACMILLAN PRESS LTD
Houndmills, Basingstoke, Hampshire RG21 2XS
and London
Companies and representatives
throughout the world

ISBN 0–333–61545–X

A catalogue record for this book is available
from the British Library.

10   9   8   7   6   5   4   3   2
04   03   02   01   00   99   98   97   96   95

Printed and bound in Great Britain by
Antony Rowe Ltd
Chippenham, Wiltshire

Contents

1   Corporate Goals and Strategies   1
Kevin Traverse-Healy

Introduction to the concepts and practice of strategic planning
for a business, relationship of public relations to the
achievement of corporate goals.

2   Planning for Corporate Communications   10
Anthony Wreford

Understanding the business objectives and strategy; agreeing
realistic communications objectives; understanding the target
audiences; developing an intelligence system; establishing
priorities for tasks and target audiences; agreeing on the
communications strategy, programme, and budget; involving
operating companies; allocating responsibilities; selling the
programme internally.

3   Marketing Communications   24
Norman A. Hart

Message cues transmitted by product, price, place and
promotion; consumer behaviour; media mix; criteria for
media choice; other message sources – outside, people and
passive; internal image audit; customers and prospects;
corporate v. brand image; 10 Ps of marketing communications;
ten point Marcom plan .

corporate relations;reputation, character and trust;
appearance and reality; corporate profiles and corporate
positioning; implementing the international profile;
defining corporate policies; dealing directly with the
outside world; identifying and reaching target audiences;
governments home and abroad; public relations in overseas
countries; international investor relations; the media;
organizing for international corporate affairs.

Development of corporate advertising; measuring results;
advertising objectives; understanding the audience; media
considerations.

Sponsorship today; why sponsor?; defining objectives; what
to sponsor; negotiating a sponsorship; maximising the
benefits; further information and advice.

Creating goodwill and understanding; how the media work;
what is news; creating a campaign; news releases; interviews;
features; media conferences; press packs; special needs of
broadcasters; television interviews; news and feature
programmes; radio interviews; working with journalists;
building company credibility.

Value of research; communications problems – messages,
audiences and media; when to use research – pre- and post-testing,
formulating strategy, tracking studies; research techniques;
obtaining and using information; value for money.

List of Figures

List of Tables

Notes on the Contributors

Michael Bland served a commission in the Army before working in Germany, Austria and Switzerland as a sales manager for Reuters Limited. After five years in finance and financial journalism he set up and ran the first PR activity for the Institute of Directors and played a key role in putting it on the map. He then spent six years as head of government relations and corporate public affairs for Ford Motor Company Limited before becoming an independent consultant in 1984. Bland is corporate communications consultant to a number of leading companies and organizations and lectures widely on a range of communication subjects in Britain, the USA and the Continent. He is the author and co-author of six leading communication textbooks and guides, numerous articles and two popular humour titles.

W. G. Byrnes, MA (Oxon) has spent most of his business life with Unilever, where he has worked as an industrial economist, a general manager, and Head of Corporate External Affairs. After reading PPE at Oxford and some years in the Computer Department of ICL, Byrnes joined Unilever's Economics Department, where he became Head of Operational Statistics, and co-authored a book on decision theory. He has worked in industrial marketing in Rotterdam, and was Chairman of Unilever's transport subsidiaries in Spain. He returned to his native Merseyside as Managing Director of Unilever Merseyside, and retired, in 1993, as Unilever's Head of Corporate External Affairs.

Colin J. Coulson-Thomas, MSc (Econ), MSc, MA, MPA, APA, PhD, FCA, FCCA, FCIS, FMS, FIPR, FITA, FIPM, Chairman of Adaptation Ltd and Attitudes Skills and Knowledge Limited. He is Professor of Corporate Transformation and Dean of the Faculty of Management at the University of Luton: also an authority on the achievement of corporate transformation. He counsels boards and management teams on re-engineering and the implementation of organizational and cultural change. He leads the European Unions COBRA project, is a member of the EU's Team '92 and holds visiting appointments at Aston and City University Business Schools, the Judge Institute of Cambridge University and the IT Institute of Salford University. He is a member of the National Biological Standards Board and the Professional Development Committee of the Institute of Directors, and serves on the Council of the Parliamentary Information Technology Committee and the board of Community Network. He has written some 30 books and reports, and also directs courses, workshops and seminars for directors and boards on policy implementation and managing change.

Peter S. Gummer is Chairman of Shandwick plc, the largest independent public relations group in the world. Gummer was educated at Selwyn College, Cambridge, and, after a period of working on local newspapers, held a number of public relations posts, both in consultancy and in-house, before forming Shandwick in 1974. He is a contributor to marketing, advertising and public relations publications both here and abroad and regularly lectures around the world. In October 1991 he was appointed Chairman of the Understanding Industry Trust. He is also Chairman of the Marketing Group of Great Britain, and the National Lottery Advisory Board for the Arts and Film. He is a member of the Arts Council of England, the NHS Policy Board and a Director of the Halifax Building Society.

Norman A. Hart, MSc, FCIM, FCAM, FIPR, is currently Managing Director of Norman Hart Associates, a marketing and training consultancy, where he specializes in marketing communications. He has been a publicity manager with AEI, a publisher with Morgan-Grampian, and a marketing manager with Unilever. He was Managing Director of an advertising agency and acted as consultant editor of *Marketing Week* and *PR Week*. Hart was for 10 years the Director of the CAM (Communications, Advertising and Marketing) Foundation, the national examination and accreditation body for marketing communications studies and qualifications. Hart is an international speaker on marketing, advertising and public relations, and author of numerous books including *Industrial Marketing Communications*, *Effective Industrial Marketing* and *The Marketing Dictionary*. He is a Visiting Fellow of Bradford University, a Course Director at the College of the Chartered Institute of Marketing, and he was the first Professor of Public Relations in the United Kingdom. He is Chairman of the International Public Relations Association (IPRA) Foundation. His current clients include IBM, BT, the EU as well as many TECs.

Roger Haywood, FIPR, FCIM, FCAM, ABC, is Chairman of Kestrel Communications Limited. He has been marketing and public relations adviser to leading British and international companies, and is also a lecturer, author and broadcaster on marketing and communications in the UK, Europe and the United States. Haywood began his career as a copywriter in advertising agencies before moving on to hold marketing positions with Dunlop and Dexion International. He was European Communications

Adviser to Air Products and Chemicals Incorporated, one of the largest US chemical corporations, before forming his own London consultancy. He has been a governor of the Communication, Advertising and Marketing (CAM) Education Foundation, Vice-Chairman of the Public Relations Consultants Association, President of the Institute of Public Relations and Chairman of the Chartered Institute of Marketing. Haywood is a Fellow of the Institute of Public Relations, and has written *All About Public Relations* and *Managing Your Reputation*, both published by McGraw-Hill.

Nicholas Ind, BA, MBA, was educated at Southampton University and Strathclyde Business School. Following eight years spent working in advertising agencies, he moved into design consultancy, specialising in corporate identity. He has conducted identity programmes for such organizations as the Royal Opera House, Kraft General Foods, Manpower and De La Rue. He has written two books, *The Corporate Image* and *Great Advertising Campaigns* and has contributed articles to a variety of journals and newspapers. His latest work is a biography of Sir Terence Conran. Ind is a visiting lecturer at Kingston University.

Angus Maitland joined the Weir Group as an economic analyst after graduating from Glasgow University, where he won the Singer Award in Management Studies. He joined Charles Barker City as the company's Director of Planning, and went onto Valin Pollen in 1980, shortly after the formation of the consultancy. In 1989 he became Chairman and Chief Executive of Valin Pollen's parent company, the VPI Group; and in 1991 he was appointed Vice-Chairman worldwide of Burson-Marsteller, the world's largest public affairs and public relations group. He left Burson-Marsteller in 1994 to set up his own strategic corporate communications firm, The Maitland Consultancy. A former winner of the Industrial Marketing Research Association's Gold Medal, Maitland is the joint author – with Professor Ronald McTavish – of one of the UK's basic textbooks on industrial marketing, and he is the author of the CBI's *Handbook on Investor Relations*.

Warren Newman is currently a consultant on corporate reputation. His career spans being Head of Corporate Relations for the UK Group of the multinational services group, Générale des Eaux, Director of Corporate Communications for the UK Atomic Energy Authority and Director of Public Relations for the National Farmers' Union. He has also been responsible for public relations in three London boroughs. He was President of the Institute of Public Relations in 1987 and was elected a Fellow of the Institute in 1986. Newman is a specialist in corporate public relations about which he both writes and lectures. He also takes a particular interest in the causes and effects of scare stories, about which he expounded in *The Anxious Society*.

Sarah Portway commenced her career in the civil service, initially in administrative and managerial roles in academic institutions. She then moved into the public service in Australia and undertook various policy roles. In 1985 Sarah was appointed as Special Adviser to the Australian Cabinet Minister with responsibility for Education and Women's Affairs. In 1987 she joined IBM Australia Limited as a consultant on government relations and subsequently was appointed as Manager of Corporate Relations before transferring to IBM United Kingdom in 1990. Portway is currently Corporate Affairs Director for IBM United Kingdom Limited. She is also the Finance Director of the Corporate Responsibility Group, a Director of the London Enterprise Agency and she holds seats on a number of other Committees.

Bill Quirke specializes in helping clients use communication to speed change in their organizations. He trained in organization development with TBA Resource Inc., in New York, and worked with them across Europe and North America. He was a board director of Burson Marsteller, and was then Managing Director of People in Business, before becoming an independent consultant. He has worked in introducing change in organizations as diverse as the British Navy, HM Customs and Excise, BP, Apple Computers, and British Airways. Internationally, he has worked, among others, with Unilever in Italy, Akzo in Holland, Price Waterhouse in Japan, and Federal Express in the USA. He is the author of *Communicating Quality*: *The Total Quality Handbook*, Butterworth Heinemann, 1992, and *Communicating Change* (McGraw-Hill, 1995). He is a regular speaker internationally at conferences on communication, customers, quality and culture change, and runs the Institute of Management Boardroom Briefing on Communication and the Management of Change.

Douglas Smith, BA (Hons), MCAM, FIPR, read an honours degree at King's College London and the LSE. After a brief spell in Fleet Street, he joined Conservative Central Office as London Publicity Officer. Later he moved into general PR consultancy before forming one of Britain's early public affairs companies. Currently he is Chairman of Parliamentary Monitoring Services and Managing Director of its lobbying arm, Westminster Advisers. Smith has been Chairman of the UK Public Relations

Consultants Association (1984–5), President of the Institute of Public Relations (1990) and President of the European Association of Public Relations Consultants (1992–4). He was local councillor in London for 25 years, holding a number of senior posts.

Kevin Traverse-Healy is Managing Director of the Centre for Public Affairs Studies Limited, London and Toulouse. He started his career with the British Oxygen Company, where he was PR executive for the company's largest trading division and then overseas with BOC International. He entered consultancy in 1976 and in 1980 was a founding director of Traverse-Healy & Regester, a firm specializing in corporate and financial public relations and investor relations, sold to Charles Barker in 1987. He was Managing Director of Charles Barker Traverse-Healy and Operations Director of Charles Barker Limited until 1991. Traverse-Healy was President of the Institute of Public Relations in 1985 and recipient of the CERP Medal for contribution to European Public Relations in 1985. He is a Fellow of the Institute of Public Relations.

Christopher West, BSc (Econ), is Managing Director of Marketing Intelligence Services Ltd, a London based marketing research and consultancy company. He worked in a variety of research posts for Shell International and Eurofinance, a Paris-based financial and economic consultancy before commencing a career in marketing research. He joined Industrial Marketing Research Ltd as a research executive in the 1960s and was appointed Managing Director in 1978. He left IMR in 1984 to form his own market research company. Chris West writes and lectures extensively on marketing subjects. He has edited two books, *Marketing on a Small Budget* and *Inflation: A Management Guide to Survival*. He has also contributed articles to the *Harvard Business Review* and the *Business Strategy Review.*

David Wragg has worked in public relations for some twenty years, before which he was a regular contributor to the business pages of the *Sunday Telegraph*. Currently working in Edinburgh as an independent PR consultant, he was previously Head of Corporate Communications for the Royal Bank of Scotland, and has held senior positions with a number of leading organizations, including the Bristol & West Building Society and the P&O Group. A member of the Institute of Public Relations, he is the author of a number of public relations books, including *Effective Sponsorship*, *Targeting Media Relations*, and *Public Relations for Sales and Marketing Management* (both with Kogan Page) and *The Public Relations Handbook* (Basil Blackwell).

Anthony Wreford was educated at Charterhouse and St Catherine's College, Oxford, where he obtained a degree in politics, philosophy, and economics. Following a two-year spell with Leo Burnett he joined Cazenove, the leading firm of stockbrokers. From 1975 until 1981 he was New Business Development Manager at the *Financial Times* and was also Director of the *Financial Times* Pension Fund. A large part of his role at the *Financial Times* was taken up with promoting the case for corporate communications. In 1981 Wreford set up McAvoy Wreford & Associates, which in 1984 became McAvoy Wreford Bayley. Since 1988 he has been working as an independent consultant advising companies on all aspects of their image. This includes communications, strategy, corporate audits and advice on special situations including crises and takeover bids. He is also a director of Pauffley & Co, the leading corporate designers, and Arts & Industry, an art sponsorship company.

Acknowledgement

Grateful acknowledgement is given to Mrs Nella Wade for the exceptional work she has done in co-ordinating all the contributors and their chapters both on time and in the form necessary for publishing.

Foreword

Management handbooks always stress that no company can survive without sound corporate objectives supported by well thought out short- and long-term strategies. Now, the necessity for involving public relations in the process of developing those vital corporate objectives and strategies is becoming widely recognized.

The Institute of Public Relations traditionally defined public relations as the planned and sustained effort to establish and maintain goodwill and mutual understanding between an organization and its publics. We have recently developed and adopted an additional definition of public relations as an alternative to our established version as the latter does not sufficiently explain the substance and purpose of public relations practice. The new definition takes account of the function of public relations in today's business and social environment and describes it as the discipline which looks after reputation with the aim of earning understanding and support and influencing opinion and behaviour.

Most business people know that the success or failure of a company does not only depend on good financial management and the skillful application of marketing principles. Today's business environment is highly volatile and anything might happen at any time and greatly affect an organisation. Whether a company achieves its business objectives, can survive a difficult time, will collapse or grow is decided by a variety of factors. However, all this is influenced by and can even depend on what people think about the company, what the company does and what it says, in short – on its reputation.

At last, more and more organizations are becoming aware of the vital need to take care of their reputation. The achievement of corporate objectives will depend on the well-planned and strategic management of this reputation and communication strategies will have to be developed alongside and in conjunction with corporate strategies.

This practical and comprehensive book is published at a crucial moment in the development of PR. It will contribute towards the process of establishing the public relations function in its rightful place – as a management discipline to be found at the highest level in all types of organizations.

MIKE BEARD
IPR President

Introduction

Public relations developed as a separate discipline some 50 years ago, and since that time it has managed to acquire a rather negative reputation as being sometimes irrelevant, and often incompetent. This has not been helped by the fact that in the past much PR practice often thoroughly deserved such a poor reputation.

The growth of PR in recent times as a management function has been rapid, as is indicated by the expansion of PR consultancies, which are more numerous, larger, and with more clients and bigger budgets than ever before.

Much of PR tended to be no more than 'press relations': public relations has taken second place. This is changing for sound business reasons, with the result that the need for effective two-way communications between an organization and its many publics is being accepted and even demanded. This 'total communications' concept, as applied to both publics and the media, is in fact little more than public relations as it was originally conceived. Even so, we are now entering a 'second generation' of public relations in which it is positioned at a senior management level, and as a separate discipline in its own right.

There are still too few practitioners with a knowledge and experience of strategic public relations, in spite of a plethora of prestigious titles. For this reason there seemed to be a need for a book that would demonstrate in practical terms what can be achieved by public relations as a major element in developing corporate or business objectives.

The aim of this book is to present PR practice in terms of strategic corporate objectives. As such, it follows that the primary target audience is chief executives and directors. Automatically it becomes essential reading for practitioners, and to a lesser degree for students and young executives.

Each chapter is complete in itself, dealing in detail with the primary PR disciplines and their associated key publics, communications objectives, and the media that might best be employed. Three particular media groups have been treated as subjects in their own right in order to avoid undue duplication: advertising, sponsorship, and press relations. Final chapters deal with research and evaluation and the emerging significance of social responsibility.

1 Corporate Goals and Strategies

Kevin Traverse-Healy

With a few exceptions, the process of creating corporate goals and the strategies by which those goals may be achieved is the cornerstone of business success. In some corporate cultures this process is highly structured and formal, while in others, equally successful, it may be informal and intuitive. In today's commercial world, however, there are few organizations that can reasonably claim to be able to ignore the basic questions of 'Where do we want to go?' and 'How (and when) are we going to get there?'

There are many elements that have to be considered by management in constructing plans that incorporate realistic goals and feasible strategies: market forces, research and development, finance, and human resources are but a few. This book will demonstrate that the way in which an organization needs to be perceived by those whose decisions or opinions will impact on the achievement of its business goals has a no less essential case for recognition within the planning mix.

In the context of this book, 'corporate identity' and 'corporate image' are the elements that require definition if we are to understand their importance in formulating an organization's overall corporate plan and facilitating its progress. There is often confusion as to what these terms actually mean, and, in fairness, corporate communication specialists in the past have not been all that successful at defining their own terminology. The definition that I prefer is provided by W. P. Margulies in an article in the *Harvard Business Review* (July/August 1977):

> Identity means the sum of all the ways a company chooses to identify itself to all its publics ... Image, on the other hand, is the perception of the company by those publics.

(Note that 'corporate identity' is not a term that is restricted to the visual element of corporate communication. The design industry has done a great deal to improve the manner in which companies project themselves in visual terms, but many have misused the term to imply only visual identity.)

It should go without saying that a company will have a corporate image whether or not it manages its corporate identity. Management almost universally has long since embraced – if sometimes with reluctance – the fundamental concept that it is going to have an image anyway so it might as well attempt to manage the development of that image through the communication of its chosen corporate identity. At last count, over 4600 organizations in Britain are currently using the services of a public relations consultancy in membership of the Public Relations Consultants Association. Many more are operating in-house departments or are being advised by non-member consultancies. Each of these companies or bodies is actively addressing the question of how it is viewed by its external audiences.

In the development of public relations over the past 50 years as a professional part of the management armoury, the function unfortunately gained in many organizations a 'bolt-on' status, as distinct from being accepted as an integral part of the overall management mix. This was due in part to the level of importance that managers, who were (and, some would argue, still are) largely untrained in this area, gave to the corporate communication process, although far greater credibility was afforded to marketing publicity. The blame must also be shared, however, by the PR practitioners, who were all too often well equipped to communicate but lacked the necessary parallel expertise of the other management processes they were seeking to represent.

While not totally removed from the management scene, this mismatch has been significantly eroded by the increase in the attention being paid to formal communications training for managers, coupled with the development of PR education and recruitment to encompass a broader understanding of other areas of management responsibility. The introduction of an MBA course at Cranfield in 1987 and more recently degree and postgraduate courses at Stirling University, the University of Wales at Cardiff and elsewhere which concentrate on public relations, and the significant increase of PR electives at UK business schools over the past few years, are representative of the strength that the function has achieved.

The development of the corporate communication function within industry and its integration into the central stream of management was highlighted by a 1987 study, *The Practice of Public Relations* by Katie Arber, then of the Durham University Business School, and sponsored by Traverse-Healy Limited. From a sample of 179 of the 500 largest UK companies, 86 per cent of companies had a defined PR policy, and of these, 76 per cent said that the policy formed a fully integrated part of a public relations plan which required board-level agreement in the context of corporate planning.

It is particularly interesting to note from Katie Arber's research that, while marketing responsibilities (including marketing communication) are increasingly being devolved to individual business unit level, this is being achieved through the development and monitoring of corporate guidelines that keep the overall responsibility for the management of the corporate identity firmly within central control. This reflects the increasing under- standing by management that there is little that cannot be devolved down to business unit level, provided central management retains control over the overall direction of the company and the role of each business unit in active support of clearly defined corporate objectives.

Later chapters will describe in detail the processes of constructing a framework for the integration of corporate communication into the cor- porate planning structure. However, in brief, what is needed is a process by which a company can first set for itself the identity that it wishes to pro- mote. To do this, it must understand the commercial, social, and political environment within which it will be required to operate. A failure to under- stand these factors may well serve to nullify the effort that will follow in defining communication objectives and in developing communication strategies and programmes that will enable these objectives to be met.

All too often, management has looked first to the tools of communica- tion – such as media relations or advertising – without considering the rea- sons for using them. It is rather like organizing a distribution system for a product not yet conceived, let alone researched and developed. Again, this has not always been the fault of management. Many corporate com- municators continue to encourage management to concentrate on the 'How' and not the 'Why'.

The need for planning and control of the communication function extends throughout its major areas of influence. These are generally taken to include all the major 'stakeholder' groups:

1. Financial public relations
2. Investors relations
3. Government relations
4. Community affairs
5. Employee communications
6. Marketing communications

To these can be added 'Issue management', which, briefly, can be described as the understanding and influence of the significant commercial, social, and political factors that ultimately may impact the ability of a responsible company to meet its reasonable business objectives. While perhaps less immediately obvious in its benefits than investor relations or employee communication, issue management offers far greater potential for the determination by a company of the environment in which it can expand and flourish.

Too many companies tend to have PR programmes of a responsive rather than proactive nature, often without a background plan or policy, with little attempt to frame a strategy, and certainly unrelated to the company's overall business plans and corporate objectives. The thinking company starts with its corporate objectives and current business plans, and the PR programme that emerges is closely related to aiding and achieving these. In the sloppy, responsive company, by contrast, corporate objectives and business plans are handed down from on high, seen more as a set of good intentions, and are never questioned until the post-mortem is held.

In the proactive company it is the responsibility of the corporate affairs professionals to question the validity of the commercial plans in the light of political and social trends that are likely adversely to affect their attainment, and of public and group perceptions of the company – since support depends upon perceptions. The secret lies in recognizing the nature of the external decision-making process, knowing who your friends and foes are, and having an early warning system in place. Simplistically, the process should be viewed as a quartered circle (see Figure 1.1). The first quarter represents the phase where the topic is emerging, the second, that wherein it is being debated, and the third, the time when it is becoming codified. In the fourth quarter it becomes accepted and is sometimes given the force of law.

Historically – almost traditionally – industry generally, and individual companies particularly, enter the process in the final arc of the second quartile or later – far too late to have real effect on the majority of issues. The aim is to enter the arena as early in quarter 1 as is possible, when ideas and options are being formulated, the preliminary drafts are being concocted, and the small print is still negotiable. The currency of this sort of contact is information, and the price paid for genuine dialogue is, often as not, preparedness to anticipate and to enter into controversy. It is worth remembering that 90 per cent of the decisions made in the public domain affecting industry are taken at administrative and executive level, not at the political level. The chances of failure increase immeasurably if the topic is thrust or dragged into the political and social arenas.

The selection of issues for corporate action is critical, and is a matter of management judgement against criteria and the understanding of the 'likelihood/significance ratio' that takes account of:

1. Will or could this issue really affect our bottom line?
2. Is the 'bad news' scenario realistic?

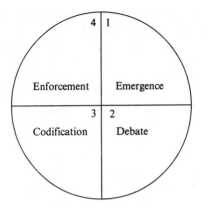

Figure 1.1 The external decision-making process

3. Could corporate action halt/amend/modify/delay the progress of the issue?
4. Will our present policies and practices stand up to public examination?
5. Are the resources to act available?
6. Is the cost to the company acceptable?
7. Is the will to act present?
8. What would be the effect of inaction?

If the corporate objectives are to be achieved, then the company is likely to need varying degrees of support at various times from stakeholders. Implicitly, this support has to be for the company's present performance and programme, its future plans, and indeed even its problems, if the objectives are to be reached.

If a company needs support, then it has to possess that most maligned of factors on the balance sheet, goodwill. Goodwill is based upon understanding. Before understanding there has to be a reputation. And a reputation presupposes that a degree of awareness exists. Behavioural research has indicated that, all other factors being equal, there is a distinct relationship between familiarity and favourability – in other words, between the degree of support a company might expect and the levels or awareness about it.

Awareness is based on the public's perceptions of an organization. These are created by statements (including visual) that a company makes about itself (or others make about it), by comments solicited or volunteered, by third-party endorsement (or otherwise) of its behaviour, and above all by the personal experience of individuals in their dealings with the company and its staff at all levels. (See Chapter 3, p. 37.)

Perceptions may be right or they may be wrong, but because they exist they become fact. It follows that public affairs and public relations are all about issue selection and issue management, coupled with the management of the corporate perception process and the correction of incorrect perceptions. Only when the range of issues has been considered can those few that are likely to affect the achievement of bottom-line targets be isolated. Only then can the decision-making models be drawn and the specific role-players, junior and senior, be nominated.

Simultaneously, the company's position has to be set out, debated internally, and agreed. The perceptions of key external factors and factions need to established, and sometimes existing internal policies and practices need to be modified and arguments reworked. Among the numerous items that remain to be considered under the heading of strategy are 'targets' and 'messages'.

By and large, the external role-players across all the selected issues become the target list for the company's contact-and-convince programme. Only when this point has been reached can a corporate communications strategy and plan be created and an effective programme be activated.

The selection and development of a corporate identity can be a most complex and exacting process, involving considerable analysis of what the company is and what it intends to be as well as what it would like to be seen to be. Statements of corporate identity include numerous value judgements (can a company be 'international' if it operates in only two or three countries? Can it be 'market-driven' if it fails to change with market needs?) which have to be thrashed out in a wholly realistic atmosphere. Often it takes outsiders to act as a catalyst to understanding the optimum corporate identity, and to produce a totally clear and concise definition of the organization that can, and should, be reflected in every detail of its communications effort.

I have often thought that the perfect example of a clear and concise corporate statement that says it all is 'The Best Little Whorehouse in Texas'. Can you think of anything relevant that it leaves out? For most companies, however, a more socially acceptable corporate identity will include elements such as 'innovative', 'market leader', 'well managed', 'profitable', 'responsive', 'responsible', 'creative', 'international', 'diversified', 'specialist' or 'prudent', and 'decent, honest, and truthful'.

The acid test of a corporate identity, once determined after hours, or even months, of agonizing over single words, is to go home and try it on your partner in life. If she, or he, rolls about on the floor in laughter, do not give up – you may not know if you have chosen the right identity, but you certainly know you have an image problem. For a corporate identity is a method of expressing a body corporate – machinery, products, factories, and effort – in human terms, and as such it must be within the boundaries of credibility of the audiences to which it will be communicated.

Once a company has defined where it wishes to go in commercial terms, the major external factors that might impact its ability to get there, and the corporate identity that will support it along the way, it needs to look closely at who it needs to be talking to in order to convert its chosen identity into a parallel image held by those who will ultimately make the decisions that will affect corporate performance.

In defining target audiences – traditionally called 'publics' by the PR profession – managers must distinguish between a variety of groups and individuals, who may or may not be interrelated or interactive, who have the ability either to take decisions that will impact the company or to influence the direction of the decision-takers through the respect in which their opinion is held.

To take a simple case by way of illustration, if a computer manufacturer wishes to sell its product, it will have key decision-taking audiences among the management of its potential customer companies, including data processing managers and possibly even their chief executives. In addition, however, a number of key external groups will exercise, to a greater or lesser extent, influence on the direction of the internal decision. In this case, these may well include external specialist consultants, the specialist computer journals and general management media, finance houses, and existing customers. All these have the potential beneficially or adversely to affect the decision that will eventually be taken by customer management. Since it is often impossible to predict precisely which individual or group is going to have an impact on each decision, it is generally necessary to communicate on a broader basis to target audiences that have been defined as closely as possible without becoming too limited.

Communication is, of course, a process that involves both the sender and the receiver of a message. It is fundamental in the management of the communication process that the company should understand the needs of its audiences, should use the language and media that the audiences understand and respect, should transmit messages that are believable to the target audiences, and, most importantly, should impart only messages that will motivate the receiver in some way – either to act, or to alter a perception of the company.

I apologize to those who find the above too obvious, but defend its inclusion on the basis of numerous encounters with managers who appear determined to communicate *their message* in *their words* through *their media*, apparently regardless of their lack of commonality with their target audience. The result has been described as 'cognitive dissonance' by communication theorists, and the suffering to corporate egos that accompanies this disease is well worth avoiding by simply following the military maxim of 'know your enemy'.

This book is unlikely, in itself, to convert any manager who still views public relations solely as some form of below-the-line marketing activity to an understanding of the breadth of contribution that it can make to the achievement of business objectives. There are some excellent publications that tackle this task, and guidance is freely available from both the Institute of Public Relations and the Public Relations Consultants Association. The book is of greater relevance to managers who have already accepted to some extent the value of managing their corporate relations and who wish to explore the processes and practices that they can use to ensure that their company will gain the maximum benefit from the professional application of this fundamental management skill.

In the end, no responsible manager can conduct the company's business without an eye to the impact on the bottom line of everything that is undertaken. Corporate communication is no exception, but with the added difficulty that here the manager is often dealing in areas of activity that defy measurement in terms that would be regarded as acceptable in other management functions. Corporate communication professionals continue to seek acceptable methodologies by which they may be able to justify, not unreasonably, the value of their activity in financial terms. A number of specialist firms, such as CARMA International, have recently emerged to service the need for definable performance monitoring. Yet, there is one truism in corporate communications that has rarely been faulted: of the thousands of companies that have decided to manage their corporate identity and annually spend hundreds of millions in corporate communication activity, there are few, in any, that have found the function of so little obvious value that they have not consistently sustained or increased the resources allocated to it – often while cutting expenditure in other areas.

Given the respect I hold for both British management and the public relations profession, I have to assume that they are not redistributing wealth from one to the other just for the sake of a 'bolt-on' service or corporate amusement. The simple fact is that effective corporate communication is neither difficult nor necessarily expensive to achieve. Rarely has its value been questioned except by those who have failed to plan and operate their corporate communication effort in a professional manner – and a number of other management disciplines have suffered to the same extent in their time.

Bibliography

Hazelton and Botan, *Public Relations Theory*, Lawrence Erlbaum.
Bowman, *The Essence of Strategic Management*, Prentice-Hall.
Cutlip, Centre and Broom, *Effective Public Relations*, 6th edn, Prentice-Hall.
Grunig and Hunt, *Managing Public Relations*, Harcourt Brace Jovanovich.
Seitel, *The Practice of Public Relations*, 3rd edn, Merrill.
Smythe, Dorward and Reback, *Managing the New Strategic Asset*, Century Business and Random House.
Regester, *Crisis Management*, Hutchinson.
White, *How to Understand and Manage Public Relations*, Business Books.

2 Planning for Corporate Communications

Anthony Wreford

The first task for the individual responsible for planning the corporate communications activities is to gain the acceptance of the senior management, almost certainly the chairman and managing director, to the principle of an active corporate communications programme. Even today, there are many companies that simply do not accept that a corporate image needs to be planned with the same business disciplines as other functions.

This resistance is often based on the false belief that corporate communications activities will provide yet another drain on the company's bottom line and hence be an unnecessary overhead. The first golden rule for initiating any corporate communications plan, therefore, is to stress to the senior management of the company that the purpose of the programme is to help improve the bottom line, not the reverse.

Fortunately most industrialists today recognise the value of a good corporate image and an effective corporate communications programme. This was not always the case as some companies were 'late for the party' and may have suffered as a result. There is, however, still some resistance and part of this negative attitude reflects the way that an ever-increasing number of companies are now structured as decentralised organisations, leaving the profit responsibility to the operating units. This inevitably means that there is a greater resistance to add head office costs, and, of course, this affects corporate communications budgets, as well as staffing levels in the central communications department.

The 1980s saw an unprecedented wave of contested takeover battles where image became an all important ingredient. Indeed research studies carried out at that time showed that corporate image was one of the areas of greatest concern to senior management. Whilst image in the 1990s still ranks high on managements list of key issues, its prominence has slightly declined as the fear of take-over bids temporarily lapsed during the recession. Nevertheless it's hard for companies to ignore the activities of others in the sector, and many reluctant communicators have been dragged in as a result of seeing the activities of their competitors. The privatisation programmes in Western Europe and the former Soviet Block States have meant whole new images being created for companies that were previously under State control. Corporate image has therefore become an essential part of corporate life in the 1990s.

This chapter has been structured as a series of steps derived from experience in planning programmes with clients, where the problems of company structure, culture, and personalities can often get in the way of sensible progress. Ten steps are suggested. Some might argue that many of the actions proposed can take place at the same time, but the real point of addressing corporate communications planning as a series of steps is to progress it as a structured plan. The great danger with corporate communications is that all the company directors will have different and preconceived ideas as to the preferred company image and the sort of techniques that should be employed. If it is possible to sell the company management the concept of a structured programme, there is one major benefit: it buys time. In other words, you will not be hurried into a particular programme of activities. It also ensures that proper and more objective thought is given to the sort of techniques that might be relevant for the audiences that need to be addressed. It further provides time to research attitudes outside the company.

The ten steps are therefore by no means commandments, but are tips based on bitter experience of what can go wrong.

Step 1: Understand the Business Objectives and Strategy

The objective of any corporate communications programme must be to help build the profitability of the company, so it is essential that the business objectives are understood before any corporate communications planning takes place.

All business plans differ and inevitably have varying priorities. For instance, the priority might be to move into new geographic areas; it might be to move into product areas where the company is not associated; it might be more narrow, in terms of ensuring that the company has a good image among the investment community prior to, say, a rights issue. Whatever the priorities, it is vital that the professional communicator is able to set the firm's objectives based on its overall business plan and priorities.

Most companies have rolling three- to five-year plans, and it is these longer-term objectives that should be taken into account. There may in addition be short-term objectives set for, say, three to six months, and these will also need to be considered but may require a separate communications programme.

A good company image usually takes several years – indeed, often generations – to build, but there is an old saying that a good image can also be destroyed overnight. In some cases images may need to be built in a much shorter period. Take-over battles are a good example of a situation that may confront the company and where a good image has to be created in a very short period. In this situation, where the company is in the limelight, there are many more opportunities to put across the company's strengths, and it is surprising how much can be achieved in a short period. Typically, those responsible for planning the corporate communications will be expected to achieve far more in a much shorter space of time than is possible. It is important, therefore, that the board of the company recognize the limitations as well as the possibilities of an active corporate communications programme.

Unless the communications adviser has direct access to the board of the company, it will be very difficult to carry out this most important first stage of planning. Senior management who recognize the importance of communications will be only too willing to share these broad business objectives with the adviser; the more cynical will not see the need.

It will be necessary to hold individual meetings with the directors responsible for the different parts of the business. These meetings should bring the business objectives to life. For example, the finance director's main concern will be the company's reputation in the financial community, and therefore his objective may well be described in terms of 'I want a higher share price for the company' or 'I want a good image so I can raise some more money.' The directors responsible for operating divisions are more likely to talk in terms of the image of the company in their particular markets. The director responsible for international activities will have a very different view, and often the most difficult request for the communications expert to achieve; this is often described in terms of 'achieving the sort of image overseas that the company enjoys at home'.

An ideal planning process must enable the communications expert or adviser to talk to all the board directors and to as many of the senior management of the operating companies as possible. Only in this way will the business plan be brought to life and the potential conflicts and the objectives be identified, and only in this way will the communicator get a proper feel for the characteristics of the company that might be promoted and those that may need to be played down.

Step 2:   Agree on Realistic Communications Objectives

Before any further planning is done, it is essential that the business objectives are interpreted as corporate communications objectives and are agreed with the company's senior management.

There is an old saying that you can sell anybody anything once, but the trick of a good salesman is to be able to go back and sell the same product to the same individual again and again. This maxim can also be used in corporate communications because it is very easy, indeed tempting, to promise the chairman a better reputation among any of the relevant target audiences in a short space of time, but, as those who have worked in this area will know, very much more difficult to achieve, and in particular to prove! So be realistic in the goals that you set for the communications programme, and resist the temptation of trying to promise something that is unlikely to be achieved. There is so much that can happen to the company during, say, a 12-month period that is totally beyond the communications expert's control, and the setting of unrealistic goals can only damage the function and reduce its credibility in the eyes of senior management. Building a good image like that enjoyed by British Airways or BP in the UK, and on an international basis by companies like Shell and Coca-Cola, takes a considerable amount of time and effort. Good images cannot be created overnight: they have to be built through a realistic commitment by the company to all aspects of its activity.

The very process of sitting down and discussing the broad communications objectives with the company management will provide an opportunity for discussing the time scale for the business, and should provide the right sort of forum for determining the priorities of the company. As such, this contact should be regular. In the process of obtaining the views of the company management, the communicator should be able to develop communications objectives and test them with the individuals concerned, so that, when the formal process of agreeing on objectives begins, all the individuals concerned should have agreed on the broad principles.

The process to date has been exclusively an internal one, in obtaining the views of the key individuals and developing a broad plan. The next step is to ascertain the views and perceptions of those outside the organization to determine the extent to which they differ from the internal view.

Step 3: Understand your Target Audiences

Many companies are reluctant to look in the mirror and conduct market research. It is important that the professional communicator overcomes this problem, for without the help of market research, some of the key information for the planning process will be missing. The key issues to be researched will include:

1. How the various target audiences view the company
2. What the perceived strengths and weaknesses are

3. Whether the company has a high or low level of awareness
4. How the competition is viewed
5. How well the management are regarded
6. What characteristics are ideally sought in a company operating in this sector

Only extensive market research can answer these and other questions. In many cases it may be necessary to conduct several studies among the specialist target audiences. Issues that may be relevant to customers, for example, will not be those that may be relevant to the financial community or indeed other opinion-formers.

There are a number of benefits to be derived from this type of research. These include:

1. An objective view of the company
2. A better understanding of the values and characteristics that are perceived as important by the target audiences
3. A check on whether the business objectives are consistent with the needs and views of the various target audiences
4. A benchmark from which to measure progress in the future

One of the most helpful aspects of some research studies is the analysis of how key audiences evaluate companies. The market research should not therefore restrict itself simply to how the company is perceived, but should study the very communications process that the target audiences go through in making their evaluation. In this context, there may be existing research studies that are available to answer some of these questions. So before embarking on any research programme, part of the planning process should be to identify all market research studies that have been conducted in the sector to ascertain what is already available, where gaps exists, and what information needs to be updated.

Some research studies are available for general use, and in many cases companies or their trade associations are willing to share market research findings with friendly or member companies. Although the topic is covered later in this chapter, it is important that the individual or group that is allocated the task of planning the corporate communications has relevant experience of market research, not only in terms of inter-pretation, but also for briefing the market research companies. A regular part of the corporate communications planning process is to keep these research data up to date and to use them to measure the effectiveness of the programme.

Step 4: Develop an Intelligence System – Information is Power

Market research is vital to determine how the company is viewed from different perspectives. But these attitudes need to be looked at together with information on the company's markets, the competitors' activities, and the other issues that may be of importance.

To plan the company image effectively, the communicator needs to be able to understand all there is to know about the sectors in which the company operates and the information needs of the target audiences being addressed. This means putting together as much published information as possible about each sector, how it is viewed, and what are regarded as the key issues. Such information is likely to come in a variety of forms. To illustrate the breadth of possibilities, the following lists contain some of the sources from two typical audiences.

1. Customers

- Industry and sector projections, e.g. CBI, IOD
- Trade press comment
- Information through trade associations
- Industry image studies
- Comparative data from overseas markets
- Reports and accounts of competitors
- Industry seminars and conferences
- Advertising expenditure figures

2. Financial community

- Business school studies, e.g. Henley, Manchester Business School
- Stockbroker write-ups
- Industry reviews
- Press cuttings
- Reports and accounts of domestic and international competitors
- Sector newsletters
- Corporate brochures and videos

In collecting information from these various sources, the communications adviser will quickly build a picture of the sort of attitudes and issues affecting not only the company, but also the industry or sectors in which it operates. One of the roles of the communicator is to be able to collect this research and to interpret it for the benefit of the company management. This analysis will help in finalizing the communications objectives, and in highlighting the particular aspects of the company that need to be researched in greater detail.

Companies whose market intelligence is thorough and up to date will often have the cutting edge in the targeting and planning of the corporate communications programme. A familiar component of today's corporate communications department is a computer with sufficient storage capacity to hold all the data required. Information must be readily available on the target audience so that it can be called up at short notice.

A regular part of this information process is to ensure that names and addresses of customers and other target groups, such as investors, are kept up to date, along with other relevant information, including their attendance at various meetings, invitations to hospitality events, special interests, etc. For this reason, the corporate communications department should be staffed with an information officer or librarian, whose sole responsibility should be to ensure that the department has access to all the information on the various markets, and that this information on the specific target audiences is kept up to date. This process has become more time-consuming with the many changes taking place among a range of target audiences. Customers, investors, and journalists move from one organization to another more frequently than ever before, and there is nothing more embarrassing for the company than a mail shot or an invitation sent to the wrong individual.

A well briefed researcher in the corporate communications department will also need to read all the newspapers and trade publications to ensure that speeches by industry leaders and commentators are picked up, that new market research information is filed and analysed, and that information on the competition is up to date and competitors' annual reports are obtained. It is not unusual, therefore, for a part of the corporate communications budget to be devoted to subscriptions. Indeed, some companies now buy shares in their competitors to ensure that all published information is obtained, ranging from the company report and accounts to corporate brochures and corporate videos, which are now sent to shareholders on a regular basis. Subscriptions to trade associations are frequently centralized with the corporate communications department to help control this information flow.

Information *is* power, therefore, but it needs to be analysed so that it can be used and acted upon. A vital part of the corporation communications planning process is to provide this interpretation.

Step 5: Establish Priorities for Tasks and Target Audiences

In developing the set of objectives, the communicator will need to identify the most important audiences to be addressed, for the objectives for each audience will differ according to their information needs and requirements.

In the early 1970s, most corporate communications programmes took a 'shotgun' approach in preaching a similar message to all target audiences. As the levels of knowledge and understanding towards business and companies have grown, so it has become necessary for companies increasingly to segment their programmes. Today an effective corporate communications programme may have four or five separate strands with specific objectives and goals. A message, for example, that may be of relevance to the financial audience will not necessarily be of the same relevance to government officials, and will certainly not be of relevance to the local community.

One of the frustrations in the planning process is trying to reach agreement on the priority tasks and the priority audiences. Inevitably, short-term considerations may often override the longer-term objectives, and one of the permanent dilemmas that will be faced in the planning process is how to reconcile the short-term considerations with the longer-term requirements. In practice, it is probably better to allocate sufficient funds behind achievable short-term tasks than to scatter insufficient funds across longer-term objectives.

It is the setting of the priorities against the various target audiences that is one of the hardest tasks in the planning process, for it can often end up as a personality debate. The finance director, for very legitimate reasons, may want to use a substantial proportion of the funds to talk to the investment community. The sales director, on the other hand, may have other ideas about a particular opportunity to talk to customers, and what can often follow is an internal debate with the communications department caught in the middle, probably being lobbied from every side. It is to be hoped that this can be avoided; a regular process to review the communications activities should ensure that these conflicts are identified long before they become an embarrassment. Ultimately, the setting of priorities has to be agreed by consensus.

Step 6: Agree on the Communications Strategy, an Outline Programme, and the Budget

By now all the relevant information should be at hand, and the communications planner can put forward a recommended strategy to achieve the agreed objectives, against the agreed set of priorities and target audiences.

In many ways this is the most difficult process of all, for committing strategic recommendations to paper inevitably brings back the structural considerations within the company. A decentralized organization will inevitably face a conflict if further corporate initiatives are suggested and if money is to be taken from operating units to fund these activities.

There has been much debate over the years as to the most effective way of funding a corporate communications programme. Operating companies recognize how management charges are set up, and a heavy loading in a particular year is unlikely to escape their notice. The other route, of asking operating companies to give up a proportion of their product promotional budget, is not really an acceptable alternative when in most cases they are being asked to achieve a bottom-line target and should be allowed the freedom to do this. There is therefore no perfect way of setting a corporate communications budget. The experienced communicator will know that any strategic recommendations will have to be digestible; and, whatever the inadequacies of the corporate structure and philosophy, unless a strategy can work in practice, there is little point in putting it forward to the management board.

The board of the company should be allowed to comment on the outline programme of activities, and on some communications activities, such as corporate advertising, they are likely to have very strong views. It is potentially dangerous at this stage to allow the board to get into too long a discussion on the precise nature of the activities, as this will need to be worked out by the communications department with their own advertising agency and PR consultancy.

The main purpose of discussing an outline programme is to sort out the monetary considerations. A not uncommon practice is effectively to split the elements of the communications programme between those parts that are truly head office considerations (for example, communications with the financial community and government) and those that are likely to benefit the operating companies (in other words, initiatives to improve company image amongst customers). The former category should be funded out of head office costs, and with the latter it may be possible to ask operating units for a contribution.

A not uncommon practice, particularly in the United States, is for the head office to start the ball rolling by putting in some money in the first two years on the basis that the operating units will pick up the costs in subsequent years. This practice is also found in the overseas operations of multinational companies, where the head office may well put in some money as 'pump-priming' in order to initiate a programme.

Step 7:   Involve the Operating Companies

For most companies, one of the important roles of the corporate communications programme will be to help improve and develop the company's image with customers. It is therefore sensible at a relatively early stage to involve the relevant individuals from the operating companies. This has to be a good principle, if only on the basis that early involvement with these key persons is more likely to provide the prospect of acceptance of a programme than if the individuals were presented with a *fait accompli*.

Most programmes are intended to help the operating companies and to supplement the existing brand or product promotions already in place. The level of involvement will depend upon the company and the type of products that are sold. Companies with a strong brand orientation will need to involve their marketing directors, whereas companies selling to industrial markets are more likely to involve their sales directors, who should be in tune with customers' needs.

There are other considerable advantages in this process of consultation. Operating companies may at some stage have to pay for part of the corporate communications programme, and they are more likely to be willing to participate in this budget if they feel they have had some input. There may also be other market intelligence or information which they can feed into the planning process. However, the most significant reason why this process is necessary is that the individuals concerned will have their own views as to what the corporate image should be and what communications techniques should be employed.

This consultation process with operating companies is a necessary part of the overall planning process if the programme is to work, be accepted, and have any chance of life beyond year one.

Step 8:   Allocate Responsibilities

One of the fundamental differences between the corporate communications departments of European companies and their counterparts in the United States is the number of personnel. It is not unusual in the US to find a corporate communications department with between 20 and 40 personnel: with the exception of the oil majors, this is not the case in Europe.

With fewer human resources, the company must decide how best to implement an active corporate communications programme. The problem is exaggerated by the inevitable front-loading that most programmes require. The sort of issues that will have to be addressed include:

1. Which board directors should be actively involved in the programme?
2. Who should be the prime spokesman on financial issues, on government related issues, and on strategic issues?
3. How much of the programme can be handled internally and to what extent will external services be needed?

4. How much involvement or help should be expected from the operating companies?
5. Should the firm use the services of agencies currently working for operating companies, or should specialist corporate communications agencies be employed?
6. Should the company buy different services from different agencies, or find an agency that can provide an integrated approach?
7. Does the company need to take on temporary staff during the early phases of the programme?

One of the principal reasons why corporate communications agencies have grown so rapidly in the last few years is due to the poor staffing within companies. The specialist corporate communications agency can be very helpful to the company, particularly in the early stages, when new systems have to be set up and where internal resources do not provide adequate depth. Indeed, with the move towards decentralization and with an increased availability of external resources, it is quite possible to keep a relatively small internal office and supplement it with services from outside.

An important consideration in allocating responsibilities is to ensure that the left foot does know what the right foot is doing and that regular meetings are held between the various consultancies, agencies and personnel who are involved in the communications programme to ensure a co-ordinated approach. Even today, when the cry for co-ordination is all too familiar, there are too few examples of companies that practise what is so often preached.

Senior management, who are inevitably very busy, will respond to precise instructions, and there should not be a problem in allocating responsibilities if the early part of the planning process has been carried out properly. Typically, the finance director will concentrate on the financial community, covering in particular the investment analysts in stockbroking firms and institutions. The chief executive and chairman will supplement the finance director, particularly when it comes to direct contact with major institutional shareholders and with the more important financial journalists. On government relations, the chairman or chief executive is more likely to play a key role except where there may be a specific scientific or technical issue, where the board director who is responsible for that operating unit is more likely to do so.

Allocating responsibilities is perhaps the simplest of the tasks. Persuading those who have been allocated responsibilities to report back on a regular basis on the outcome of their discussions and the impressions seen and created, or indeed to pass on other relevant information, is altogether another problem. Some form of regular debriefing must take place if the programme is to be adequately monitored and controlled once the individuals have been allocated responsibilities.

Step 9: Sell the Programme Internally

This chapter has so far ignored the employees and any consultation process wider than either the board directors or key operating personnel. It is time to redress the imbalance, for employees are important if the programme is to have maximum impact.

Most employees appreciate why their products or services have to be promoted through advertising, on television or the press, or through other communications techniques. What is often more difficult for them to grasp is why the company should spend substantial sums of money on promoting its name and its image. This can be a particularly sensitive issue at a time when the company may be engaged in negotiating either the closure of a plant or the annual wage review.

Very few companies take time to pre-sell the corporate communications programme to their employees and keep them informed about its activities. If the programme is to be accepted and, more significantly, supported by employees, however, it should be sold to them before it appears externally. This is not an exercise in damage limitation, but goes back to the basic premise that the best (or indeed worst) form of corporate advertising for any company is the employees themselves. This is supported by many research studies and shows why a well briefed employee can often be the most effective communications tool the company possesses.

One example demonstrates how this should work. Several years ago, when Dunlop were starting their corporate advertising programme, a short video was prepared explaining the reasons for the campaign. A sample of customers and members of the public were shown being interviewed and asked what they thought of Dunlop. The results were presented on the video as background to why it was important that major customers and the buying public have a better understanding of the range of Dunlop products. The video was shown in all Dunlop offices several days before the first television commercial appeared. Coupled with the video presentation were details of the viewing times of the TV commercial in the relevant ITV regions. The response was very encouraging. Employees reported back to their families and friends and were proud to be able to discuss the reasons behind the new corporate advertising for Dunlop.

Although Dunlop has now been taken over, this does not invalidate the process that the company went through to pre-brief its employees. This is a principle that has since been followed by many companies and is essential if the corporate communications programme is to gain internal support. It is particularly important if the company is embarking on corporate advertising or any form of sponsorship which may be highly visible and not immediately understood by the rank-and-file in the company. Regular updates are also important, preferably with simple research findings, such as new customers or press comments. All of this can be a very helpful way of demonstrating the value of the corporate communications initiative.

Step 10:   Don't Stop Planning

It would be easy to form the impression that the communications planning process is a once-and-for-all process. This far from the truth, for communications planning is a regular process. Discussions with senior management need to take place on a regular basis to ensure that the communications department is up to date with corporate planning, changing market conditions and, indeed, the economic, political and social issues that inevitably face every company.

Part of this regular planning process of course can be linked with the market research programme which has been discussed and which is covered in greater detail later in the book. Customers' attitudes change, so do those of investors, and it is important that these changes are fed into the planning process so that it can be fine-tuned.

Time scales inevitably differ between companies, but a regular review process at least twice a year should ensure that the programme remains in touch with external developments and is consistent with the company's own corporate plans.

Remember, the purpose of any corporate communications programme is to help the company be more profitable.

CONCLUDING REMARKS

In many ways this subject is not an easy one, since the corporate communications function is relatively new, certainly to most European companies. The resources put behind corporate communications have not been as great as many have felt desirable, and the commitment of the company management has in many cases been, at best, questionable. We are all still learning the best way of approaching this area, and the ten steps that were outlined above should be taken as guiding steps rather than a definitive approach.

I have deliberately avoided reference in this chapter to what is often known as the communications audit. I feared that to discuss the communications audit would in many ways detract from the practicalities of planning the corporate communications function. The audit, which is described elsewhere, is a very useful process to take account of all the communications activities that a company is engaged in, and as such it should be part of the overall corporate communications planning process. Indeed, the approaches that I have advocated are in themselves some form of audit.

The success or failure of the communications planning process will at the end of the day rest upon two key factors: the commitment and energy of the top management, and the willingness of other individuals to share their experience and expertise towards a common interest. Too often, these factors are sadly missing, because the corporate communications function either is not high enough on the chairman's agenda or, alternatively, is in conflict with the interests of the operating companies.

Corporate communications planning requires determination, common sense, a little politics, and a great deal of patience!

Bibliography

D. Bernstein, *Company Image and Reality*, Holt, Rinehart & Winston.
C. Heathcote Parkinson and N. Rowe, *Communicate*, Pan.
W. Oleins, *Corporate Identity*, Thames & Hudson.
A. Ries and J. Trout, *Positioning: The Battle for Your Mind*, McGraw-Hill.

3 Marketing Communications
Norman A. Hart

Considerable confusion exists concerning the roles of public relations and advertising in relation to the marketing function. This stems largely from the ambiguity of the term 'public relations', which has two distinct interpretations, one conceptual and the other practical. The former is well stated in the definition given by the Institute of Public Relations:

> Public Relations practice is the planned and sustained effort to establish and maintain goodwill and mutual understanding between an organisation and its publics.

Clearly, the achievement of such a broad objective implies the sending and receiving of messages along the most appropriate channels of communication to reach the many diverse publics upon which the success of an organisation depends. And the publics include customers and prospects just as much as employees and shareholders, while the channels of communication include advertising and direct mail just as much as editorial publicity and sponsorship.

In spite of the very clear definition given above, practitioners and top management alike continue to interpret PR in its practical application as being little more than press relations leading to editorial publicity. What is overlooked is that advertising and editorial publicity are both 'media', and are as relevant to the achievement of marketing objectives as they are to the achievement of public relations objectives. Advertising, then, is a subset of public relations, and not a competitor. It carries messages that may relate to financial matters, personnel, purchasing, or indeed marketing. The same can be said of editorial publicity.

The purpose of this chapter is to identify and discuss briefly all the various message sources and channels that are likely to impinge upon the minds of customers and others who might have a role to play in the purchasing–selling interface. For convenience, these are all brought together under the term 'marketing communications'. Here, alas, there are a number of definitions giving alternative interpretations, from a narrow perspective to a broad one.

The generally held view is that marketing communications is simply the non face-to-face promotional activities of advertising, publicity, direct mail, exhibitions, and sales promotion. While in practice this is exactly right, for the purposes of this chapter it is necessary to move a little further into the ultimate objective, and here another definition helps: 'Marketing communications are normally across-the-board communications ... to help move a potential customer from a state of ignorance towards a position of decision and action.

In other words, a prospective customer goes through a series of stages of acceptance in the process of adopting a new product, and it is the purpose of marketing communications to facilitate and accelerate that movement. This procedure is referred to as the 'adoption process' and can be broken down into five stages.

1. *Awareness*: the individual becomes cognizant of the innovation but lacks information about it.
2. *Interest*: the individual is stimulated to seek information about the innovation.
3. *Evaluation*: the individual considers whether it would make sense to try the innovation.
4. *Trial*: the individual tries the innovation on a small scale to improve his or her estimation of its utility.
5. *Adoption*: the individual decides to make full and regular use of the innovation.

Clearly, marketing communications encompasses any form of communication that contributes to the conversion of a non-customer to a customer, and subsequently to the retention of such custom.

A model that has stood the test of time can be seen in Fig. 3.1. Here are not only the stages of the adoption process, but also the positive and negative factors which will accelerate or decelerate the rate at which the process will take place. It should be noted that the sales force is not usually considered to be part of marketing communications.

MESSAGE CUES

Within the marketing mix, provision for marketing communications may seem to reside in the fourth of the '4 Ps':

1. Product
2. Price

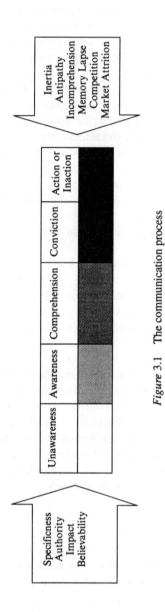

Figure 3.1   The communication process

3. Place
4. Promotion

This, however, is now regarded as inadequate, since by compartmentaliz-ing 'promotion' a number of other important opportunities can be missed. One authority makes this point:

> The promotional mix has long been viewed as the company's sole com-munications link with the consumer. However, this kind of provincial-ism can often lead to suboptimisation of the firm's total communications effort. Because if viewed in isolation, promotion can actually work against other elements in the marketing communications mix. Other communications elements with which promotion must be co-ordinated are price, product, retail outlets, and all other company actions which consumers might perceive as communicating something about the company's total product offering.

Before examining the role of promotion as such we should look at the message cues that might be transmitted by the other 3 P's – product, price and place.

Product

The fundamental marketing concept postulates that a customer does not buy a product but rather a produce performance, or more to the point, a satisfaction. In the consumer field it has been said that a customer does not buy *soap*, but rather *hope*: similarly, in industrial marketing the customer buys *holes* rather than *drills*. Furthermore, the customer bases purchasing decisions upon the perceived benefits that will be received as against the actual physical product attributes.

The total product offering is not what the supplier offers, but what the customer sees to be on offer. It may well be that packaging and present-ation constitute the key factor in a purchasing decision, particularly with the increasing number of undifferentiated products. Indeed, with some of these – for instance, cigarettes, cosmetics, and drinks – it could be argued that the package is the product. Increasingly, what comes inside the pack is identical as between one brand and another, and that where that is so, the package is the single most important purchasing influence. With products that sell in supermarkets, this is particularly important.

An interesting example of packaging and presentation concerns a range of divan beds where the mattresses were finished in a variety of fabrics from the traditional to the very modern. A further variable was that the finishes on offer were of a soft plain surface, a quilted finish, or the rather old-fashioned button-type fixing. The customers unhesitatingly chose a quilted finish in the traditional fabric, notwithstanding the fact that all the mattresses were physically identical.

Research evidence shows that the buyer is influenced to a critical degree by the size of a product and its shape, colour, weight, feel, typography, and even smell. The successful package is the ones that appeals to both conscious and unconscious level of the consumer's mind. The conscious mind recognizes just the product, whereas the unconscious mind is motivated by the package.

It must not be supposed that 'presentation' of product applies only to the consumer field. The study of 'organizational buyer behaviour' shows clearly the many subjective factors that enter into a purchasing decision. Gone are the days when a handful of components was bundled into a black box, and all that mattered was that the performance matched the specification. The appearance of an industrial product sends out signals. The design, shape, colour, and so on, all combine to create an impression on the one hand of a dynamic, innovative, go-ahead company, or on the other of a traditional or maybe a backward one. It is important to realize that it usually costs no more to put a conscious effort into good product presentation, whereas to create the same effect by means of conventional promotional media is often very expensive.

Consideration must further be given to brand name as part of the total product offering. Any product is going to be called something by its customers and users, so it might as well be a name of the company's own choice, and one that brings with it certain positive attributes. Does it have or imply a favourable connotation? Is it short and memorable? Can people actually pronounce it? Does it support the claims being made of product performance? And then there is the graphic symbolism or the associated logotype: a good brand name can evoke a feeling of trust, confidence, security, strength, durability, speed, status, and the like.

Price

For many if not most products, the signal given by price, and thus the effect on purchasing, follows the normal economist's law of demand. As price falls, so demand increases. With everyday products, where price levels are common knowledge, the message conveyed by price is indicative of good or bad value for money: hence the success of supermarkets in being able to offer heavily branded products at a lower price than the local grocer, and, going one stage further, the success of own-label products which undercut the established branded ones.

For some products, however, the normal rules do not apply, as is shown for instance in Figure 3.2. In this case, price is taken as signalling quality or prestige, and within limits creates a desire to acquire which increases as the price increases. Without delving into the ethical considerations, the fact is that in some circumstances a reduction in price will signal a reduction in quality and vice versa. This is particularly so where the customer is unable to make a judgement on any other basis – a watch, for instance, or a hi-fi set, or cosmetics in general. There are other factors, of course, such as appearance and availability, but in the main, the assessment of quality in such items will be based heavily upon price.

The same price–demand relationship is found in products that are purchased as gifts. Here a higher price may be paid largely as a compliment to the receiver of the gift, or for that matter to enhance the prestige or satisfy the ego of the giver. Once again, it is a matter of perception on the part of

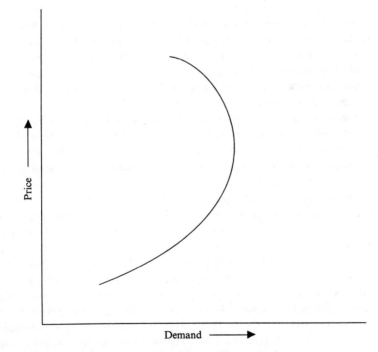

Figure 3.2   Where price is taken as signalling quality or prestige

the buyer. It matters little what message the seller intends to convey: the purchase will be determined by the way in which the buyer interprets the message.

An example in the field of services was in a programme of seminars where, in order to attract larger numbers to a particular subject area, the price per day was dropped progressively over a period of years: the numbers decreased. The sponsor in desperation offered the seminar free of charge. No one attended. At the other end of the scale, an advance course of instruction was offered at a much higher price than hitherto, and higher than the competition: the number of registrations went up.

Over and above simple price levels, there are many price offerings that can give positive signals without involving the price-cutting that leads to a price war. Credit facilities, quantity discounts, prompt payment discounts, special offers, trade-ins, free delivery, sale or return, and so on can all provide a competitive edge without necessarily incurring a high cost.

Place

Physically, of course, there is a well defined correlation between market share and the number of outlets. This can be seen in car hire firms, for example, or petrol service stations. But there is also a psychological factor, and that is that every retail outlet has a perceived reputation or image, and if this is positive then it is likely to bear an influence on the sales of the individual products it carries. The products will stand to benefit from what is known as the 'halo effect' of the store.

The store image or personality will vary from one group of people to another. So an expensive high-fashion store might evoke a feeling of confidence, reliability and comfort to people in the higher-income bracket, whereas to people on lower incomes it might communicate extravagance, waste, and snobbishness.

The location of a store is perhaps the starting point. It may be situated in either an up-market or down-market part of a town. Furthermore, the exterior of the building will signal ancient or modern, small or large, elegant or drab – even the name and facia will convey an impression. The interior of the store is even more important. The size of gangways, displays, colour, sound, smell, temperature, decor, and lighting will all play a part. Added to this is store personnel, all of whom will be trasmitting messages depending upon their age, sex, race, speech, product knowledge, friendliness, and helpfulness. In the personnel field it is most easy to swing from a very positive perception to a very negative one just for lack of staff selection, training, and motivation.

In putting together a marketing communications mix, the question here is, to what extent might 'place' be important in enhancing a product perception in such a way as to increase sales? Let us take an example of two extremes. In one case take a new Russian wristwatch being offered by a soap-box salesman in Woolwich market. He claims that its accuracy is greater than any other watch owing to the application of new technology. The price is at a bargain knock-down level of £49.00 including gold bracelet. Now take the same watch and the same claims and price, and put it in the window of Harrods in Knightsbridge. Which 'place' is likely to be most successful? An interesting reflection on the reputation of Harrods is that, referring to the previous section, if the price of the watch were put up to £149.00, the sales might well increase.

Promotion

It is unreasonable to discuss promotional media before first examining the nature of the market with which it is intended to communicate, the people that go to make up that market, and their purchasing motivations.

In the first place, there is very little evidence to support the contention that any purchasing decisions, even those of consumers, are largely irrational. Purchases are made to provide a perceived satisfaction, and as long as they do just that, such an action can hardly be held to be irrational. What they are in fact is subjective, but that is quite a different matter. The confusion arises out of the basic purchasing motivation. What we have had drilled into us is that people buy things to satisfy their 'needs'. This is not so. They actually make purchases for the most part to satisfy their 'wants', a fundamentally different human characteristic. What a person 'wants' is a highly subjective matter and varies from individual to individual regardless of whether the decision is within the framework of a family purchase or a company (organization) purchase. Indeed, since the number of people known to be involved in the latter is so much larger, so also is the likelihood of decisions being all the more subjective and complex.

The change from a philosophy of 'needs' to one of 'wants' can be quite profound throughout the marketing process – in product design, in market research formulation, in pricing strategy, in selling, but above all in promotional propositions and promotional media. This is not to argue that objective factors do not enter into purchasing decisions. Quite the opposite: they enter into all such decisions to a greater or lesser extent. What is argued, however, is that there is also a high degree of personal motivation – to satisfy the self in all purchases, whether for company, family, or indeed self.

CONSUMER BEHAVIOUR

'Consumer behaviour', whether personal or organizational, is governed by what might be termed internal and external factors. The former are largely outside the control of the marketer and comprise innate personality factors plus early acquired behavioural patterns such as attitudes, beliefs, cultural and social mores, ego deficiencies, and the like. External factors are much more current and dynamic influences; they contribute to people's continuous development in terms of preferences, aspirations, activities, and indeed their perceptions of themselves – how they would wish to be seen by their contemporaries and their peer groups.

Thus, in terms of buying behaviour, the messages reaching them will be from a vast variety of sources, some of which will be acceptable and others not, but all from one standpoint: the buyers themselves. And this must be the key to successful marketing information formulation. The starting point, then, of the buying process is the buyer and the buyer's perceived wants.

THE MEDIA MIX

All markets are amenable to segmentation, especially industrial ones. And in each market segment there will be a multitude of quite different decision-making units, each comprising a number of individuals having their own particular egocentric motivations. Not only will the selling message need to vary from one to another, but, even more important, so will the media necessary to reach any target group. And a target group may vary between a few tens of people to millions. For effective communication, therefore, it is unlikely that just one or two media can be relied on: rather more likely is the need to select by methodical analysis an optimum combination of media categories to achieve the desired effect on the buyer in the form of any of the classical marketing communications models such as attention, interest, belief, intention, desire, purchase. All the indications are that, in order to make a thorough and positive communication with all the purchasing influences in a particular market segment, what is required is a 'media mix'.

Inter-Media Comparisons

To arrive at an effective media mix presupposes the availability of data upon which to make comparative judgements. In consumer advertising there is a relatively wide range of research material available to assist the media planner, but, even here the task is not easy. In the industrial sector it is difficult to obtain even the most elementary information. Thus, if guess-work is to be avoided, some form of logical grid should be devised against which each possible medium can be evaluated and given a comparative rating.

Figure 3.3 is an example of a typical grid. The list of promotional media is by no means exhaustive, and will differ from one company to another. In the same way, the criteria for media choice may vary depending, for instance, on whether the target market is a consumer or an industry. The following 12 factors and the use of a matrix are regarded as no more than an aid to planning for the marketing communicator.

1. *Market size*   The total size of a market segment and all of the people within it must influence the choice of media. With a market size of 10 units, there is clearly not much room for anything more than personal contact and whatever back-up might be required. Move to 100 units and the situation hardly changes. At 1000, the personal contact must become selective: here one can add direct mail, specialized press, editorial publicity, literature, and perhaps sponsored films and audio-visual (AV) material, local

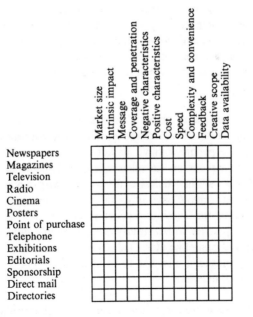

Figure 3.3   Promotional media grid

demonstrations, or telephone selling. At 10 000, the value of personal selling lessens and press advertising and other non-personal media take over. Public exhibitions have a particular merit here, combining unit economy with the benefits of face-to-face contact. At this point, direct mail sometimes becomes difficult to handle, but editorial back-up is well worth full exploitation. At 100 000 it is possible to move into the mass media, with television, radio, national newspapers, and posters replacing, or heavily supplementing, the media already listed.

2. *Impact* The extent to which a promotional message is transmitted, received, stored, and can then be recalled with accuracy is vital. Each medium has its own intrinsic impact potential. Clearly, a medium that facilitates two-way communication is top of the list, so personal selling, exhibitions, demonstrations, and telephone selling are all worthy of a high rating. Direct mail, properly conceived, can expect to perform well here, as can editorial publicity, sponsored films, and literature. All the research evidence we have on page traffic and Starch (USA) measurements would indicated that press advertising performs least well in achieving impact. Television, on the other hand, has a high, if transitory, impact potential.

3. *Message* What is the nature of the selling message? Is it simple, or a reminder? Is it complex, technical, or innovative? In the former case television, press advertising, point of purchase, posters, and radio will do well. For a complicated message, however, the need is for demonstrations, seminars, feature articles, literature, sponsored films, and for the efforts of the sales force.

4. *Coverage and penetration* This is the breadth and depth of a medium's capability. In breadth the question is, What proportion of the target audience (i.e. people within a market segment) is covered by readership as opposed to circulation (in other words, will have an 'opportunity to see')? In direct mail this could be 100 per cent; with a national newspaper, perhaps 60 per cent. Commonly, an in-depth coverage of around 80 per cent is aimed for. Turning to penetration, certain media are known by long-standing practice to penetrate decision-making units even where the people involved cannot be identified – a major trade fair, for instance, or a weekly trade magazine that has to be seen by anyone who is anyone in order to keep up to date.

5. *Negative characteristics* Some people resent advertising, and it is as well to check before using a particular media group whether this could be

in any way counter-productive. Most people in the UK dislike advertising messages on the telephone or salesmen at the front door or on the street corner. They also dislike loose inserts, and direct mail that is too intensive or repetitive: for many, radio and television commercials are intrusive. It depends on many factors – just check it out.

6. *Positive characteristics* Is there an added plus which comes over and above the basic medium itself? Examples are with an advert in a very prestigious publication, where to be seen in good company lends an extra credibility to an advertising proposition. With an exhibition stand, a comfortable lounge can be a welcome oasis after the formal business has been completed. An in-house exhibition or seminar might draw together people with common interests who have not met for some time and welcome the chance of informal discussion almost as much as they appreciate the event itself.

7. *Cost* There are two costs to be considered, and also price. The first cost is the total capital investment involved and whether this is compatible with the cash flow position and the other major expenditures in marketing activities. Second, the cost per contact must be evaluated, ranging as it does from the latest estimated call cost for an industrial salesman of over £200 to just a few pence for a mass medium. Media planning decisions are often made on the outcome of aggressive media buying, and this is where price comes in. All rate cards have their price, and 10 per cent off quoted rates can be a lot of money.

8. *Speed* Television, radio, newspapers, direct mail – all, under pressure, can transmit messages within 24 hours or less, and to a very large audiences. The sales force can respond even more quickly, but at a rate of just a few people a day. At the other extreme, it might be two years before an appropriate trade fair takes place. Thus, if the time for activating consumer/customer behavior is a critical factor, the choice of media must be influenced by this.

9. *Complexity and convenience* Nothing could be simpler than to advocate a half million pound appropriation to a single commercial network on television, and the balance to full pages in national newspapers. Such a media strategy may even be right. This is in stark contrast to the complexity of a multi-market multi-shot direct mail campaign, coupled with regional presentations and tied in with local PR, back-up sales visits, regional press, supporting literature, and posters with a culminating business gift. The choice of media just might be influenced by ease of use (idleness), coupled with such

other non-professional factors as good or bad agency commission: is there any possible justification for some media nominally paying commission and others not? Media choice within an agency, therefore, must have some regard for the amount of effort required to service each medium (a cost) in relation to the income and aggravation it is likely to receive.

10. *Feedback*   Examine any advertising medium and you will find that the greater majority of advertisements invite no explicit response in the way of a direct feedback, and so receive very little. Hence press advertising, and television, are essentially one-way communication systems. Since impact is greater where a dialogue can be established, there must be an intrinsic advantage in all the face-to-face media, and even with direct mail and editorial publicity where there are some instances of feedback. It is worth noting that many of the popular sales promotion techniques heavily involve the customers' participation.

11. *Creative scope*   Should a medium be chosen for its creative scope? This is increasingly regarded as a major factor, but within the rather strict limits of availability of colour or movement. What is meant by creative scope is the opportunity for some quite novel or extraordinary approach that could be made entirely as a result of the medium being used. In press relations the creative opportunities to set up an extremely newsworthy event are limitless, and needless to say this would be done in such a way as to involve the product or company inextricably. With direct mail there is complete freedom on material, size, shape, colour, smell, timing, audience, and frequency. Exhibitions also have an almost infinite variety of creative opportunities. Particularly where the product itself is mundane, the choice of media for creativity is especially relevant.

12. *Data availability*   It is inexcusable that large sums of money should be invested into promotional media which in turn cannot be bothered to provide basic data on the audience they are reaching. A good deal of information is available regarding television and the press and their coverage of the various consumer market segments. It follows that the more a marketing company can feel sure of its facts about a particular medium, the safer it will feel in using that medium.

In general, as audiences become narrower and more specialized, so the data available becomes less reliable. In technical journals, for instance, and in exhibitions there is usually very little information available.

OTHER PROMOTIONAL ACTIVITIES

In any marketing textbook, the promotional ingredient of the 4 Ps will be shown to comprise four elements: advertising, personal selling, sales promotion, and publicity (the latter being the American term for editorial publicity and the like). There are a number of items which should be added to those already mentioned, and most of these come under the heading of sales promotion:

- Coupons
- Premiums
- Trading stamps
- Contests
- Incentive travel
- Discounts
- Branded offers
- Samples
- Co-operative advertising

MESSAGE SOURCES

A new concept in planning for marketing communications is to consider incoming messages from the perspective of the receiver. Just how does a prospective customer learn about a product or a company, and what are message sources that lead to the forming of an attitude and eventually to an intention to buy, followed by an actual purchase? Clearly, all those activities listed under 'promotion' play a major part here, as do the important message cues received from product, price, and place. But where, for instance, does 'personal recommendation' come in? In many purchasing transactions, particularly first-time buying, this can be more important than any amount of advertising or packaging.

The fact is that there are tens or even hundreds of other messages sources which have been neglected in the past and are now emerging as important contributors to the development of perception by customers. They can be considered under three headings: outside message sources, people message sources, and passive message sources. These are all in addition to the 'active message sources' summarised above.

Outside Message Sources

Opinions about you or your product expressed by what might be called 'third parties' are always more powerful and credible than your own claims. Messages from customers and/or users of a product are possibly more effective than any other message source, and yet the main thrust of any promotional campaign seems to be at prospects to gain new business rather than encouraging recommendation by reassuring existing customers that their purchasing decisions were right ones. i.e. overcoming any 'cognitive' or 'past-purchase' dissonance in which a customer has second thoughts about the wisdom of the purchase. Recommendation by a retailer, agent, or distributor is equally important. Such people are seen to be largely unbiased as well as perhaps slightly better informed than oneself. The value of considering the messages transmitted by people outside the organization is that in the first place they exist, and to ignore them is foolish, and in the second place they will be regarded as credible. What is being said, then, by one's competitors, suppliers, and local communities? And what also by relevant trade associations and institutions and special interest groups whose point of view can have a major effect?

People Message Sources

Obviously, the sales force is in the forefront of sending messages about a company and its products, and it is worth while examining these messages to make sure they are in every way positive and supportive. To a greater or lesser degree, however, every employee develops an attitude, good or bad, and has the opportunity at least occasionally to express a view.

What impression does the chief executive give when speaking in public? Indeed, is there a proactive programme of speaking engagements to help raise the company's visibility and the regard with which its top management is held? How about other senior management? Are they encouraged to be seen and heard in public, and do they give a good account of themselves? Are they trained to do so? Receptionists and telephonists are in the front line and are recognized as being so, but is the same consideration given to the public interface of service engineers and delivery drivers? How are the complaints and enquiries handled, and (to take an extreme example) what kind of an impression is given to applicants for jobs, and in particular those who are eventually turned down? Shareholders are a potential source of good news about an organization, but to what extent are they cultivated and informed so as to ensure that they transmit favourable messages?

The answer to all these questions is that in the past much has been left to chance: if anything, the involvement of employees in outside activities has been regarded as being of dubious value. There is now a growing realization that, not only is there a benefit to marketing, but also, the benefit can be greatly enhanced if a properly planned programme of participation is produced and implemented. Membership of trade associations, learned bodies, chambers of trade, CBI, etc., can all contribute to the overall corporate perception.

Passive Message Sources

Every company has a company cheque, with its name printed on it. As such, the cheque serves its purpose of making payments to its creditors. But, like it or not, it is also a message source. A well designed cheque costs no more to print than an indifferent one, and even though the potential audience is both small and specialized, it can surely only benefit the company and its products that they are seen in the best possible light. There are many other objects and activities whose functions are not remotely connected with marketing as such but which inevitably contribute to the total marketing communications offering: obvious ones like sales letters, or indeed any letters, house magazines, labels, house styling, business cards, and annual reports; less obvious items such as instruction manuals, price lists, delivery notes and invoices, calenders and diaries, wall charts, notice boards, showrooms, and the appearance of the factory.

Then what about the company name and logotype, the reception area, the way visitors are received and entertained? Each company differs in its range of relevant message sources. It is simply a matter of taking action to capitalize on a much under-utilized resource.

INTERNAL IMAGE AUDIT

The value of one particular message source as against another can vary widely, so it is necessary to give some kind of weighting to each. Taking each source in turn, we need to ask. Does this message source create an impression that is favourable, neutral, or unfavourable? This is not a difficult or expensive exercise, and it can result in a profile that shows clearly where attention is needed.

Going one stage further, a check-list can be produced in which each item is classified according to its importance. An overall measurement can then be obtained which can act as a benchmark for comparisons in the future. Such an example is given in Table 3.1. The 'rating' number is the maximum that should be scored against a particular item if it is thought to give a good impression in every way. If on the other hand it is thought to give an inferior impression, then the score allocated should be marked down accordingly as far as zero. In this example, if the score is above 100 then the company image is well above average; in the range 70–100 the image is fair to good; below 70 calls for some action, and from the score sheet it is obvious which particular elements need attention.

Table 3.1   Typical message sources

Item	Rating	Score
1. Company name	5	_____
2. Letter heading	6	_____
3. Head office building	2	_____
4. Reception area	4	_____
5. Sales literature	7	_____
6. House style/logo/trademark	5	_____
7. Switchboard response	6	_____
8. Price list	2	_____
9. Company car	2	_____
10. Notice boards	2	_____
11. Entertaining guests	3	_____
12. Product performance	8	_____
13. Product range	5	_____
14. Product appearance & packaging	4	_____
15. Distribution & agents	3	_____
16. People outside your business, e.g. trade associations	4	_____
17. Chief executive speaking in public	5	_____
18. Salesmen	6	_____
19. Sales service	6	_____
20. Delivery times	7	_____
21. Applicants for jobs	2	_____
22. Advertising	7	_____
23. Press releases	4	_____
24. Exhibitions, displays, receptions	5	_____
25. Visual aids, films, photographs	3	_____
26. Business gifts	2	_____
27. Direct mail & letters	3	_____
28. Charity support	1	_____
29. Directories entries	1	_____
30. Invoices, delivery notes, documentation	1	_____

Most factors are so obvious that judgement can be made by a small group of senior 'internal' staff without the need of expensive 'outside' consultants. And the checklist should number at least 100 sources.

CUSTOMERS AND PROSPECTS

In considering public relations activities aimed at influencing customers and prospects, it is inevitable that there will be an overlap into what may be considered the marketing area. For instance, is prestige advertising PR or marketing communications? This question also applies to editorial publicity about new appointments, technological advances, large contracts. Indeed the closeness of these facets of publicity would tend to indicate the need for some form of central control.

Overall, one may say that public relations is concerned with creating a favourable image, or, to use a less emotive word, a favourable reputation. Evidence of the value within a marketing context is provided by Dr Theodore Levitt in his study *Industrial Buying Behaviour* for the Harvard Graduate Business School:

> One of the venerable questions in marketing, and particularly the marketing of industrial products, is whether a company's generalised reputation affects its ability to sell its products. With the great flood of new products in recent years, the question has been focused more sharply around the extent to which a company's generalised reputations affects its ability to launch new products. While nobody claims that a good reputation is an adequate substitute for a good product supported by a good sales effort, the question remains as to what contribution a good reputation can make to a good selling effort. Thus, all other things being equal, does a relatively well-known company ... have a real edge over a relatively obscure company? Would it pay for a relatively obscure company to spend more money to advertise and promote its name and general competence or to spend more on training its salesmen?

Following this question, the study goes on to identify sixteen areas in which a good reputation can be shown to have a positive benefit. It concludes: 'Having a good reputation is always better than being a less well-known or completely anonymous company.'

The emergence of reputation as a factor in the marketing mix leads onto the extension of the classical 4 P's into Five. The fourth P of promotion (which more properly anyway should be 'perception') now has to be considered as those activities which are involved with the product (brand image) and those concerned with the company (corporate image). It can be said then that whether or not a product is purchased is dependent on five factors – the product, its price, its availability, the brand image and the corporate image. Each one of these variables can act in a positive or negative way but the net effect must obviously be positive for a purchase to take place. Thus a product might be very good (positive) but the price rather high (negative) and not too readily available (negative). The brand name might be unknown (negative) but the manufacturer highly regarded

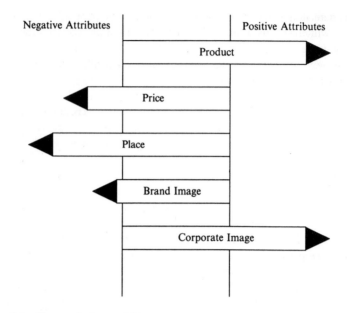

Figure 3.4   Five marketing variables

(positive). The product benefits and corporate image in this case must clearly be strong enough to overcome the 'price', 'place' and 'brand image' barriers. See Fig. 3.4.

The attractiveness of the total product offering is diagrammatically illustrated by the example above which demonstrates both the polarity of each factor (positive or negative) and the intensity of each. A series of such diagrams facilitates the comparison of all competitive products in a market segment, and highlights their strengths and weaknesses.

Such an analysis enables a strategy to be selected for increasing market shares of one's own product simply by considering which one (or more) of the five factors is likely to be the most cost-effective in beating the competitors.

Alternatively one can look at a constant market share but a trade off of one factor against another one e.g. price could be increased but corporate image strengthened without loss of sales. In so far as PR is the function which builds reputation or corporate image it can be seen then to have a direct correlation to sales and hence to profit.

Corporate v Brand Image

There is an increasing awareness that there is likely to be a synergistic benefit in capitalising on both a strong corporate image and also an equally dominant brand image. There will continue to be products such as detergents which will have just a brand name without a supporting corporate name. Equally there are successful products which go under the corporate name only without a separate brand. But the trend is firmly in favour of having both, hence Ford and Fiesta, and Nestlé and Polo mints.

This differentiation between brand and corporate leads to a rather convenient simplification in which marketing communications is tied to product promotion, and thus brand image, and the broader and more strategic function of public relations is concerned with corporate image.

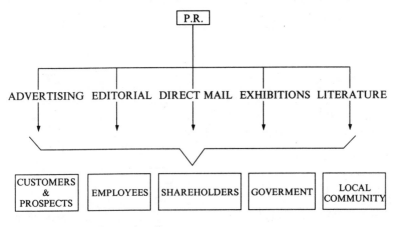

Figure 3.5   PR audiences / media

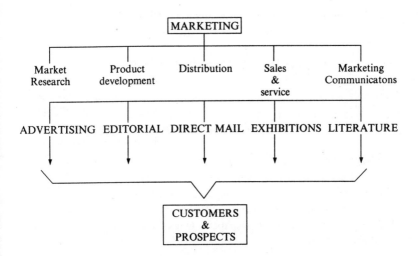

Figure 3.6   Marcom audiences / media

If such a differentiation is accepted then public relations can be seen as a new and separate function which makes use of exactly the same channels of communication as the function of marketing. Whilst the same media are available to serve both marketing and public relations, the essential differences are to be found in the different target audiences and of course the messages sent to them. (See Figs 3.5 and 3.6.) Referring back to the 'adoption process' the two, functions can be considered separately through 'awareness' and 'attitude/perception' but come together to stimulate 'behavioural intent', leading to 'behaviour' and thence to repeat purchasing – the ultimate goal of all marketing activity, as shown in Figure 3.7 below.

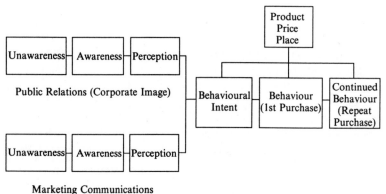

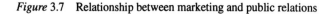

Figure 3.7   Relationship between marketing and public relations

THE 10 P'S OF MARKETING COMMUNICATIONS

It will be seen that in planning for marketing communications there are ten quite separate areas to be covered. These are as follows, and for convenience, and with a little cheating, they all begin with a 'P'.

1. *Product cues* – packaging, presentation, brand image, guarantee.
2. *Price cues* – List price, credit, other financial factors.
3. *Place cues* – Quality, location, and number of retail outlets, direct response media, delivery times, distribution.
4. *Paid-for advertising* – newspapers, magazines, TV, radio, outdoor, ie all above the line.

5. *Promotion* – Direct mail, exhibitions, competitions, financial offers, samples, literature, ie all below the line.
6. *Personal selling and service* – Field sales force, service depots and engineers, merchandisers.
7. *Publicity* – press relations and all activities leading to editorial coverage both news and features.
8. *Third party messages* – What other people outside the organisation say about the company and its products.
9. *People message sources* – All those verbal and non-verbal messages from employees.
10. *Passive message sources* – Those which were never intended to send messages to customers, but nevertheless do.

THE TEN POINT MARCOM PLAN

It might be said that whatever kind of marketing communication's plan is produced, its purpose must be to fit into a marketing plan which in turn looks to a business plan for its overall objectives. It is important therefore to understand the inter-relationship of these three plans which in turn can best be demonstrated by comparing their respective objectives and strategies.

THE STRATEGIC CASCADE

The following list gives the objectives of each plan, and a number of examples of the strategies which might be adopted to achieve them.

Business Objective – Profit

Possible Strategies:

Financial (e.g. cost cutting)
Production (increased productivity)
R & D (new technology)
Marketing (increased sales)

Marketing Objective – Sales/ Market Share

Possible Strategies:

Acquisition
Price reduction

Product development
More outlets
New markets
Stronger promotion

Marketing Communications Objective – Awareness/Perception

Possible Strategies:

Advertising
Editorial publicity
Exhibitions
Direct mail

NB Another communications strategy must be to increase the personal selling effort. Strangely, though, this function is not encompassed by the term 'marketing communications' even though it is clearly embodied in Promotion, the fourth P in the marketing mix.

What will be noted from the above list is that strategy at one level turns into an objective at the next one down. Hence the term 'strategic cascade'.

A Marcom Plan can be broken down into discrete steps as given below. Some might argue that the opening stage should be research rather than objectives, and that is a fair point. If, then, all the necessary information for compiling the plan is not available, it is clearly necessary to conduct research into the market, and indeed into any other topic as is required. Given this to be done, work should proceed as follows:

Step One – Objectives

These should comprise a clear statement of the aims of the marcom plan, having regard to both the marketing and the business objectives. They should be simple to understand, unambiguous, and most importantly, quantified. So many plans in the past have set out to achieve "an increase in awareness" of a given product. What must be asked is by how much, by whom, and by when. There is clearly no way in which a campaign can be evaluated unless there is a tangible, and thus a measurable, objective. Furthermore, how can a budget possibly be set without knowing precisely what the benefit is going to be.

Step Two – Issues

The question here is are there any issues, internal or external, which would undermine the achievement of the objectives? The state of the economy might be an important factor, as might be unhelpful staff attitudes. If the communications' objective is to establish a firm as the technological leader in the field, this will be of no avail if one of the product range has a poor performance. Indeed it may be necessary to change the objectives in view of the existence of certain issues.

Step Three – Strategy

There should be no confusion here of the difference between objectives, strategy and plan. Quite simply the objective is what we aim to achieve, the strategy how we aim to achieve it, and the plan the details of the programme of activities which are to take place. The strategy then sets down in brief the policy for reaching the objective i.e. 'by means of'. It derives perhaps from the military meaning in which the objective is to 'take the hill' and the strategy is by means of using 'the infantry at night'.

Step Four – Audiences

In order to achieve the greatest cost-effectiveness of a marketing communications campaign there are two essentials here. First there is a need to fine tune each market segment or niche market into those narrow groups which have the same homogeneous characteristics, and in industrial or business markets this means identifying the people belonging to the decision making unit, and not just the organisations. The second and equally important ingredient is to quantify the people concerned .

Step Five – Messages

It is important to understand that these should not be a statement of the 'attributes' of the product or its function or performance. Rather it is a matter of identifying customer benefits. One can even argue that customers only buy 'perceived benefits' and so if a customer **thinks** he or she is getting satisfaction then to all intents and purposes he or she **is**. Thus, messages must be transmitted to satisfy the 'needs' or 'wants' of a prospect which more usefully might be termed 'requirements'. And messages need to be prioritised and tailored to fit each person in the DMU.

Step Six – Media

These are the channels of communication through which the messages are to be sent to the target audiences. Here then is the guts of the plan showing how each of the component parts relates to the others in both time, messages, and what might be termed brand identity. They will be matched to each of the target audiences for minimum wastage. Channels will include advertising, editorial publicity, exhibitions, direct mail, seminars, road shows, etc.

Step Seven – Timetable

This usually spans one year which can be on a rolling basis. A shorter timescale might be employed, and it is certainly useful to give some indication of a longer period ahead. In practice one can see how a direct mail campaign will support an exhibition, and how a press release is timed so as to avoid being scooped by an advertisement carrying the same story.

Step Eight – Budget

Following the plan is the earliest stage in which it is possible to produce a budget. There is no sensible reason for starting out with a sum of money, and figuring out how best to spend it. It may be far too much or far too little. But by working progressively and logically through each of the steps, having regard to the 'task' to be achieved, the production of a budget is simply a matter of costing all the various items which have been built into the plan.

Step Nine – Measurement

Campaign evaluation is both vital and simple providing the objectives are clear and quantified. Furthermore, it is important to carry out some form of tracking in order to make adjustments to the campaign if targets are not being met. It is necessary to stress that the only relevant criteria are the communications objectives as opposed for instance marketing objectives. Thus to measure 'sales' is quite unacceptable since they will have been influenced by other factors such as product performance, price, delivery, and indeed the efficacy of the sales force. Typical communications objectives are awareness, perception, and of course sales leads.

Step Ten – Resources

This relates to human resources, both in terms of the number of people to be involved in implementing the campaign, and in their professional capability to carry out the work involved with maximum efficiency. This part of the plan should also take in the use of outside services such as the advertising agency and PR consultancy. Here also is where any training needs and expense should be covered.

Bibliography

D. Berstein, *Company Image and Reality*, Holt, Rinehart & Winston.
N. A. Hart, *Industrial Marketing Communications*, Kogan Page.
N. A. Hart and J. Stapleton, *The Marketing Dictionary*, Butterworth-Heinemann.
R. Haywood, *All About PR*, McGraw-Hill.
W. Howard, *The Practice of Public Relations*, Butterworth-Heinemann.
P. Hutton, *Survey Research for Managers*, Macmillan.
N. Stone, *How to Manage Public Relations*, McGraw-Hill.

4 Financial Public Relations

Peter S. Gummer

INTRODUCTION

Financial public relations has done more for the respectability of PR in general and the PR practitioner in particular than any other single factor. The success of financial PR has forced many chief executives and their financial officers to reconsider the role of PR in their businesses and, in many cases, to accept that public relations today is as important a corporate weapon as media advertising, market research, or any other modern business skill.

This re-evaluation has taken place against a backdrop of intense activity in the City of London. The Big Bang in October 1986 marked the start of a roller coaster. This included a bull and bear market, a string of corporate take-over battles followed by sales to help ease debt burden, rights issues, Black Monday and Wednesday, the EC, the Cadbury Report on corporate governance, high profile company collapses, etc, etc. The list seems almost endless.

The rise and fall of secondary and tertiary markets have all put communications and financial PR in the spotlight.

Initially the Big Bang threw the traditional roles of market-making, dealing and banking into confusion so for financial PR to grow up at this time was both good and bad. It was good because at the time the traditional rules and ways of the City had been broken, providing an opportunity for those with the reputation and entrepreneurship to have a go. On the other hand, these executives have been able to move into areas that are not by rights their own preserve. For example, certain aspects of the role of the merchant banker and the financial PR executive are too blurred and confusing to the market being served.

The chief executive, therefore, who is reviewing the firm's current financial PR advice or, more importantly, is bringing financial PR on board for the first time, must be perfectly clear about what the PR role is to achieve for the company and how it will interface with other advisers.

There is only one satisfactory way into and through this problem. Chief executives (and 99 per cent of the time this role cannot be delegated) must set down clearly what they believe financial PR can achieve in the normal course of events – particularly in handling the financial calendar. This should be agreed with the other advisers – the merchant bankers, stockbrokers, etc. – and with the internal finance director, company secretary, and PR officer. It is only when this has been agreed that the more high-profile roles in flotation, privatisation, take-overs, and mergers can be considered.

So who are financial PR people trying to influence, and what would a typical programme of financial PR consist of?

THE KEY TARGETS FOR FINANCIAL PR

In most PR activities, and financial PR is no exception, detailed attention and an analysis of the key target groups to be influenced bring great benefit to both the evaluation of the programme and its cost efficiency.

Key targets to be included in any list for a financial PR programme would be:

1. Financial journalists
   - Newspapers/electronic media, etc.
2. The City
   - Stockbrokers
   - Merchant bankers
   - Analysts
3. Shareholders (existing and potential)
   - Private
   - Institutional

The priority given to these targets will depend somewhat upon the programme being written and the objectives to be reached.

Let us consider how these target groups relate one to another when planning a financial PR programme to support the financial calendar.

THE FINANCIAL CALENDAR

General

Every public company of whatever size, from the smallest USM to the largest multinational, must provide information for the Stock Exchange for public digestion at certain times during the year. Ideally, many substantial private companies, particularly those planning flotations or take-overs, should be disciplined to undertake a similar programme of disclosure. The more effectively this is undertaken, the better the communication between the company and its existing and potential shareholders is likely to be.

The basic schedule of work is outlined below. It provides a useful step in establishing a PR programme, whether a company is using its internal department, external advisers, or a combination of both. It is the basis for an identifiable set of tasks which can easily be evaluated on a qualitative basis. Most important of all, it establishes personal relationships between a company's chairman or chief executive and the key people in the PR department or PR consultancy.

For the PR team, the financial calendar provides an opportunity to understand in detail how the public company operates and therefore ensures that, in times of crisis such as take-over bids or defences, the PR team can hit the ground running.

Half-Year Results/Interims

Generally speaking, the half-year figures are a low-publicity item unless a public company is in the FT 100 or is itself a very high-profile business. There is little advantage in holding a press conference to present these results.

The PR agency/internal department should fulfil four key functions:

1. It should be responsible for the preparation of the relevant press release and should be prepared to argue about detailed content to ensure that it properly represents what the journalists wish to know. This is not always an easy matter. Company chairmen often wish to make different points in a very different way!
2. After providing copies of the press information to the Stock Exchange, the PR executives are responsible for further distribution. The circulation of a financial press release should not be limited to the media, although they are very important. The release and any supporting information should also be delivered to banks and brokers – both those of the company and those of other interested parties – and in some circumstances to key institutional shareholders.
3. The company must be thoroughly briefed on likely questions and answers from any of the above target groups. There is nothing more embarrassing for the chairman of a company, having released information and indicated at the foot of the release that he is available to answer questions, than to find that he is inadequately briefed. It behoves PR advisers to ensure that this never happens.

4. Ideally, the press release should go out as early as possible in the day. The good PR executive will ring around the key journalists to ensure that any questions which can be answered can be dealt with quickly, thereby gaining a position to advise on likely questions and model answers. The cardinal rule is that access to the chairman of the public company should be facilitated by the PR executive, not hindered.

Preliminary Results

The publication of the preliminary results of a public company is the highlight of the financial year. It is the moment at which the City, the shareholders, and the media can all evaluate the company's performance. It therefore has high publicity value for all listed and unlisted public, and large private, companies.

To the chairman and chief executive, this is what it is all about! They and their teams have worked very hard to make the results happen; the tendency – particularly if they consider the results good – is to expect them to have a higher publicity value than in fact they merit. The pressure is often put on the PR people to arrange press conferences, run advertising, and do all manner of other things to make these results a media event.

It should be remembered that the results of a public company are usually announced on a day when plenty of other public companies are also active – not just with results but with news of public enquiries, rights issues, personnel changes, etc. PR executives must give due warning that preliminary results can fall on good or bad days and should encourage the client to plan accordingly. The media, as will be shown later in this chapter, will discuss results with the brokers. If the results are good (or even bad) but in line with market expectations, they will tend to receive more modest coverage than if they are really hot news – i.e. unexpectedly good or bad.

Try not to have a press conference. Instead, try to encourage individual journalists to follow up the detail on a one-to-one basis or on the telephone. There is no point in planning a press conference, which will always take up more journalistic time than is readily available, unless the company news really justifies it.

The PR agency or internal department have some very important tasks to perform when the preliminaries are due.

1. Obviously, as with the interims, they are responsible for the preparation of the press documentation. This will include the press release and a statement of the figures, together with whatever the company and its auditors consider relevant to a real understanding of the press statement. Financial

PR people are reliable professionals, and they should be involved early in the preparation of this information with other advisers such as auditors, merchant bankers, and stockbrokers. If a company does not feel that it can involve the PR people on this confidential basis, then it has the wrong PR team; any doubts about their ability to handle such information should immediately result in their dismissal or resignation.

2. A similar circulation should be arranged for the preliminaries as for the interims.

3. The client briefing should be as thorough as possible. A review of recent press coverage and brokers' circulars, particularly the interims and the previous annual results, will help to prepare for likely questions. Those are the sources, coupled with the annual report, to which most journalists will refer in order to update themselves before interviewing the chief executive.

4. An early circulation to the Stock Exchange, the media and the brokers is recommended. Most key journalists will talk to the brokers in order to gauge the City reaction before writing their own articles. These are intimate relationships and feed off each other. They are mutually supportive.

5. Most public companies tend to talk to the media before they talk to the brokers. Experience suggests that this is incorrect. Briefing brokers early in the day before the media start compiling their articles is to be encouraged. The message will then be the same in the City and in the next day's press.

The Annual Report and Accounts

Normally this is a very low-interest item. The annual report simply confirms what the preliminaries have already indicated. It is around this time that some public companies choose to implement corporate advertising. If there has been a failure to get the message across in the editorial columns at the preliminary stage, then there is a case for advertising the annual results, highlighting that key message if only to put the record straight. Advertising the annual results through the purchase of space usually does little more than repeat what the media have already covered in the editorial columns and what the City already knows and is therefore reflected in the share price. It should only be used when it is necessary to correct facts or ill-balanced reporting. The PR role regarding the annual report could normally be considered as follows:

1. PR people are inevitably involved in the design, layout, and content of this document. Indeed, their input and knowledge is very considerable, and they should be encouraged to help in any way possible.

2. PR has a unique role in the preparation of the chairman's statement, and yet PR executives often are not consulted or involved until too late. However, they should have their ears close to the ground and should advise their chairman on particular announcements and points to emphasize in the annual report.
3. The chairman and the PR adviser should decide between them whether they want a high-profile annual report or not. By introducing items that will interest the City or the press, the PR executive can present the chairman's statement in such a way that it will make news or not as the case may warrant.
4. The circulation list for the annual report should be as comprehensive as possible. This is the document to which all commentators will refer, whatever their interests, in preparing future articles, brokers' circulars, etc. The fullest possible circulation list should be maintained and updated year by year to encourage wide and informed comment.

The Annual General Meeting

For most public companies, the AGM is an anticlimax. This is a sad reflection on the owners of the business, the shareholders. It is only when matters are at crisis point that meetings are well attended. PR people believe, in general, that shareholders should be encouraged and invited to take an active part in the interests of the company which they own. For the company secretary and the finance director, therefore, the AGM is an important PR platform. Their main tasks are:

1. To establish a time and date which allows shareholders to attend from around the country; if there is a strong geographical concentration of shareholding members, it is better to hold the AGM in the centre of that conurbation.
2. To establish the format and timetable. This is, of course, the company secretary's domain. PR people should be a party to those discussions and should undertake to arrange the entertaining of guests in an appropriate manner.
3. To review carefully the circulation lists for the annual report, and the interim and preliminary results, when inviting people to the AGM. In most cases the merchant bank, accountants, stockbrokers, and other company advisers will wish to send representatives. This is an ideal opportunity for the board of directors of the public company to meet these advisers and discuss plans for the future.

4. To advise on the impact of any proposed statements that might be made at the meeting. There is great pressure on the chairman to make statements additional to those included in the annual report. Inevitably, the AGM takes place at the beginning of a new financial year, and therefore it is too early to make statements which later events may prove ill-founded or hurried. The impact of any such public statements should be discussed with the PR people before they are made to ensure that they are going to have the desired effect. Company chairmen often feel the need to talk before it is necessary so to do.
5. To provide some basis for staff, pensioners, etc., to attend. With wider share ownership among employees, this is now an important company event.

THE ONGOING FINANCIAL PR PROGRAMME

General

Although the financial calendar provides an ideal opportunity for a public company to develop its relationship with its public relations advisers, there are three main areas of ongoing work which should be thoroughly undertaken throughout the year.

First and foremost there should be a scheduled plan for communicating with the City, including the brokers and institutions. Second, the area that usually receives most attention is the communications programme with the press. Third, the area that is least considered is the need to ensure that the staff, whatever their number and wherever their location, are fully informed of the financial statements that are being made about their company and its financial stability and growth upon which their employment depends.

Let us consider each of these three areas in turn.

Communicating with the City

The principles

When establishing the policy for a public company's communication programme with the City, it is important that the public company adheres to certain key principles.

First, the City hates surprises. As a community, the requirement is for a public company to move inexorably through its financial calendar, meeting or significantly exceeding the brokers' forecasts and therefore supporting the share price upon which they are predicated. Of course commercial and financial life is not like that. In effect, however, this idealistic scheme really requires the existence of an orderly market. The responsibility of the public company is to be prepared to adopt an honest stance, particularly with the stockbroker and analyst who follow its shares.

Second, a public company must be prepared to share both the good and the bad news with the brokers and the institutions, either in face-to-face discussions or through selected intermediaries such as merchant bankers or PR people. This places a very heavy burden of responsibility on the PR people.

Third, it is only very rarely that public companies get away with being less than honest with the City. Occasionally this may be possible, but in the vast majority of cases misleading the City means that your card is marked. The City has a long memory, and often the share price will suffer for many years to come.

Recognizing the needs of the key targets

There are three key targets for the majority of public companies: brokers, institutions, and private shareholders.

Stockbrokers live on a steady flow of information, both planned and rumoured! This is the basis for their circulars and the analyses upon which they wish to recommend shares for purchase or sale. Similarly, attention should be given to the market-makers responsible for the shares in the public company. These probably number only two or three firms.

Institutional shareholders wish to see a return on their investment based on an ongoing relationship. Full information of a detailed kind is vital. Institutions tend to become disenchanted with those companies that consider their needs as shareholders only in situations of crisis. Many public companies could have spurned unwelcome take-over bids with ease if only they had developed relationships with those key institutions who own their shares. Nobody likes being called upon for support only when trouble is brewing and their help is urgently needed.

Private shareholders rarely own the business in which they invest. It is the institutions that invariably carry most shareholding muscle. However, the programme of privatization and the marketing of the stock market have all made the private shareholder a very important element in the mix. A regular, but not excessive, flow of information from a public company to its private shareholders, over and above that required by the Stock Exchange in the form of annual and interim returns, is an essential part of the communications programme.

Establishing lines of communications with the City

Most of the financial PR community would argue that an open door policy is a cornerstone of a satisfactory relationship with the City. Willingness to deal with questions and devote time to nurture relationships is essential.

Invariably, public companies become concerned about the number of requests they receive to give brokers' lunches and similar City platforms. They also complain, simultaneously, that they do not obtain an adequate City rating. The truth is that, with the exception of the very large public company, one person at main board level must be prepared to devote some time and effort to these City events, in order to present the company's case. Moreover, as the City buys the future of a company and not its past, such presentations should be forward-looking and, above all else, honest.

These events, and particularly the stockbroker lunches, are really selling exercises for the stockbroking firm. They provide an opportunity for the broker to introduce an interesting public company to a number of institutional investors. It is the task of the public company to enable the stockbroker to do deals as a result of such a lunch. This is a selling opportunity; it should be prepared for on exactly that basis.

The relationship between stockbroker and the media has already been discussed. If brokers find the share of a particular company and the style of its management attractive, and if they believe that the share is undervalued, then inevitably the company will receive sympathetic coverage in the media. The role of the PR team in preparing a complementary message for stockbrokers and the media is therefore essential.

Institutional communications

A regular analysis of the shareholder register will indicate the numbers of institutional shareholders in any company. It is the responsibility of the company secretary to note changes in the register, usually on a fortnightly basis. Such an analysis will lead most public company boards to the conclusion that they are owned by City institutions. A regular programme of meetings with these institutions on a face-to-face basis, therefore, will bring considerable benefit in creating shareholder loyalty in good times and bad. This is a task that should never be delegated or put on one side simply because of the pressure of other short-term obligations.

Communication with the private shareholder

It has long been argued that the private shareholder is disinterested in the annual report – all that he looks at is the salary of the chairman and highest paid director! While this is clearly not the case, there is more than a germ of truth in the thought. Most private shareholders do not understand, and have limited interest in, the flood of company material that pours through their letterboxes, particularly during crisis situations such as take-overs. Their real interest is in the dividend or capital growth of the stock.

However, shareholder loyalty cannot only be bought: it should be sought. A regular flow of press clippings and interesting information helps to bring life to the shareholders' investment. If the company produces products, gifts, and services at a discount which may be of interest to a shareholder and can be offered at a preferential rate, then this too may create longer-term loyalty.

In general, however, there is no substitute for good financial performance and making the shareholders feel that they are part of a company that cares.

Communicating with the Press

The principles

Most PR activity is unfortunately reduced to media relations. It has already been demonstrated that financial PR entails much more than simply dealing with a few financial journalists. This is not to denigrate the role of media relations – it is important and vital. However, it is not the only role of financial public relations.

Professional communication with the press involves a time commitment. Above all else, public company spokespeople must be accessible. Whether chairmen, chief executives, or finance directors, they must be accessible not only as far as their own diaries are concerned, but also as far as the journalist is concerned. The journalist has different priorities, different deadlines, and different schedules to meet. These must be recognized and accepted if good media contacts are to be established.

Being accessible is the keynote of all that follows.

Second, public company spokesperson should ascertain from the outset of a conversation the exact status of the discussion. Is it on or off the record? Is the quote attributable? Most journalists will abide by these conventions, but only if they are clearly stated at the outset. For some reason, many people who talk to the media are self-conscious about establishing this at the beginning of a conversation. This is precisely what the less scrupulous journalists want! They do not ask the question themselves, but will assume that everything is on the record unless told that this is not the case. All spokespeople should establish the status of the conversation before discussing an item which, when the paper appears the next day, they may regret.

Third, know exactly who your friends are. Help good journalists to do their job better; give them the direct line that rings on your desk, your home telephone number, your weekend number. Expect them to do the same. Reciprocate their attention. Invest in that trust.

Awareness of the media role

The financial journalist has a responsibility to his or her reader, not to the chairmen of the companies about which he or she writes. This is an over-simplification of a complex relationship. However, in essence, journalists want a good story which preferably no other newspaper is carrying. They want their readers to make, or at least not to lose, money. Where situations are going wrong, they want to ensure that their readers sell stock before the losses become really damaging. Remember that this is what keeps the financial columns of the national press alive. Providing financial journalists with information to help them fulfil their role is a key part of the com-munications programme.

Journalists are not their own masters. They are always subject to the editorial position of the newspaper that employs them. The *Daily Mirror* clearly takes a different political line from *The Times* or *Telegraph*. Con-tentious issues will have an effect on the way a newspaper positions a story.

If any public company spokesperson ever reads a story about the com-pany or watches it on television or video and then sits back and says, 'I did not mean to say that', or 'She did not understand what I meant', then that spokesperson has not yet understood the role of the media in reporting a public company's activities.

Building on existing contacts

Accessibility to journalists will inevitably develop relationships which will spill from a business into a social environment.

Trying to persuade people through a vigorous exchange to give their individual endorsement to your point of view requires an investment of time. Only superficial commentators require limited attention - and their opinion is hardly worth the paper on which it is written. So, if you are going to persuade leading financial journalists to take up your case, you must know and respect their points of view. These journalists may well become close allies or even close friends.

As the relationship develops, you will find that it may become relaxed and easy-going. A word of warning, however. Many company chairmen have found that, in developing the relationship, they have forgotten that their confidants are journalists. They have not remembered to establish the status of their conversation, and the result has sometimes been the breaking of a confidence. It is then too late to shout, 'I did not mean to say that' or 'That was not for publication.' Never forget that the journalist is a journalist. As in all matters, remember the status of every conversation you have.

Question of timetable

Press relations is ultimately about copy in the paper, pictures on a screen, or words from a radio. Serving the journalist therefore entails understanding in detail the timetable that leads up to that deadline. It is not enough to know roughly when the copy goes down: you must know whether it is going down at 6.10 pm or 6.30 pm.

Why is timing so important? In situations of crisis a late comment can often be very useful. For example, in a take-over bid a late statement from a predator may just make the morning editions, but there might not be time for the adversary's point of view to appear in the same edition. Nothing confirms this as finally as the journalistic line stating: 'Mr XYZ was not available for comment.'

How and when to use a press conference

A press conference provides, in financial PR terms, an opportunity to promote a single message which can be clearly put forward to a number of people who will then be able to ask good questions in lively debate.

Press conferences, however, have one drawback, which is often catastrophically underestimated. There are now far fewer financial journalists on national papers than there were some years ago. The pressures on their time, the variety of companies they need to follow, and the lack of specialization that has resulted mean that the mix of journalists who appear at a press conference vary, from the very good to the very bad. This means that a good question from a good journalist can be heard by everybody else present and is often misinterpreted by the less able media representatives. In addition, if the chairman of a public company makes an error in answering a particular line of questioning, it is not just one newspaper that is being told, but ten or twenty different media representatives.

If conversations are usually or always conducted on a one-to-one basis and are carefully reviewed with the PR advisers directly afterwards, there is always the opportunity of putting right a particular point in conversation with the next journalist with whom one speaks.

Sometimes a press conference is vital, but it should be held somewhere easily accessible for the journalists rather than the public company board. Even a press conference at 3 pm in the Hyde Park Hotel, Knightsbridge, London SW1, is likely to have a low unqualified turnout unless the content is of earth-shattering importance!

Formulating a financial press release

A financial press release has to be newsworthy. There is financial news that is important to the boards of public companies but has little or no significance to the majority of journalists. The PR adviser must be ruthless in identifying what should go out and what should not. Infrequent but newsworthy press releases give a much higher standing to any public company than regular, low-news-value stories which are spiked as often as they are read.

Always ensure that, wherever possible, the press release can be easily subdivided into short and long stories. Some newspapers have little financial space and one or two paragraphs is all they can use. Other more specialist publications, such as the *Financial Times*, may be able to use seven or eight paragraphs. Long or short, however, better stories include a quotation which adds colour and quality to the release.

Any financial release will usually have an effect on the share price, and therefore it has to be right in every respect – a decimal point can send a share price through the floor or the sky. Proof-reading should never be left to one person or simply to the word processor operator. The cardinal rule is for the final draft release to be signed off by an officer of the company, preferably the finance director or company secretary.

Broadcasting

It is now a truism that nobody reads any more! Most people receive most information from a screen, a little from a radio, but hardly anything through the written word. If a public company is to make itself understood in a colourful and lasting way, then it is vital that its spokesperson learns to use broadcasting media.

Training, training, and more training is the *sine qua non* of success in this area. Doing mock interviews for the annual report or in preparation for crises helps enormously when the real event arises.

If television or the radio invite you to appear, grasp the opportunity with both hands. Take it and use it to the best advantage. If in the midst of a take-over bid, make sure that the take-over panel is content with the decision to appear. What can and cannot be said in these circumstances is divided by a very fine line. Whenever possible, go on live; prerecorded programmes can suffer quite a lot in the hands of editors.

Keeping the initiative

In all that is done in financial press relations, it is necessary to be open and to keep the initiative. A defensive position under scrutiny from the financial media invariably leads to disaster. Keep coming forward in the discussions and sharing with the media the problems and opportunities in which your business is placed.

There are many PR people who unfortunately still indulge in dirty tricks. This reprehensible behaviour may lead to short-term gain, but experience suggests that those who play dirty tricks fall by dirty tricks!

Communicating with the Staff

The principles

There will be only very limited disagreement about the principles that apply when communicating with employees at all levels. Unfortunately, the acceptance in theory is rarely carried out in practice.

The fact is that staff know very much more about the financial situation of the company than the chairman and board ever believe. This is hardly surprising. Staff have to deal with suppliers that do not get paid or are kept waiting; staff hear rumours of lay-offs or short working. They have a sharp-end understanding of the ebb and flow of business life and often a simple housekeeping approach to financial matters which runs close to the truth. Any communication with employees therefore must assume a very high level of pre-knowledge, albeit of a rather unsophisticated kind.

Always communicate with staff by preparing answers to the questions *they* want answered. The temptation is to present a case to employees which boosts the ego of management but leaves a feeling of dissatisfaction among the staff. Think carefully what questions need answering, and even try them out on two or three groups before wider circulation.

It is essential that management makes every effort, however expensive and difficult it may prove to be, to inform all employees before they read about their employer or company in the press. It is *their* company; they work in it, and they should be given a priority. To allow them to read in the press or see on TV stories about their company before they have been consulted or informed is asking for trouble.

The order of the day is clear: get to those who work with you first; deal with them honestly, and be prepared to view the financial performance of the business from their point of view rather than your own.

It is an ongoing process

The temptation to regard financial communication with employees as a once- or twice-yearly exercise is, of course, too easy. Financial communication is really about having an ongoing dialogue on the financial performance of the company. The financial timetable is obviously helpful in this. A video, house newspaper, financial seminars, and so on are all helpful in getting the information across.

Consider structuring these activities by using journalists, who approach problems in the same way as the workforce. Invite the City editor of a national daily to interview the board on the financial results so they can be circulated to the workplace. Video the interviews. Encourage discussion. The sharing of financial information rarely does any harm and greatly helps in disposing of rumour and defusing situations.

This is particularly true when dealing with the trade unions. Keeping them informed encourages a genuine understanding of the decisions that have to be made to keep businesses moving forward in the light of new technology, reducing workforces, and so on. Frank discussions with employees' unions, employee committees, etc., help in planning major changes in a company's fortunes.

SPECIAL SITUATIONS

Most financial public relations professionals will enjoy developing an ongoing programme with a public company. The special situation, however, sends blood coursing through their veins. Mention the words 'privatisation', 'flotation', 'take-over', or 'defence' and they know that their skills will be tested to the full.

These special situations are always best handled by PR advisers – internal or external – who know a company's business, have good relationships with its officers and other advisers, and know the media, stockbrokers, etc., who follow the company's fortunes. Hence, establishing the relationship with PR professionals is best initiated with a commitment to the ongoing financial calendar. Then they are up to speed for the special situation.

The three examples chosen – flotation, take-over defence, and attack – require skills peculiar to only a handful of agencies and even fewer internal departments. Make sure that your company employs these skills, whether you need them now or not. If yours is a professionally run business, you will almost certainly need them in the future!

Flotation – A Public Relations Plan

In the following section a PR programme for a company flotation is identified. Naturally, it is general rather than specific, but it provides a checklist for the PR tasks that need to be considered.

1. AN Company Limited – Background information

1.1 *Name* A statement of the name of the company before and after listing must be clarified, particularly where a new company is being formed and the business of this operating company is subsumed in a new entity.

1.2 *Details of the issue* A clear statement of the intention to float the company, either by placing or by tender, needs to be presented. The timetable is important in establishing the target date as early as possible.

1.3 *History* A detailed statement of the history of the company needs to be agreed with the client so that PR advisers can talk with authority when briefing journalists, brokers, etc. This should include details of main products and services provided, main offices throughout the UK, export and other trading details, etc.

1.4 *Competition* Details should be provided of any competitive company, particularly if listed, so that comparisons can be made, dates identified, and satisfactory explanations given to intermediaries.

2. Public relations objectives

A clear statement of the PR objectives needs to be agreed between the company, its PR people, and other advisers.

3. Target groups

Although these groups will vary depending upon the nature of the industry and the size of the company involved, a list of probable targets will include the following:

3.1 *Media*
- National and regional financial and business press
- National, local, and provincial press
- Specialist trade press
- Financial and business correspondents on national and local radio and television

3.2 *Investment community*
- Stockbrokers
- Market-makers
- Investment analysts
- Institutional investors
- Banks
- Finance houses

3.3 *Employees*
- Management
- Staff

4. Methods

4.1 *General* In view of the fact that these notes are intended as a guideline towards the launch, for purpose of clarity a section is included with a timetable of activities in which the week of the launch is nominated as 'week X'.

4.2 *Media* A balanced and informed media is of prime importance to any company planning either a full or USM listing. Effective media relations involve the development of mutual respect and confidence between the individuals concerned, which necessitates the devotion of time by senior management in making itself available to the media both in face-to-face meetings and on the telephone.

It is always to be recommended that any company in this situation undertakes a carefully orchestrated programme of media liaison in order to establish awareness of the company's activities, its history, successes and future potential as an investment medium. It is important to guard against the dangerous effects of overkill in such a programme, and so it is recommended that a limited number of quality editorial features be sought in the appropriate media.

5. Programme and timetable (week X = week of launch)

5.1 *Introduction* The programme that follows assumes a period of notice of up to three months. In some cases it could be much longer, probably up to a year. The longer the period, the more opportunities are presented to control the weight of publicity, particularly in the company's own trade and technical media.

5.2 *Week commencing*

X – 10

- Carry out in-depth briefing with AN Company Limited
- Establish existence of, and obtain current market research relating to, the Group's activities and markets
- Liaise with company and brokers on preparation of corporate brochure and prospectus
- Prepare press information folders and press release paper

X – 9

- Continue liaison on preparation of corporate brochure and prospectus
- Start preparing brief company profile and biographies of key directors
- Arrange photography of key directors for press purposes

X – 8

- Continue liaison on preparation of corporate brochure and prospectus
- Prepare detailed media distribution lists
- Prepare list of selected financial journalists for individual interviews and start scheduling meetings for week *X – 6*
- Continue preparation of corporate brochure and prospectus
- Arrange press cuttings' monitoring service

X – 7

- Identify appropriate brokers' investment analysts for company's sectors
- Obtain current brokers' circulars on company's sectors, if available

X – 6

- Start programme of press interviews for feature stories
- Start making arrangements for investment analysts' presentation in week *X – 1*
- Agree final proof of corporate brochure
- Identify, in conjunction with brokers, appropriate potential institutional investors
- Press information folders and press release paper ready

X – 5

- Prepare first draft of press announcement for circulation by company and brokers

- Make preparations for potential institutional investors' lunch in week $X - 2$

X – 4

- Assist company in preparing 'box' advertisement for one newspaper or as required for full listing
- Company to book advertising space for ('box') advertisement
- Continue liaison on preparation of prospectus
- Continue arrangements for investment analysts' presentation in week $X - 1$

X – 3

- Issue invitations to selected journalists for press conference during week X
- Issue invitations to investment analysts for presentation in week $X - 1$
- Prepare draft press announcement of launch
- Corporate brochure ready
- Continue to liaise on preparation of prospectus
- Submit proposals for ongoing corporate and financial public relations support

X – 2

- Finalize press announcement
- Finalize contents of press folder, including photographs, biographies of key directors, corporate brochures, etc.
- Prepare list of likely press questions and answers at press conference
- Prepare list of likely analysts' questions and answers
- Liaise on final proof of prospectus
- Agree final copy for ('box') advertisement
- Arrange for *Financial Times* and other appropriate newspapers to carry share price in New Issues/USM column
- Lunch for potential institutional investors

X – 1

- Prospectus available
- Investment analysts' presentation
- Distribute press announcement of launch with press (information folders, under embargo if appropriate)
- ('Box') advertisement appears in selected press

X

- Monitor and assess all press comments

- Monitor and assess brokers' reactions/circulars
- Monitor share price at start of dealings
- Prepare report on first day's dealings
- Assess required level of press follow-up

X + 1
- Prepare report on public relations aspects of launch
- Undertake agreed corporate and financial public relations programme
- Continue to monitor share price movements
- Establish new shareholder profile

Defence or Attack – Some Key Rules

Every take-over attack or defence is different. Much of the earlier discussion on developing a strong financial PR programme on an ongoing basis will stand most public companies in good stead when these crises occur.

There are nine key areas, however, which every public company should consider with its PR people, whatever its own plans or size:

1. *Define the audiences* Always review the audiences – media, investment community, and staff – and be certain there is clarity among them as to the company's intentions and long-term plans.
2. *Evaluate image* Perceived reality is far more important than reality. Spend time and money researching the key audiences so there is genuine knowledge – up-to-date knowledge – of how the company is perceived.
3. *Clear channels of communication* Make sure that the lines of communication are known and open – particularly throughout the organization to the staff.
4. *Form a control group* Always have at the ready a control group with board authority to react to any given crisis. This group should include seconded advisers from the bank, brokers, and PR firm.
5. *Logistical aspects of communications* Crises rarely happen in office hours! Does the switchboard operate late at night? Is it easy to gain access to the office outside office hours? Is there a full list of directors' home numbers? Is there a duty secretary who can work the fax machine? These, and many other questions, must be asked and answered in preparation for a crisis.
6. *Tone of voice* Every company has a character – an image, if you prefer. In crisis, panic can set in and result in behaviour that is 'out of

character'. Determine and understand how to behave in character at times of crisis.

7. *Review strengths and weaknesses* The control group should always review the company's strengths and weaknesses, as these will change with the market and the perceptions of the key target groups.
8. *Analysis of predator or target* As the company's strengths and weaknesses change, so does the view taken of a predator or a target. Remember it is the perceived strengths and weaknesses that are more important than the reality.
9. *Assess political factors* The Monopolies Commission, the employment effect in marginal constituencies, and many other political facts can make or break a major bid situation. Analyse these in relation to each situation, whether as target or predator.

CONCLUSION

Financial public relations is here to stay. This chapter has illustrated its role in handling the financial calendar, its ongoing role, and some key elements of communication in special situations.

In the final analysis, however, financial public relations is about the quality of people who do it. Essentially, it is a creative function at general management level with all the financial discipline that implies. It is the duty of every public company to ensure that it enjoys the quality of financial PR help it deserves.

Bibliography

B. Bruce, *Images of Power*, Kogan Page.
T. L. Harris, *The Marketer's Guide to Public Relations*, Wiley.
R. Hayes and R. Watts, *Corporate Revolution*, Heinemann.
F. P. Seitel, *The Practice of Public Relations*, 4th edn, Merrill.
C. Simcock, *A Head for Business*, Kogan Page.

5 Internal Communication

Bill Quirke

INTRODUCTION

There is a cultural deregulation going on, where barriers to the free flow of ideas are being challenged and dismantled. The shift is to a firm where ideas, rather than information, are the currency. In his book, *Post-Capitalist Society*, Drucker argues that the primary resource of the post-capitalist society will be knowledge, not capital, and the manufacturing productivity revolution is over. Now it is the productivity of non-manual workers that matters. The various classes of the old capitalist society are being replaced by just two – knowledge workers and service workers.

In such organizations the flow of ideas, information and knowledge around the organization will be crucial to success. The role of communication as the process by which this flow is achieved is central to the management of the organization. However, given that the pressure is already on to change the nature and effectiveness of internal communication, it is sobering to see how far organizations have to catch up. Research shows that for all the millions spent on internal communication over the past 10 years, employee satisfaction has barely improved. MORI's tracking studies over 20 years show only a 2% increase in employee satisfaction with communication.

The message should be clear – organizations are failing to meet even the communication needs of their past, while they are being rapidly carried into the future. Not only are the goalposts shifting, but we never even mastered the old game.

The pace of change in most organizations is rapidly increasing, fuelled by demand for the creation of distinctive competitive edges in order to survive in an ever changing market place. Organizations need to meet rising expectations among customers, to create better quality, cost effectiveness and customer service, to get motivation and commitment amongst their employees.

This has brought internal communication to the fore. Communication will become the competitive edge of organizations tomorrow. As product life cycles shorten, and competitors catch up more quickly, success will require the ability to feed experience quickly back into the organization from the market, and the key competitive edge will be speed of response.

Most organizations recognize the need for good communication with their people. Over the last few years, that battle has largely been won. Managers want, and organizations need, more from communication than before. While there may be a general agreement that communication is important, that consensus masks the very different perceptions of why it is important, what is its role and how it can help the organization succeed.

The nature and role of internal communication is changing, driven by the changes taking place both outside and within organizations. Information technology is driving change in the structure of organizations, in the same way as the automation of manufacturing processes led to the reduction in manual workforces.

Formal and informal communication is shifting from the vertical to the horizontal, from the line management chain of command to networks of colleagues, suppliers, collaborators and customers. The focus on customers, greater cross-department cooperation, process re-engineering and Total Quality mean that the focus is increasingly on links that run laterally across the organization. These are usually between people of similar rank and power, with no line power over each other, and so rely more on collaboration and cooperation. Increasingly then communication – especially informal communication – runs laterally between equals, while the formal channels run vertically.

Communicating in All Directions

The organization chart of an enterprise may nominally reflect the lines of accountability, but they rarely reflect the lines of communication, and day to day dealing. There are a greater number and variety of channels for communication, and more constituencies with which to communicate.

While organizations may be shrinking in terms of numbers, and layers may be being removed, life inside is becoming more complex. Confronted with change on every front, the typical organization will have strategic action teams, cross functional task forces, supplier quality groups, and new product development project teams galore. Most of these will, by definition, operate across functional and departmental lines, and managers will be members, simultaneously, of a number of teams. They may owe more allegiance to these than to their nominal line boss, and operate outside the formal chain of command. The drive is to internal alliances and cross departmental cooperation, with a greater onus on the quality of relationships. Cross department collaboration means greater interdependency, and greater sharing of objectives and problems. To work together effectively, areas have to be able to think beyond their own priorities, and to see situations from their colleagues' viewpoints.

As the need for better communication increases at an accelerating rate, the problems that beset it increase. The changing attitudes of the consumer, and the fragmentation of media will have a major impact on communicating to people at work.

Given that everybody recognises communication as central to success, and they also recognize the problems in dealing with it, why is good internal communication so difficult to achieve? While there is common agreement that effective communication is a vital part of change, and an intellectual acceptance that well planned communication can help tap into employees' energies and ideas, communication strategy is rarely included in the business planning process. The dilemma that organizations face is that while internal communication is central to success, managers tend to regard it as peripheral, or as an optional 'bolt on' to their real job, something to be done when there's time and leisure, or something to be delegated to the communications department. There is a low understanding of what communication involves and low commitment to getting it right.

Communication Equals Information

There's a belief that communication is a question of mechanics and delivering messages. This usually shows up as a desire to build the Chief Executive a bigger megaphone, on his assumption that if people aren't doing what he wants them to, it's because they can't hear him. Typically, this involves shopping for new media and imitating the technology employed by another organization, without the spirit that made it work.

Similarly, attention is paid to pumping out news of new developments that may interest the Board, but aren't relevant or interesting to the people it's addressed to. Information is based on what should interest people, not on what people actually want to know.

Communication is an Event

When there are redundancies, or when there's a drive to cut costs, or when a new strategy is launched, senior managers feel there should be a communication programme to get the message across. Once that need has passed, and the programme is completed, it is business as usual, and communication wanes.

Telling the Troops

Senior management often translates communication simply as 'telling'. There tends to be an in-built assumption that the right to communicate lies with those at the top of the organization. Leaders want to deliver a stirring speech, and ask 'what shall we tell the troops?' Decisions are taken at senior levels, then passed down the line to the internal communicators to be packaged and distributed as well and as appropriately as possible. There is little consideration of how communication issues should affect and shape decisions themselves, and the process of communication is a reactive and a limited one.

This picture of an assembly line of communication, in which discrete messages are produced by the specialists, crafted, packaged together and sent out, contrasts oddly with the management philosophy of simultaneous engineering, Total Quality and process improvement. It relegates the communication function, at worst, to the despatch department. If a production mentality underlies communication, so too do the assumptions of a hierarchical approach, where your importance depends on your rank, and information becomes a badge of status, and a means of exercising power. The role of internal communication becomes that of pushing information down to the troops rather than listening to staff. Passing down information has been largely limited to communicating the company's stance on particular issues, rather than providing context for decisions, or responding to issues raised by employees. Communication tends to be, in short, a product crafted to the satisfaction of the supplier, rather than necessarily of value to the customer.

The role of the communicator has been to plan and manage any communication, so that it is presented to the appropriate people in the most appropriate way. It has also focused on keeping employees up to date on developments within the company.

Broadcasting into the Culture

Companies reviewing their communication spend too much time deciding what it is they want to say, what are their core messages that they want their employees to receive. While it is important to be clear what the messages are, this is only one side of the equation. They do not spend enough time trying to understand how their employees **listen** to the messages. Without an understanding of employees' **listening**, companies, however efficient their dissemination of information, are only in control of half the communication equation. Employees 'decode' all communication they receive, listening for the 'real' message. How people listen depends on the organization's culture. In the public sector, for example, there is an acute sensitivity to 'business speak' – and the suspicion that it shows a betrayal of old values. Culture 'refracts' communication. You may say one thing – but they hear another. If you do not know how your employees listen, you're not in control of your communication.

The central skill in managing today's organization has gone from 'telling the troops' to fostering and facilitating communication. This means bringing the same respect and disciplines to communicating with the employee as is brought to communicating with the customer. It is as much a question of attitude as of technique.

For the business to succeed you need to connect those who know what needs to be changed, to those who have the power to make change happen. Senior managers have a dilemma – how to get people to speak up, when they've been trained to keep their heads down. Communication is the way of making that connection – it's not simply about letting those below know what those above have decided.

THE AIM OF COMMUNICATION TODAY

A business can only achieve its best when everyone's energies are pointed in the same direction and are not at cross purposes. Employees need to have a clear picture of the overall direction and ambitions of the company. Each employee has to have a clear sense of where he or she fits in and how he contributes to the company's goals.

For any number of people discussing communication within an organization, there will be at least the same number of different definitions of the word 'communication', and different mental pictures of what good communication looks like. The aim of communication for strategic advantage should be to align attitudes, share knowledge, and manage information. People are not blank sheets of paper on which management can inscribe their thinking, nor are they passive recipients of messages which attach themselves uniformly to the brain. We still operate day to day on a mechanistic approach to people and a production oriented notion of communication.

Messages are crafted and honed, refined through draft after draft, and then distributed to the consumer via various channels of communication.

Traditionally, the role of communication would focus on some of the following:

- The announcement of management conclusions
- The working of management thinking into messages which are then efficiently distributed via communication channels
- Ensuring consistency of information and making messages easily comprehensible, and easy to disseminate.

Communication could be seen as a means of ensuring informed compliance with instructions. While some older, production oriented organizations in mature markets were establishing cascade briefings as a way of passing on information, others were discovering that they needed more from their people than simple compliance. The drive to engage the thought, creativity, energy and commitment of employees, which involves a significant shift in the basis of the employer/employee relationship, changes totally the assumptions on which communication is based, and the job it is intended to do.

The additional objectives communication has now to fulfil include:

- The stimulation of thinking, participation and ideas
- The networking of know how and learning across the organization
- The involvement of all employees in improving processes
- The identification of ways of providing additional value to customers
- The expansion of what all employees believe is possible

Internal communication is still largely viewed as being mainly the dissemination of information or messages. Some organizations are however starting to use communication as a key means of empowering and galvanising their people.

This can be seen in the shift from the use of a limited number of one way distribution channels – memos, announcements, noticeboards – issued from behind the closed door of the manager's office, to the proliferation of interactive communication channels, such as company meetings, management forums, speak up lines, videoconferencing, satellite broadcasting, electronic mail, and conference databases. The role of communication is shifting, and shifting rapidly, because lessons being learned about customers, and about processes within the business, are being applied to communication.

Since even product superiority is no guarantee of competitive edge, the culture of the organization, and how people interrelate, is increasingly seen as a way of differentiating service in a way that cannot easily be matched. As people become familiar with principles of quality, process improvement and customer value, they will need to approach communication as a process that needs management, and continuous improvement.

In this process of evolution, different organizations will find themselves at different stages, with different objectives. While organizations can learn from each other in terms of good ideas and sound communication practice, it is easy to become product focused, and to try applying someone else's good idea which may be wholly inappropriate for you.

The role of communication becomes not the top–down dissemination of management thinking, but the bottom-up means of connecting those who know what needs to change to those who have the authority to make change happen. The Chief Executive trying to create change will want a flow of ideas suggestions and feedback, but may find he has to use communication practices that suppress precisely what's needed. The irony is that the debate about internal communication has revolved around what it is that employees need. Today, the greater urgency is felt by senior managers, who want communication to give them what they need to make the business succeed.

DEVELOPING AN INTERNAL COMMUNICATION STRATEGY

Organizations have enthusiastically thrown themselves into a world of change. Managers network with other organizations to learn their lessons and to adopt their ideas, attend conferences to pick up transformational tips, and experiment at home with new philosophies of management.

In terms of communication, the practice of team meetings, video-conferencing, electronic mail, and business television have all been adopted and spread throughout organizations under the impression that all improvement in communication must be good. However, the enthusiastic embracing of communication practices is itself a danger, as organizations adopt ideas developed in industries other than their own, which have developed in cultures very different from their own, and which were designed to further business strategies opposite to their own.

Communication is a means to an end, and to arrive at the best strategy, you first have to start with the business strategy, and define the end. What kind of company do you want your communication to support? It should take into account how the business has chosen to serve its customers, the stability or volatility in its environment, and the pressure on it to change its current stage of development and what it next needs to become.

An employee communications strategy will be different for different types of organizations, and needs to be based on an awareness of the business gaps communication is designed to bridge. Business can range from the established market-leading Goliath to the flexible and opportunistic David – each of which will need, and adopt, a quite different focus to its communication strategy.

In a stable market, slow and methodical organizations that consistently follow established successful procedures, thrive. Adopting approaches internally that run counter to this methodical approach, may actually endanger the business's survival. Adopting communication processes that do not fit the stable, hierarchical organization may detract from its success, and breed dissatisfaction and diversions. In a stable market, the inclination will be to maintain existing practices, and communication will centre on keeping people happily doing the same job they have always done. Discussion about the quality of communication will stem from concerns about employee morale. Attitude surveys will be used to test for levels of employee satisfaction, and consultation procedures will exist to give employees a voice, and an opportunity for contact with senior management. The focus of communication will be on reinforcing a reassuring feeling of belonging within the organization.

In a flexible and adaptive corporation, attention is on staying tuned to the environment, responding quickly to new demands and being able to change direction swiftly. Here communication will concentrate on focusing employees' attention on the world outside. It will make people aware of competitive pressures and the organization's need to achieve a competitive advantage. Communication will feed in information about markets and customers and that levels of customer satisfaction, quality and service will be tracked and reported.

Communication tends to grow and change as the organization develops, and the role it is expected to play will differ between businesses which are different ages, in different industries, are at different stages of development, and have a different competitive positioning, even in the same market. Trying to introduce communication approaches from say the banking industry, and from a business that is a mature market leader, to a small start up fashion retailer will not work. Communication practices usually evolve as solutions to internal problems – simply adopting someone else's solution, when your problem will be different will not produce the results wanted and will create confusion. Any business adopts a competitive positioning in terms of the value it offers for the money it charges. But it also chooses to cater to a particular type of customer, and caters to that customer's particular balance of price, value and quality. Organizations can't be all things to all people, and while choice proliferates, companies focus selectively on what they will offer and how they will go about providing it. Tracey and Wiersema have divided the competitive positioning of companies into three categories:

- operational efficiency
- closeness to the customer
- product leadership

The job that communication has to do will differ according to which of these routes an organization chooses to follow.

Operational Efficiency

Operational efficiency means providing customers with reliable products or services at competitive prices and delivered with minimum inconvenience. Companies continually try to minimize overhead costs, to eliminate steps in the service or production process, to reduce costs, and increase effectiveness. DHL is typical of this kind of process improvement company, using a bus to pick up parcels, and using the time between pick up and airport to document the package and enter it into the system.

Communication focuses on creating greater understanding of roles and priorities across boundaries. Team meetings discuss ways of eliminating snags in the process, and are updated on measure of efficiency, progress on costs and the implementation of the team's ideas. Meetings are run by the team leader, assisted by a facilitator from elsewhere within the business, and representatives from other neighbouring areas attend, to alert the team to upcoming changes, to hear about problems that have arisen from their areas, and to feed back remedial actions.

Closeness to the Customer

Closeness to the customer means segmenting and targeting markets precisely and then tailoring offerings to match. Those pursuing a strategy of closeness to the customer invest to build long term customer loyalty, and look at the customer's life-time value to the company, not the value of any single transaction.

For this business strategy, communication has to stress flexibility and responsiveness. Communication systems are tailored to meet the different needs of different departments' and functions, rather than there being a single regimented model for all. Selection, induction and training programmes stress the creative decision-making skills needed to respond to individual customer needs. Internal information, in directories or on disk, is designed to speed customer service and problem solving.

Communication focuses on feeding the views and attitudes of the customer into the organization. Team meetings focus on customer feedback, complaints and commendations. Customers are brought in regularly to provide feedback directly. Employees from the supplier visit, or are seconded to customers, employees from traditionally back room departments man the stands at trade shows. Upward feedback sessions are run at which front line staff update senior management on customer reactions, needs and requests. Employees are given the authority to make decisions to solve problems, and are empowered to spend the necessary money to do so. Communication focuses on stories of employees' ingenuity in solving problems, and who put themselves out to help customers.

Product Leadership

Competing as a product leader means offering customized leading-edge products and services. That takes creativity of ideas, applicability of those ideas and speed in getting them into the market. Creativity means recognizing and embracing ideas that originate outside the company, so communication focuses on feeding ideas from elsewhere in, and keeping track of competitors' activity. Team meetings include feedback on customer experiences and problems, competitors' advances, and brainstorming exercises. Internal seminars on technical developments are complemented by overviews of social trends. Outsiders are regularly brought in, supplier forums are held to identify areas for improvement, together with advisory panels, and customer user forums.

To increase the speed of getting innovative ideas into the market, internal departments spend time familiarising themselves with each other's roles, and identifying ways of accelerating the development process. Marketing and Research and Development hold team meetings together, and communication is organised along project team lines with the project leader co-ordinating lines of communication.

Stages of Development

While the business strategy will dictate how communication should best be organized, communication strategy will also be affected by the organization's stage of development.

Organizations can enjoy long periods of relative stability and growth, only to be confronted by change that is driven by their environment – a sudden change in competition, or a slower change, such as the progressive deregulation of an industry. They may also be spurred to change by the pressures of having outgrown the systems and style which has served them well in the past.

In a developing business, responding to a changing environment, no strategy and structure will be forever. Whatever is found to fit and suit the organization today, will become constricting and uncomfortable as it develops. The challenge is to identify those communication practices which conspire to keep in place the constrictions of an outgrown structure and style, and to change them into practices that will enable the organization to sense and respond to its environment.

At the outset, organizations begin from a set of circumstances and ambitions which change during the course of their development – going from infancy to maturity – or to premature senility. In periods of calm environments and stable markets, an organization might stay at any one stage for an indefinite amount of time, only being pushed onward by problems arising out of an increasing mismatch between how it operates and what it is trying to achieve.

The first step to developing a strategy for communication is to assess where an organization is on that path, what problems are forcing it to develop further, and how communication should be used to help it reach the next stage.

Not all organizations follow the same path, some are created fully formed at a stage of development, rather than growing into that stage over time, some may be created by legislation rather than by entrepreneurial opportunism. For the purposes of illustration, however, the following organization travels through each stage of development.

Growth

Two partners found a company based on a good idea they think they can exploit. They spend all their time working on the new product, and hire in friends and colleagues with similar attitudes and passions. They talk all the time, and communication happens informally, since there is little distinction between work and play.

The business knows how well it is doing – the product works well, or distributors are agreeing to stock it. Colleagues use flip charts in the coffee area, and whiteboards in the meeting room, to discuss developments and exchange ideas. People join the business who are attracted to its dynamism, are excited by the product, and reflect the attitudes and values of the founders.

As the business prospers, and the number of people in the organization grows, the problems begin. Informal communication that depends on frequent contact and interaction between colleagues starts to fail. People are now on different sites, and working on specialized functions, so individual pictures of how the business is doing fragment, and confusion begins. The founders acknowledge that they do not have the necessary management skills, and bring in a more rounded and experienced business manager to provide structure and direction for the business.

Systemisation

Clear roles, responsibilities and accountabilities are established, and the business is organized around a functional structure. Communication becomes focused on the function, and becomes more formal and impersonal. Contact and meetings happen within the department. The overall business picture is neglected for a clear picture of the function's role and purpose, and communication shifts away from relationship toward task-focused information.

The perceived need for clearer direction and control establishes the new business manager and the executive team as those who decide strategy and set direction. Middle managers now have less power, and less say and are expected to fulfil specialist functional responsibilities, within a framework set for them by the leadership.

As the business continues to grow, enjoying a period of relative stability, the tension between the senior manager group and their subordinates increases. The leadership are seen to be less in touch with the markets and the needs and attitudes of customers, while those at the sharp end feel they are better placed to know what is really good for the business. While they may acknowledge the desirability of consistent standards and uniform procedures across the business, they increasingly pursue their own initiatives tailored to local needs. Communication shifts to focus on the local unit or division. Team meetings stress the performance of the business unit, and corporate news and messages are filtered out as uninteresting or irrelevant. Newsletters for the unit spring up, and new individual logos are developed for the unit.

Lower level managers start to push for greater autonomy, and the business begins to allow greater delegation of responsibility, while talking more of local empowerment. At this time of tension and internal competition, the senior management response is to resist the temptation to reassert authority, and to delegate greater responsibility to the divisional managers, the factory production directors, and the market sector sales managers.

Decentralisation

Senior managers in the division are allowed to get on with the job, reporting regularly to the centre on progress against agreed budgets. Managers at the centre maintain a hands off approach, and focus on identifying opportunities which can be rolled out across the divisions.

Communication at the unit level fosters familiarity across, and strong identification with, the unit. Open days are held for employees' families, and social events are subsidised for employees to get to know each other. Long service awards are presented by local management. Communication from the centre tends to be only occasional, the Christmas letter from the Chairman, or the employee annual report during the financial reporting season. Senior managers visiting the divisional locations see only the senior management team, and the feeling of the centre being the corporate 'them' grows, as the centre implicitly assigns ownership of the employees' loyalty and allegiance to local management.

This stage of greater delegation allows greater closeness to the customer and faster responsiveness to the market. Employees can see who they are working for, and greater identification and loyalty makes for greater motivation and productivity.

Problems begin as divisional managers are seen to be going too far in their local initiatives without enough regard to the interests of the business as a whole. One declines to use a fellow division's manufacturing capability, preferring to contract a competitor to build products he can then badge with the company's name. Another manager runs an advertising and press campaign that cuts across corporate identity guidelines. What started as healthy decentralisation now seems to be toppling into fragmentation, and managers at the centre worry that the benefits of being a single business are being lost.

Unit managers begin to quote the Chairman's speeches on the desirability of operational autonomy, and argue about the nature of the strategic framework within which that autonomy is supposed to be exercised. Pressing on with their local objectives, operational managers initiate things within their own fiefdoms without thinking how to, or being willing to, co-ordinate with the rest of the organization.

Autonomy creates a parochial attitude, and an unwillingness to sacrifice local interests and benefits for the good of the whole business. Employees focus on local issues and priorities, and do not appreciate the wider picture. Internal familiarity with other divisions decreases, and the opinion of other divisions' effectiveness declines at the same rate. Internal competition increases, and divisions are found to be reinventing wheel after wheel.

Individual divisions hold separate management conferences, and have individual newsletters. Divisions' successes are highlighted against the perceived failure of sister divisions, and sensitivity grows among 'scapegoat' loss making, or high investment business units. Some divisional managers feel colleagues at other divisions are getting away with murder, and begin complaining of growing separatism. There is little communication between the divisions, and managers see their careers progressing within their division, rather than within the group.

Central co-ordination

In a bid to maximize the benefits of having divisions within the same group, a bid is made at the centre to halt the fragmentation. Decentralised units are merged into product or market sector groups, and more formalised planning and review procedures are established Return on capital invested becomes an important criterion used in allocating funds, and each group has to compete for, and justify, the allocation of corporate funds.

Corporate function staff are increased at the centre to develop and implement company-wide programmes of control and review for line managers. Some specialist functions, such as information technology, are centralized at headquarters, while daily operating decisions remain decentralized. Centralized purchasing is adopted to take advantage of group negotiating muscle and bulk discounts.

Consistent processes for selection and recruitment are established. Group wide management training programmes are created, and managers from across the divisions are brought together for induction and development programmes.

The corporate centre reasserts its ownership of employees, and standard contracts, terms and conditions are introduced across the Group. Share options, employee share ownership and company-wide profit sharing are used to encourage identity with the firm as a whole. An employee annual report is designed to make the financial workings of the business more easily accessible to the workforce.

Communication is coordinated more strongly from the centre. A cascade briefing system, from the Group Chief Executive down, is adopted to ensure employees in the units are fully aware of corporate messages. Corporate videos are regularly distributed, and a weekly press clipping service is established to keep everyone up to date on any developments affecting the Group.

Annual management conferences for the management teams of all the divisions to come together are staged. A corporate identity manual is circulated detailing corporate guidelines, and outlawing any deviant abuse of the logo in the units. A corporate newspaper is created, and an electronic mail service helps to link separate sites together. Job openings within the group are advertised on noticeboards and circulated in the mail. The Group corporate logo now features prominently on internal communication, and local newsletters are phased out in favour of locally tailored editions of the Group newsletter.

All of these new co-ordination systems prove useful for achieving growth through more effective allocation of a company's limited resources. They prompt managers to look beyond the needs of their local units, and to feel a part of a greater whole. Employees still identify with their local units, but are bolstered by the security of being part of a financially strong group, and the kudos of working for a well known corporate name their friends recognize from the advertising campaign.

Managers retain much of their local decision making responsibility, but spend more time accounting for, and explaining decisions to the centre. The proliferation of functional staff at the centre and the increase in initiatives on all fronts sponsored by the centre starts to erode the time managers have to do their jobs. Lines of communication become entangled, as functional managers at the centre bypass the operational line management chain and go direct to their dotted line, functional reportees in the units with requests for information, market statistics and progress reports on initiatives. Local management team colleagues complain about conflicting instructions, competing claims on their time, and lack of coordination between functions at the centre.

Bureaucracy overload

The increasing number of systems and programmes begins to exceed its usefulness, and the initiatives begin to seem a diversion from the day to day business of serving the customer. The choice is forced between serving the external customer, and supplying the internal customer at the centre with reports, information and updates. As the message to become market led spreads down the business, and corporate standards of quality are pursued, local managers become increasingly disenchanted with functional managers at the centre pulling rank to force them to do things at the expense of the customer. Since those at the centre are not familiar with day to day operational pressures and local pressures, their requests inevitably appear insensitive and untimely. At the centre, functional staff are equally exasperated at local managers' lack of responsiveness, grudging compliance with requests, and their lack of understanding of pressures and demands put on the corporate centre.

Parties on all sides complain of a deluge of paper and criticise the bureaucracy that has grown. One man's bureaucracy being another man's system, the apparent consensus on the bureaucratic overload masks the fact that bureaucracy is the word that each gives to the other's system, and conceals the lack of shared objectives and definitions of value.

Managers who have been around for a while are able to build up a shadow network of informal contacts, and can get things done by using relationships and contacts rather than following what they perceive as increasingly cumbersome procedures. Managers use their informal networks to make up for the shortcomings of the formal structures and systems. When cooperation between divisions is needed, people do favours for each other and put themselves out for the sake of the relationships.

When the perceived bureaucracy goes too far, the informal process assumes greater power and importance, as managers use it to bypass the frustrations of the system. Managers take pride in knowing who to contact, and what strings to pull. This works well to get things done to meet tight customer deadlines, but it also acts to bypass official lines of communication and thwart any management initiative for change.

Networking

Once the organization and the markets it serves have grown too complex, for regimented systems, formal procedures and controls are seen as too inadequate to manage the complexity of the business. There is a need to use more of the informal power of relationships to make the organization work. Faced with the erosion of their hierarchical power, and only having line power anyway over people below them, managers start consciously to form their networks, and to engineer informal contacts.

Working with their teams, managers help them identify the networks of influential colleagues whose help and support is needed. Departments who are critical to their success are identified, and their people invited to sit in meetings, updates and presentations to get some understanding of different perspectives, pressures and priorities. Breakfasts and lunches are hosted to allow people within departments that rarely meet formally to get together, in the expectation that contact will create greater familiarity, a higher rating of each other's effectiveness and greater cooperation.

The move to managing a network, rather than a hierarchy, requires a more flexible approach to management. The focus is on solving problems quickly through bringing together teams from across functions. Teams are assembled to meet a particular problem, and disband once the problem has been addressed.

Communication centres on building networks as a means of creating cooperation and sharing knowledge. Conferences of key managers are held frequently to focus on major problem issues. Business forums are held to keep people up to date on industry issues, customer plans and activities in other divisions. Senior managers tour the units to listen to employees in informal sessions, and upward feedback is seen as vital to progress.

People who need to cooperate with each other are brought together both for social occasions, and to discuss business issues. The aim is to create contact and familiarity, and so increase trust and goodwill. Managers from areas across the business are brought together at off site sessions and are trained in behavioural skills for better team work and resolving conflicts.

Communication is organized across the network as well as within units. Forums are held in which colleagues from different divisions present and discuss solutions to common problems. Functional networks are established, so that professionals who do not share the same reporting lines can come together to discuss relevant technical and professional issues. Electronic discussion databases allow them to continue debates and pool views, approaches and experience, despite geographical separation.

Typically, the formation of a strategy begins with the question of what it is that employees want from communication. It has proved better to take a different approach – ask not what your people want from communication, ask what your strategy requires of your people. Start with the business strategy, and begin looking at what was required from which people within the organization, before looking at what communication approaches might help achieve it.

From the point of view of achieving the business strategy, the organization asks itself the question 'What is it we need from our people, right now, and in the future?' This allows them to map out the people within the organization on a range of objectives, featured as steps on the Com-

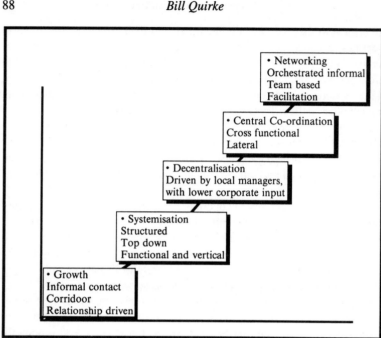

Figure 5.1   Stage of development and communication style

munication Escalator. This approach focuses on what is needed **from** employees, not what is needed **by** employees.

There are different groups of employees from whom different objectives are required for a given time period. Some may need for the moment only to be aware, others to be wholly committed. For the best investment of scarce time and resources, there will be a need for the organization to differentiate between employees, and to prioritise from whom it needs what over a time period.

Different organizations will find themselves on different steps, and will aim to move up by a different number of steps. They may aim, as a priority, to be selective, and take some, rather than all, of their people up the escalator, at different rates. Representing this as an escalator is done for a number of reasons. It is a continual dynamic process, and the idea is to keep all members of an organization moving up it.

There is a fast growing emphasis on two way communication, changing one way team briefings to two way meetings, and the practice of managing by walking around. The shift is toward more informal, less structured communication at the level of the level of the immediate line manager and his

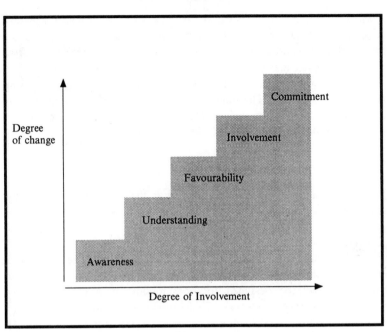

Figure 5.2   The communication escalator

team. Socially, there tends to be less formality and distancing between manager and subordinates, and a recognition that it is the quality of the relationship rather than hierarchical power that makes the team work. Away from the line team, however, communication is less a function of relationship than of technical execution.

It is tempting to be drawn in to the intricacies of technology and media, focusing on execution rather than the soundness of strategy and the appropriateness of methods being used. The most frequently used means of communication identified by employee attitude research and communication reviews suggests that there is a clear mismatch between what is needed and what is used.

- Newletters
- Memos
- Team briefings
- Departmental meetings
- Noticeboards
- Video
- Electronic mail

Most of these are processes that are aimed at creating awareness, and, on a good day, understanding. Add to this that the greatest source of information that employees report is the grapevine, while preferring to hear things from the immediate line manager, and the scale of the mismatch becomes clearer.

Different communication channels and tools achieve different communication objectives. The more the organization needs an employee to move toward the upper end of the escalator, the more face to face communication is needed, and the more time is involved.

Awareness

Means of creating awareness will range from the corporate identity, press coverage, announcements on the bulletin board, internal and external advertising campaigns, to payslip inserts, memos, continuous strip displays, direct mail, and employee annual reports. They may also include video, computer disc, and electronic mail. These media will generally be at arm's length, call for little interaction or response, and allow for little feedback. They will be designed for consumption by a broadly defined audience, with little tailoring. Their production will require mainly executional skills, expertise in imaginative design and production quality, accessible writing, and efficiency of distribution. The test for communication will be did people either receive, or get a chance to see the message in a form they found appropriate.

Understanding

The shift from awareness to understanding is one of feedback and additional information, tailored to the needs of a more closely defined group of people. Communication may be more face to face, and more interactive. The aim here is not simply to present messages, but to provide rationales, get feedback and refine the communication until it gets through. It will also focus on getting feedback to check for understanding.

Such processes could include management conferences, roadshows, satellite broadcasting, videoconferencing and customer feedback forums. Meetings will tend to be presentations, with a small number of people presenting to audiences. The focus will be on striking a balance between professionalism of presentation, a degree of interaction, and communicating to large enough groups to make an efficient use of time. There will be a disciplined format in which the presenters retain the initiative to communicate, and interaction is through question and answer sessions at the end of presentations.

Support

Pursuing the more ambitious objective of support means a significant shift in interaction. It is not enough here to get people to understand what is happening, and what its implications will be. The aim is to elicit acceptance, if not of the change itself, then of the need for, and the rationale behind, the change. Employees may not like what is happening, but they can accept why it is happening, and support the logic with colleagues, family and customers.

The focus will be more on education than presentation, with input from outside the organization, a review of parallel trends in other industries, and a review of the changing dynamics of the business. Such sessions could include business forums, training events and customer seminars. A guest speaker from another organization may share relevant experience, or a management guru may be asked to chair discussion and challenge thinking.

Numbers will be limited, and the room will be arranged to foster interaction. Presentations will be less formal, with continual discussion, rather than set question and answer periods.

Involvement

The aim is as much to get employees to share their pre-existing reactions, concerns and objections as it is to provide them with management thinking. These processes will be far more of a dialogue, with the avowed aim of sharing thinking, assessing implications, exploring alternatives, and reviewing best means of implementation. There will be a greater recognition that communication is a dialogue between partners, with the aim less of getting the message across, than listening to reactions and pooling experience and expertise across hierarchical boundaries.

Communication will not be limited to a conversation between managers and subordinates. Colleagues within specialities and across functions will gather to talk independently, and exchange ideas and information either face to face or at arm's length.

Team meetings will be used not only to disseminate management thinking, but also to identify and solve issues that prevent the team working effectively, improve processes and reduce costs.

Cross functional project teams will work to solve issues identified by the team meeting process.

Feedback forums will be called in which employees feed back to their managers the issues that are proving to be obstacles, and requesting they resolve the issues with their own colleagues.

Speak up programmes will be used to encourage the raising of issues or concerns that stand in the way of the business.

Interactive conferencing will use IT systems to continue the debate, to share information and to set agendas prior to meetings.

Commitment

Commitment comes from a sense of ownership, and ownership from having participated in the development of strategy and solution. Gaining commitment will entail a high degree of working through the pressures affecting the business, reviewing possible competitive scenarios, and the strategic options open to the business. High degrees of interaction and participation, flexibility for expansion of particular points, and ensuring everyone is clear and has the opportunity to contribute, makes this a time intensive process.

There will be time spent in syndicates and breakout sessions for colleagues to share thinking and check each other's perceptions. Feedback will be in shirtsleeves sessions, airing concerns and challenging management thinking. The forums will be relatively informal, with a loose agenda, and room for employees to set the pace and the issues for discussion. There will be a facilitator, rather than a presenter, and the focus will be on ensuring people feel safe to raise issues, and that the debate is aimed at a constructive resolution of perceived problems.

The style of meetings will focus on openness, and feeling safe to raise issues. Talkback sessions in which the Chief Executive meets with people from all levels of the organization, informally at lunch, or more formally through invitation to team meetings, will demonstrate a willingness to accept feedback without retribution and in a spirit of constructive enquiry.

At the bottom of the communication escalator, the focus is on the distribution of information, one way, to a passive audience. Toward the middle, the balance shifts to greater dialogue, and face to face communication. At the top end of the escalator, the focus is more on management willingness to listen, and do less talking. Toward the bottom of the escalator, the focus is on the task of communication, and the efficient distribution of information. As you climb toward the top, the emphasis shifts to the quality of the relationship.

It may simply be too much to try getting everyone up the same steps of the escalator. Organizations which lack the simple pipework of communication – sound and credible information channels, directories, pay and benefits, etc., may need to spend time getting the basics in place before pursuing innovative technologies or radical sharing of views and opinions.

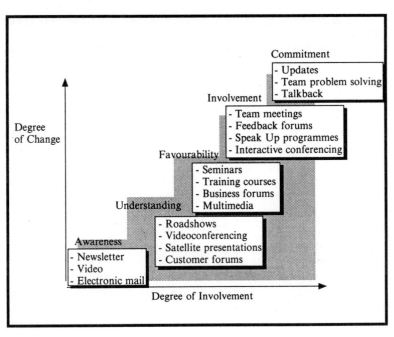

Figure 5.3   Matching processes to objectives

CONCLUSION

The communication expertise needed for the future may continue to include technical knowhow about production tools, but it will certainly demand the ability to identify how communication can help achieve the business strategy, and a knowledge of the variables that affect communication within the organization. The internal communicator will need to be both a consultant in the communication process to the internal customer, and an expect scout familiar with the cultural landscape of the business.

Bibliography

P. F. Drucker, *The Coming of the New Organisation*, Harvard Business School.
J. R. Katzenbach and D. K. Smith, *The Wisdom of Teams*, Harvard Business School
W. J. Quirke, *Communicating Change*, McGraw-Hill.
J. Smythe, C. Dorward and J. Reback, *Managing the Corporate Reputation*, Century Business, Random House.
K. Thompson, *The Employee Revolution*, Pitman Publishing.

M. Tracey and F. Wiersema, *Choosing Disciplines or Choosing Customers*, Harvard Business School.

F. Trompenaars, *Riding the Waves of Culture*, The Economist Books.

S. Vandermerwe, *From Tin Soldiers to Russian Dolls*, Butterworth-Heinemann.

6 Community Relations

Warren Newman

I start with two statements which the Institute of Public Relations Board of Management has decided will supplement its long-standing definition of public relations:

> Public relations is about reputation – the effect of what you do, what you say and what others say about you.

> Public Relations Practice is the discipline that looks after reputation – with the aim of earning understanding and support, and influencing opinion and behaviour.

The essence of modern public relations practice is first to deserve a good reputation; then, by planned communication, to enjoy the reputation you deserve. Nowhere is the principle more clearly applicable than in the field the profession calls community relations. Community relations is about being a good corporate citizen.

WHAT IS CORPORATE CITIZENSHIP?

What do we mean by being a citizen? It implies a relationship with a community which offers benefits but also carries responsibilities. As a citizen you can vote and are entitled to the protection of the State via a system of law and order, social security and healthcare provision. In return you are expected to work, pay taxes and help raise the next generation. The good citizen also contributes in other ways – by participating in communal decision-making (local politics) or by making donations to charity. The *very* good and wealthy citizen establishes Trusts and seeks to ensure that the community is a better place as a consequence of his involvement. Such individuals offer patronage to the arts or commission the best architects and artists to design and adorn their homes and offices.

Corporate citizenship is based on the notion that business corporations have similar legal and moral responsibilities to those of individuals. This is not a question of pure corporate altruism. In a very inter-dependent society it is sensible for business to get involved with communities for reasons of enlightened self-interest. In this chapter I hope to illuminate the benefits to business of planned and managed community relations policies.

STAKEHOLDERS

In the jargon of current business-talk the word stakeholders is taking root and it is a valuable idea. It reflects the realization that companies have responsibilities beyond shareholders, notwithstanding their legal obligations to their shareholders. We now ask who are the people – individuals and organizations – on whom the future of the corporation depends? Put that way it is clear that employees, suppliers, customers and the community in which a company trades do have a stake in its prosperity and are affected by its behaviour towards, for example, the environment. We hold therefore that corporations should be socially responsible and be held accountable for their lapses. Society expects business to make a profit, but not at any cost. It expects the corporate citizen to give as well as take.

WHAT DOES A COMMUNITY NEED?

If we look at the needs of a typical community evidently some things are beyond any company to provide. Business can only pay its local and national taxes and rely on government to supply such things as law and order; schools; healthcare and social services.

Business can play its part in making a community prosperous so that its people can be gainfully employed. It can contribute expertise and money to enhance education. It can look after the health and well-being of employees while they are at work and contribute to the provision of recreation and cultural amenities that they might enjoy in their leisure hours. It can avoid polluting the water in which its stakeholders might swim. It can set a good example by having socially aware employment policies.

The company that wants to earn a good reputation will take care to nurture the surroundings in which it does business. The young people it wants to recruit will be impressed by its social responsibility towards the community and the environment. They will certainly be better educated if business has made clear what it expects from schools and colleges and has made a contribution towards achieving those results. Local government and other organizations might make better informed decisions because business is involved in some way.

Large firms that deliberately try to source their needs from local small suppliers will be helping develop a prosperous community. Companies that encourage participation in all aspects of local affairs will be spreading their reputation while helping. They might also be giving their people a special form of training by allowing them to spread their wings in a different environment.

Graham Millar, Managing Director of Nestlé Rowntree, confirms the benefits of planned community relations programmes: 'Reputation and goodwill are vital to our business. By actively contributing to the community we have developed and earned a reputation with people, with our customers and with our employees, as a respected and responsible company.'

COMMUNICATING WITH YOUR LOCAL COMMUNITY

Good deeds will earn their rewards but the shy corporation will only get part of the benefits available. Having earned the right to a good reputation a corporation needs to let people know about their community-friendly policies and actions. The local media – newspapers, radio and television – are different from national level. Their readers or listeners naturally have a great interest in local individuals and businesses. Their journalists know they have to be able to return again and again to reliable sources of information and therefore will see themselves as community leaders – involved and approachable and dedicated to accuracy. Indeed the principle of enlightened self-interest means that they want a thriving commercial community that can afford to advertise and, through paying salaries, enable readers to be able to afford to buy their papers.

Within any community are people that the senior managers of businesses should get to know. Members of Parliament represent constituencies and do like to be kept in touch with commercial success or problems. A working relationship will pay dividends should difficulties arise that require legislation to be promoted or resisted. Similarly ward councillors should be nurtured as political friends on the local authority: the first time you meet them should not be when you apply for planning permission for some controversial plant.

Officers of the council may turn out to be even more important to you than elected councillors. Invitations from big business to be briefed on how a company is doing are likely to be accepted by chief executives or their staff responsible for planning, development or finance. They want early warning of financial difficulties in a large local company that might cause political controversy. They do not want to arrive at their office only to find that a large source of jobs and income to the council has disappeared – and they did not know it was likely to happen.

In any community there are leaders of thought whose view of an organization is important. They include bankers, professionals like solicitors, doctors and teachers, trade union leaders, community workers and other business people. There are also activists who may take an interest in your business because of the nature of what you do. They may be local branches of national environmental organizations or local protest groups worried about emissions from your factory chimney.

Learn a lesson from the nuclear industry. Operators of plant that worries people maintain regular contact with local opinion leaders, produce newssheets, hold consultative committees and make sure the local authorities never forget how many jobs are involved in their business. The nuclear operators need public permission to operate and want to be seen as safety conscious and reliable. The key is to maintain relationships and become indispensable to the broader running of the community

An award winning case study of community consultation and information went to a brilliantly conceived programme by Derek Dutton of British Gas (North) who walked away with the 1993 IPR Sword of Excellence. He had to prepare the community for a pipeline across Hampstead Heath in North London. So many famous people and politically active figures use the Heath that the secret was meticulous research to identify every person and organization who might be affected and keep them fully briefed every step of the way. Derek and his team turned a problem into a triumph by talking to people, listening to them and responding to legitimate concerns.

GETTING INVOLVED WITH THE COMMUNITY

So community relations programmes mean you have to get involved with local life. It is part of the job of senior managers, as ambassadors for their organization, to give time and expertise outside their business. Involvement means joining in the work of organizations for, or representing commerce and industry. Examples are the Rotary Clubs and Round Tables; Chambers of Commerce; regional offices of the CBI or Business in the Community. Of these it is Business in the Community that dedicates itself to energizing the commercial world to involve itself (and uses royal influence as an engine of encouragement). It believes that business leaders should participate in economic development, education, environment, employee volunteering and equal opportunities programmes. In

1986 HRH The Prince of Wales launched The Per Cent Club under the auspices of BiTC. Its sole activity is to bring together once a year the chairmen or chief executives of member companies who sign the pledge! The undertaking is to donate no less than half a per cent of pre-tax (UK) profits, or one per cent of dividends, to the community. Included in that giving can be financial assistance such as cash, sponsorship, loans and venture capital funds, secondment of staff, professional expertise, time given voluntarily by employees, and the donation of goods, equipment, buildings, and the use of company facilities. Involvement may be with any charitable organization, or community or development activity, such as employment, job creation, local regeneration, education and training, the environment, arts and music.

This is a very broad definition of company charitable activity and covers all the options discussed in this chapter. Members of the Per Cent Club are encouraged to talk about what they do, especially in their annual reports. They like to feel part of a growing elite of large companies who are making their community programmes an integral part of their business and see mutual benefits in their involvement.

Neil Shaw, Chairman and Chief Executive of Tate & Lyle plc, voices the commitment: 'We have long valued the concept of partnership between business, the public sector and volunteer groups. Our community activities both in the UK and abroad, focus particularly on initiatives in the localities of our plants and the provision of direct assistance for individuals seeking further educational attainment. In addition, we also encourage secondment of employees to particular projects in the belief that, not only can this make a worthwhile contribution to community activities, but in doing so, the experience will enable volunteers to develop their own management potential.'

Robert Clarke, chairman of United Biscuits and another founder member explains: 'Our commitment to community involvement stems from our strong sense of social responsibility combined with the realization of the commercial benefits that it brings. Good operating principles – involving ethical dealing, strong people values and a generous and far-reaching sense of community responsibility – are essential to effective long-term business performance.'

Management consultants Bain & Co in a study of corporate community involvement, reported that companies have found that the more they operate their programmes as an integral part of their business, the greater the impact they are able to have on the community and the more they benefit themselves. The most commonly cited benefits, reports Bain, relate to employees.

'Companies are finding that community involvement can successfully and cost-effectively help build employee morale, create the right employer image and assist the development and recruitment of staff.'

GETTING INVOLVED IN LOCAL GOVERNMENT

You might release staff to take part in local politics. To be chairperson of a committee of a local authority or to be its mayor, is very time consuming. Unless business encourages its staff to stand for election to local authorities, the ruling bodies of communities will be dominated by geriatrics or unemployed young activists. There is a mutual benefit in getting involved. The staff person on the council is getting to know what is happening locally and can act, without charge, as your local government consultant. You will have easy access to public papers that may act as leads for business development.

With a little thought firms will discover that they have facilities that local voluntary organizations crave. The chance to use your photocopiers or computers out-of-hours, can bring enormous gratitude at little cost.

Employers moan about the state of the nation's education system but they can do more than moan. They can become school governors and bring the insights of business to the teachers who have never been exposed to the commercial world. You can develop links between your company and one or more schools. In the London Borough of Tower Hamlets business gives an incentive to young people to turn up at school regularly by offering a guaranteed job as a reward. One of the favourite schemes gives opportunity for trainee managers and teachers to swap places for a while. Both get a better understanding of the each other's worlds. Pupils might be given work experience opportunities while managers give time to schools to teach about their company.

It is even possible nowadays to have a school with your own name by financing the successors to City Technology Colleges. The new scheme specifically empowers a voluntary-aided or opted-out school to change its name to meet the needs of a sponsor. (Other schools need not apply.) With the government expecting industrial sponsors to put up the first £100,000 it is just as well they can offer something beyond a place on the Board of Governors. Business has rightly been cool about investing in the earlier City Technology Colleges which would benefit a small elite while antagonising most of the education world. Government has become too ready to expect commercial interests to pay for things that are properly the financial responsibility of the public sector. You should be very sure that there is a sound commercial reason for getting involved in any project. Donations that are politically controversial can alienate as easily as they create goodwill.

CHARITABLE DONATIONS

Which leads to the thorny subject of charitable donations. Simply giving money is of dubious benefit. It becomes a matter of the whim of the organization's top management who gets money, since you cannot support every good local cause. One way around this problem is to involve employees in raising money and in deciding who will be the beneficiary. Allied Dunbar, for example, matches the fund-raising efforts of its employees in its headquarters town of Swindon and releases their time to get engaged directly in the charity. For example, their employees might raise money to give young handicapped people an outing *and* organize the event. This approach turns charity into real community involvement. The Business in the Community organization can tell you about member firms who have successfully adopted this approach.

The Managing Director of Texaco was asked to explain why they had gone for staff involvement with a single charity of their choosing. He agreed that for an oil company of his size he could easily have reached into a drawer and written a cheque. But he would have missed the great opportunity for staff development as people at all levels of the company revealed hidden talents through managing fund-raising activity. People got pleasure by being deeply involved.

EMPLOYEE VOLUNTEERING

Employee volunteering has now started to become common with its own Community unit within BiTC. Prince Charles launched the initiative in 1990 to encourage employee involvement. The idea is to combine community needs with employee skills under a formal and managed scheme. American Express says employee volunteering is its most substantial involvement in the community and it likes the dual benefits of helping people while developing its employees. It also builds a high profile in the community as a good corporate citizen. Big name companies like ASDA Stores, IBM, Royal Mail Letters and Whitbread are active supporters of this route to community involvement. IBM Public Affairs Manager Sarah Portway explains: 'Encouraging employees to be involved in their local communities seems to us to be a winner all round. The community gains access to our most valuable asset, our people. Employees learn valuable skills that can enrich both their professional and personal lives. We gain from a more motivated workforce.' Another organization active in this field is The Prince's Trust Volunteers which runs schemes for employees to become involved in training courses for unemployed youth. Employees gain an understanding and appreciation of the views and feelings of young people from different ethnic, cultural, social and regional backgrounds. They also develop their team-working skills. Business in the Arts encourages senior executives to help arts managers tackle projects. The arts community benefits and managers get to test their capabilities in a new and often exciting environment. 'Business people and the arts together are a vital creative force in the community' says Colin Tweedy, Director General of the Association of Business Sponsorship of the Arts (ABSA).

Above all, companies can discover hidden talents among their staff when they release them to volunteering projects. Freed from the formal constraints of hierarchical organisations it is surprising how much talent we manage to suppress at work!

GETTING THE COMMUNITY INVOLVED WITH YOU

You can gain valuable goodwill by bringing your community to you. Hold an open day to let people see what you do; or plan routine plant visits with, perhaps, a retired employee as a guide. For some organizations open means open to everybody. For others it means separate invitations to councillors or teachers or local magistrates.

A water company held consultative meetings to discuss future investments. The people who came said they did not want publications: they wanted to see for themselves where water comes from. In fact all the water came from underground sources and could not be seen. But the company laid on exhibitions and displays at their head office and the crowds flocked in. No longer were they an anonymous 'water board'.

As an employer you should be sensitive to the needs of minorities in your area and try to give some jobs to people from ethnic minorities or who have disabilities – like being aged over 40! Do you really need an all graduate workforce? One large company adopted that policy and saw its staff turnover soar as frustrated young people sought promotion to more challenging jobs with other organisations. Yet the company was depriving the opportunity of work to hundreds of non-graduates who were perfectly capable of doing most of the jobs and instead were consigned to the dole queue.

BUILDING ON CORPORATE SPONSORSHIP

When I selected an arts' organization for my group to sponsor I was very careful to assess their ability to contribute to community relations activities by operating companies. Générale des Eaux uses its sponsorship of the London Mozart Players mainly for corporate hospitality. But we have taken the orchestra to play in regions where we trade; have run a family concert for the customers of a local water company and have provided our local education authorities with the chance to run music workshops in schools (including schools for the disadvantaged.)

PLANNING FOR EMERGENCIES

All the good you do with community relations activities can be brought to a crashing halt if you mishandle an emergency. Disasters can be anticipated and emergency responses rehearsed. You will be developing your community relations if you involve local emergency services in your thinking and practising. If appropriate you should involve the fire brigade, police, ambulance service and local authority emergency planning officer in your deliberations. Even the local newspaper might welcome being involved in your simulation of how you deal with a bomb scare or glass found in drinks.

EMPLOYMENT RESPONSIBILITIES

For many companies the decision to relocate shows most sharply the responsibilities they unavoidably have to a community. Some towns are effectively company towns, relying too heavily on the jobs and income from a single large employer. Organizations like British Steel became adept at helping such communities manage the transition by encouraging alternative employment strategies and providing seed financing. The neighbourhood you move to may not be quite so distressed but you will be watched as a big newcomer and will have to earn respect through a proactive community relations policy. The people you take with you will want help in integrating into the new location and planned corporate involvement will help them make new relationships.

An example of a potentially hostile community won the Best Corporate Community Involvement Campaign award in the 1992 PR Week Awards. News International was moving to a new multi-million pound printing plant outside Knowsley in Merseyside. Its community relations intentions were hampered by locals who had been enraged by *Sun* newspaper reporting of the Hillsborough disaster. PR Firm Mason Williams was asked to develop a programme to integrate employees into the community and introduce News International to the area. Their solution was The Greenforce Initiative – an environmental scheme involving several community projects. One helped a school turn its disused playground into an environmental garden. Greenforce brought together the Government-backed Groundwork Trust and community groups. It involved 2000 schoolchildren and 27 schools in the projects and planted 1000 trees and 4000 bulbs. News International worked with the local council on the project and used press coverage to establish its role as a community-friendly employer.

SUMMARY

Big organizations might develop corporate policies for handling community relations. Smaller enterprises will react instinctively to local needs and opportunities. In both cases their actions will derive from recognition that commercial organisations are part of communities rather than detached observers. It is a symbiotic relationship and therefore one of the deepest most organisations will have.

There will be time when corporate money is needed to solve intractable problems like deprivation in Liverpool and other inner-city areas. There will be times when corporate management skills will be the most useful response. In other places the build-up of small involvement will best meet local needs. This chapter has suggested that it is a senior management responsibility to respond to local needs and creatively. To manage your enterprise you have to be involved in influencing the environment in which it operates. By working in this way you will expand business contacts, improve the local environment, help expand the local economy and help build pride and confidence in the communities you serve.

Public relations counsellors often say that an organization cannot decide whether or not to have a reputation: only to choose what effort it puts into developing a good one. Community relations is bit like that. You have corporate relationships with your local community whether you like it or not.

Whether such relationships enhance your company reputation is up to you to manage.

Bibliography

Cuthip, Centre and Broom, *Effective Public Relations*, Prentice-Hall.
R. Haywood, *All About Public Relations*, McGraw-Hill.
W. Howard (ed.), *The Practice of Public Relations,* Heinemann.
S. Sleight, *Sponsorship: What it is and How to Use it,* McGraw-Hill.

and various publications from:

Business in the Community and The Prince's Trusts, 8 Stratton Street, London
    W1X 5FD.
Institute of Public Relations Library: Sword of Excellence Case Studies.
Involvement & Participation Association, 42 Colebrooke Row, London N1 8AF.

7 Parliamentary and European Union Relations

Douglas Smith

Success in government affairs – commonly called lobbying – has four principal ingredients: good advance intelligence; skilful timing; a mature, realistic presentation of one's case; and finally sustained pressure, the ability to fight it all through. One could well argue that these qualities lie behind every successful business activity. It is therefore remarkable how frequently such a commonsense approach is neglected by those who, whatever their personal feelings, simply cannot afford to ignore politicians and the political world in which we live.

Constantly I meet businessmen who believe that occasional meetings with MPs or peers – even having some of them grace their board of directors – are adequate to keep themselves both informed and fully protected against any legislative moves that might arise. Others rely upon their trade associations or unions as an efficient early warning system or fire service, should such be needed. In some cases their trust is well reposed. The National Farmers' Union, for example, does not miss any tricks; we all know how well food interests have been defended both in Britain and in the European Union (EU) over the decades. But other industries are not as efficiently served: indeed, by relying upon trade groups, they have neglected to properly alert themselves. High penalties have been paid for such sloth.

The principal reason for failure is an inability to recognize that political change is a long and slow process but one that can, nonetheless, suddenly catch up with you. A famous statesman likened politics to a tortoise; it hardly appears to move, but seems to travel hundreds of yards if you take your eyes away for a few minutes.

Equally, it is not easy for people outside the world of government to realize how the system works. Indeed, some innocent souls have spent a lifetime in Parliament itself – and picked up their knighthood at the end – without appreciating half of the interrelating factors involved. This is because there is, of course, no set pattern in the body politic, any more than there is for the human body or the law. There are, however, good rules to follow, and one does not need to be a constitutional expert to appreciate them.

LONG-RANGE INTELLIGENCE

First, there is the need for advance intelligence. By this we do not mean simply the monitoring of parliamentary activity, significant though it can be: one has to look a great deal further back than 'The Week in Westminster'. In democracies, change is wrought through political parties. Their policies are formed most frequently when in opposition; in government, politicians tend to be rushed off their feet with difficulties of the day – implementation rather than formation. When governments support new legislation in a hurry it is invariably half-baked – the poll tax being a striking UK example. So it is a wise person who, realizing that no party can rule forever, keeps an eye on what opposition groups are about and makes friends there as well as in the party of government.

Some wild ideas quickly gain ground among opposition parties. Inevitably they are looking for policies that contrast with those of government; indeed, they rightly commence their thinking from a different standpoint. Academics and theorists abound in this area. Often there are fanatics as well, in Winston Churchill's definition of the fanatic as a person who 'never changes his mind and never changes the subject'. Once a policy is hammered out in some arcane and distant discussion, it can gradually become part of the party manifesto, loudly applauded by further groups of enthusiasts at conferences and embodied in the Queen's Speech should that party gain power, without once being firmly exposed to reality. The hazard is then far more difficult to resist.

Clearly, great issues of policy – the nationalization versus privatization argument, for instance – will not be easily influenced by any one interest group, however powerful. Yet more detailed application of such policies can be amended (or even killed) by judicious action in the earliest stages. An example is the privatization of the bus services in England and Wales. Fundamental Conservative thinking here was well set in the late 1970s with the proposal to push back previous policies of nationalization. Yet it was the National Bus Company that was chosen for dismemberment and private sale, rather than the more costly British Rail, not only because it was a simpler process, but also because one particular academic gained the ear of one particular opposition spokesman at key moments in the manifesto–making process. It is perhaps amusing to speculate how a proposal to impose local charges for farm properties, haystacks, and the like would fare in Conservative circles. The argument would run that these properties are protected by police and fire services like all others, and such services are supported out of our taxes: so why should they not be equally, or at least partially, open to levy? One suspects that this notion would not even reach the floor of a party conference before being firmly dismissed as illogical and certain to raise food prices. Farmers' profits would, of course, not be mentioned at any stage.

The importance of intelligence as against simple monitoring should be plain. It pays to have sources back at the roots of policy formation, in Whitehall and the EU as much as in British political parties, who are able to scent danger at the earliest stage, when it is far easier to defeat. Equally, there are opportunities for positive moves to be made influencing policy and effecting change: again, these need to be planned early and promoted discreetly.

Such in-depth monitoring poses difficulties for busy executives and all but the largest organizations. If a company belongs to an efficient trade association or union, then one of these should be carrying out the task – not simply monitoring the daily flow of paper from Westminster but also studying Select Committee proceedings as appropriate, or policy-forming reports to government and opposition. Such groups, or specialist units within the major companies, will also have their own teams of experts developing research and support policy with skills equal to (or even surpassing) those within government itself.

MONITORING HELP

The average chief executive cannot, however, hope to have these resources at his disposal. Staff and material costs are high, and are hardly justifiable in covering an area where action could well be required only occasionally. Yet management might very well not wish to rely solely on trade association information, which will, of course, be equally open to the firm's competitors. Fortunately, an alternative exists: specialist companies can be employed to provide both daily monitoring and high-level intelligence services. By acting for a range of clients, such consultancies or monitoring groups can meet information needs at modest cost. As with any press cuttings agency, the fee depends upon range of subjects covered. But a similar same-day, or next-day, service can be provided, with urgent news passed on directly by phone. The consultancy might well make use of POLIS, an information-retrieval system set up in 1978 by the Commons Library and the Central Computer Agency. External users can input into this system to check on references to them in Parliament, and companies sensibly do so.

An efficient monitoring agency could also provide political information summaries as part of the service. These are most helpful to the busy executive. They include appropriate articles from influential media as well as a digest of political developments, broken down into subjects. At key moments in the political year – Budget time, for example – more detailed reports might be provided. In short, there are several routes available to gain an adequate background, enabling you to know not only when to move but also what current issues are about when you do. Placing an individual problem or opportunity into political perspective is often as important as identifying it in the first place.

The major error of many even large concerns is their failure to have a purposeful strategy in the public area, to set out company objectives and then test them coldly against present and likely future political scenes. If a realistic plan of action can be forged and contacts built in advance, then success is frequent. As an illustration of the nature of such advance contacts, all-party groups are important. They exist on nearly every major subject in Parliament, some far more active than others; if there is not one covering the desired area of activity, it can be formed. A small group of MPs and peers with greater knowledge of an industry or topic and, more important, a real interest can be invaluable, first as a sounding board for any campaign, then as allies in the fighting of it. Such support can be equally valuable in simply gathering information or sounding out government reaction. There are some 70 000 written or oral parliamentary questions asked by MPs every year. Many are party-political in aim, but others are a small part of various lobbying campaigns.

Information alone will not, however, influence decisions, nor will simple internal agreement on a corporate strategy. Timing, persuasion and pressure – the three other principal ingredients of lobbying success – are also necessary.

TIME SPENT IN RECONNAISSANCE

Let us assume that we are now armed with accurate information and our arguments are clear. We must then ask: are they achievable and, if so, on either a short or a longer term? There really is no point in assailing civil servants or politicians if the moment is not right: better by far, in such circumstances, to plant seeds for future germination, or move towards a far more limited initial objective.

It pays to be quite ruthless in assessing the changes of success or the degree to which it might be gained. There will always be voices recommending action at once, with all cannons firing, drums beating and troops advancing on a broad front. Political reactions might be more genteel than the machine gun in repelling such an approach but repelled it will be nonetheless.

Before attacking, your skilled general will, in any event, have engaged in reconnaissance. It should not be entirely factual. Friends made well ahead of any campaign are able better to assist you. For example, if you have bothered to meet and brief some involved civil servants on your background – and there is always an excuse so to do – then useful advice on detail could well be provided in times of need. Assuming that you have the good sense not to pressurize from the first but simply to open up friendly lines of contact, their response later might be crucial. The same applies to Members of Parliament. They are concerned mainly (apart, of course, from wider matters of government or specialist committees upon which they serve) with their constituencies and in most cases also with their careers. Accordingly, they will be attracted to people who can assist them in both, and do so with maximum economy of effort for all concerned.

The approach taken by a large American computer specialist over recent years is a model example to consider. The firm was aiming to expand in Britain, but was equally keen to win business from government as from private concerns. Yet its policy was deliberately long-term and down-key. Members of the firm met and briefed all MPs where they had offices or factories without once asking favours. Indeed, by skilful publicity of local visits from their MPs, they built a useful bank of goodwill. Evidence was offered and freely provided to inquiries being conducted in Parliament on matters of mutual concern. This brought close contact with civil servants as well as MPs and peers who had a specialist rather than simply constituency interest. An all-party group had events sponsored, again most modestly. In short, the American concern was increasingly perceived as British, and built up a core of understanding, with sympathetic friends both Westminster and Whitehall. So when it faced a real crisis the fire engines were ready and waiting to assist.

This brief example of competence prompts other advice for those dealing with parliamentarians. Indeed, speaking with MPs and peers is likely to be a task for chief executives rather than any advisers. A poor impression is created if politicians do not have the opportunity to hear arguments at first hand, however much they appreciate the role of any advisers in organizing the occasion or framing a brief.

Too frequently one hears it said that back-bench MPs and peers are mere cyphers, and that time spent with them is wasted. This is not so. Of course, it is civil servants who handle matters of detail and also, with Ministers, issues of policy. I have already stressed how connections with them should be cultivated. But if only a few MPs and the properly informed peers pursue an issue, it cannot be neglected; nor need one rest with any departmental brush-off. It is all a matter of judgement and balance. To pursue any case solely by way of parliamentary protest is to risk offending those who are fundamentally important; on the other hand, if you place yourself entirely in civil service hands, without pressure potential elsewhere, you are running needless risk.

Light Socket Rescue

Another example proves our point. Several years back there was a major revision of electrical safety regulations. The new code was, of course, drafted by civil servants, one of whom was consumed by the belief that our usual light sockets, if within easy reach (like standard lamps), presented a real hazard to safety. He recommended that such lamps should be fitted with an Edison screw rather than the common bayonet socket.

The industry learned of these proposals far too late. Their intelligence was poor, and they had not been fully consulted. Certain manufacturers were therefore faced with the expense of major retooling of equipment to meet the proposed standard, and this was linked to a likely fall in sales because of increased complexity in fitting.

A consultancy was called to advise and act. They quickly identified a dozen MPs from the three main parties who had constituency interests – those places where the manufacturers concerned were based. A suitable time was chosen for a meeting with these members in the Commons. It was explained how damaging the proposals would be to the industry but that they were needless in any event. Home accident records had been combed to demonstrate that very few accidents occurred by fingers, even probing juvenile ones, being thrust into live lamp sockets. A succinct, written brief set out all these arguments. It also gave an indication of immediate action, since a Committee was looking at the proposed regulations only the following week. Members were convinced. A number promised to attend the Committee to put their constituents' case.

It was here that the consultants were wily. They knew the minister who was leading the Committee to be a reasonable and intelligent man. They guessed that he did not appreciate the full extent of any disturbance that might be created. And they wanted to alert him to the proposed objection because ministers who have traps sprung on them can well turn obstinate, regardless of the force of arguments employed. The minister's parliamentary private secretary – a fellow MP who acts as his eyes and ears in Parliament – was briefed and conveyed the message. When the Committee met and objections were raised, they were sympathetically received; the proposed clause was taken back for review and subsequently dropped.

Of course, the manufacturers saw that all credit was given locally to their respective MPs, who had responded with such energy and good sense. The minister was also pleased at having avoided making an obvious error, and at being recognized by colleagues as a man who was capable of flexible action.

Clearly lessons emerge from this modest example of democracy in action. MPs were carefully selected and skilfully briefed – a short statement of the case, backed by figures and indicating what action they might then take. All the parties were involved; this was not a political issue. One person was selected to put the manufacturers' case (although others were present), and one person again constructed the brief. It was therefore a concise presentation. And when victory was achieved due recognition was paid to those who had helped, which created warm feelings all round. The cost of this lobbying exercise, incidentally, was reckoned in hundreds of pounds; it saved the industry quite literally millions.

I could match such a story with others less successful. The tale is told of a captain of industry who, feeling threatened, similarly called together a group of MPs. He hectored them for half-an-hour not only in detail on his particular problem but also on faults in government policy as a whole. There was no written brief to back his words. And he wore his wartime medals clanking on his chest as he spoke. Do not be over-elaborate. MPs are quick to grasp points but cannot be experts on all subjects. They are, however, good at asking questions and skilled at tactics, if given proper time to act. Do not enter into broader political argument, however strongly you may feel. Keep with the subject. Respect MPs' busy time schedule – and recognize their efforts, win or lose.

Their Lordships' House

I referred earlier to the briefing of peers. Frequently the Upper House is forgotten entirely in lobbying approaches, which is unfortunate and ill-advised. There are more than 1200 peers in the Upper House (compared with 651 MPs), of whom about one-third are life peers. Active membership is, however, far lower – around 700, of whom 300–400 could be described as regular attenders.

Their Lordships differ fundamentally from members of the Lower House. They are, of course, older but often far more experienced. Many have been leaders of industry, commerce, the unions, and the civil service. There are senior scientists, medical people, and soldiers. Party politics has its place but debates on sweeping issues are less significant; reasoned argument on points of detail is more common and much sensible amendment of the intestines of legislation results therefrom. Government whips hold less sway here, nor does government always overturn changes made to Bills in the Lords.

Accordingly, it pays to brief peers who have an interest in your field Their knowledge and support can prove equally helpful. They are often stimulating and extremely well informed company, and should not be treated lightly. Lords' committees are also more receptive to evidence offered than similar groups in the Lower House. And, because of the people involved, their reports can carry weight in government or policy-forming circles.

Their Lordships are best approached by letter and subsequent meeting in the Upper House. Since they do not have constituents to concern them, peers are often more free for visits to premises or for lunch. With MPs meetings in the constituency itself are usually more sensible on local issues. Peers will especially welcome back-up facilities if they concern themselves with campaigns. Most do not enjoy even the modest secretarial support of their Lower House counterparts.

Meeting the Minister

There is one further area where direct chief executive involvement is likely in any public affairs activity. This is when meeting a minister directly. Such an occasion will almost certainly have been preceded by contact at a lower level with the civil servants most involved. But if progress is not being made here and a policy decision is required, then an appeal to the minister concerned is sensible. Few civil servants will resent such a move, provided it is courteously approached.

Unless the company in question is large, in which event contact can be made direct, quite the best route to any minister is again through one's constituency MP – or several of them, if they can properly be mustered. It is better if they are of the same political persuasion as the minister, or otherwise reasonable people not likely to embroil one in doctrinal disputes. But there are few ministers who will resist a meeting, arranged through their Private Office, with a group that has sensible points to raise and members to support them.

Again, groundwork is vital on such occasions. Too often delegations sail in, are most courteously treated by the minister and his attendant staff and are then ushered out with polite words of reassurance and future action. At the end they have only a cup of civil service tea to show for their pains. If resistance is anticipated, then a parliamentary question or two in advance is sensible, not simply to establish some facts ahead of the meeting itself but also to give due warning that you are serious and are prepared to press your point. Once more a briefing note should be brought with you and placed before the minister at the start of your discussion. It will be short on opinion but hard on fact. This will be the basis of your meeting. Do not be deflected from it. Ideally, use a single spokesman, supported by colleagues. Never, never disagree in front of the minister. At the conclusion, courteously ask when and how you will hear the minister's decision. Too serious a delay should not be accepted, and reasons should be on hand as to why a prompt response is necessary.

I must stress that, however well any concern is organized, changes in government Bills and certainly in policy are not achieved quickly or easily. On major issues governments are rarely deflected, but on matters of detail and practice there is usually room for change. The skill lies in identifying and exploiting this marginal ground, using all the machinery described plus other techniques too numerous to list. Discretion is equally necessary in the selection of your allies. Some MPs can do you more harm than good on certain issues. They are not always the people you might imagine – so be sensible and diplomatic in taking advance soundings.

To return to the basic point, it is preferable by far to ensure that ill-conceived legislation does not reach Parliament in the first place, which takes us back to fundamental intelligence work and civil service grassroots contact. 'Prepare, prevent' is a sound motto for every lobbyist. It applies even more when your aim is the procurement of business rather than any campaign as such. Here there are rules to follow and pitfalls to avoid which can be successfully approached only by planning. This applies as much in the EU, which we now examine, as in Britain.

EUROPEAN APPROACHES

Lobbying in the European Union has become increasingly important to all commercial concerns, and at last proper attention is now being paid to it. There remains a tendency in Britain to devalue the role and importance of the EU. Many MPs at Westminster, and sadly not a few civil servants in Whitehall, are keen to do this, principally in defence of their own position and power. It is foolishly naive. Both constitutionally and politically, the EU already plays a strong part in governing Britain. Wide-ranging decisions are taken in the Union which now pass directly in UK law or have to be introduced into it by the government. Indeed, over half UK legislation starts in Brussels. The areas covered are considerable – from company law to VAT – and fast-growing. They cannot be ignored. Yet monthly one hears reports of lavish receptions called at Strasbourg that clash with a Budget vote; glossy brochures arriving long after the key debate; a costly presentation neglecting some important EU languages. British firms in particular need to guard against cosy lobbying analogies with Whitehall and Westminster. Indeed, it is American firms, with their experiences of the complex Washington system, who often present their cases best in Brussels.

We must start with some basic facts. First, power within the Union is diffused. The right to initiate legislation lies with the Commission of the European Union in Brussels, which also has executive power and the right to enforce policies already agreed. It can therefore take legal action against, and fine, companies breaking EU rules.

The Commission has 17 Commissioners, serving four-year terms, and controlling 11 000 executive staff recruited from member states. Here is the Union's largest legislative source, managing the Community budget (half agricultural) but also holding others powers. For example, anti-dumping action, competition policy, the classification of goods, and the free movement of goods are Commission responsibilities, all of which are exercised more and more frequently.

Then there is the European Parliament, elected directly in five-year terms, and currently (from 1994) consisting of 565 members, of whom 87 are from the United Kingdom. The Parliament is there to advise but is steadily acquiring greater ability both to block and to amend legislation and even to initiate it. Over 85% of amendments by the EP to Single Market legislation were adopted into the final text. It has also, of course, traditional powers to vote the Budget and sack the Commissioners.

Since the Maastricht Treaty we also have the Committee of the Regions as a third force. It is too early yet to judge its impact but without doubt it will greatly strengthen the regional, grassroots voice of the European Union.

The Council of Ministers is perhaps best known to the British. Theoretically, it has the last word on legislation, and also takes decisions on matters like farm price reviews. But the Commission is not the Council's civil service; that must be clear. In Council meetings ministers aim to win decisions in their own government's favour but there is a spirit of compromise abroad. All 12 member states are represented on the Council; the UK has 10 votes, as do France, Germany, and Italy. There are 76 votes in all.

More important perhaps than the individual ministers themselves are the national permanent representatives which, when they meet together as COREPER, undertake much of the political bargaining and detailed drafting. Although there is only one Council, in practice it meets in many forms according to items under discussion. UKREP is Britain's office with COREPER; it comprises some 60 officials drawn from various Whitehall departments.

The European Court of Justice, sitting in Luxembourg, is to many the most powerful institution of all. It is the supreme constitutional authority of the EU. The Court – never to be confused with the European Court of Human Rights in Strasbourg – hears Commission cases against firms or governments, as well as appeals against Commission decisions and fines. It also interprets Union law on behalf of national courts. And its rulings are final.

Those seeking finance should not ignore the European Investment Bank, which has invested £7 bn each year across the Union in the form of loans EU and administers a variety of EU borrowing and lending operations.

Finally, there are the various national authorities implementing Union laws – governments, regional and local authorities, agricultural intervention boards, bodies like the Manpower Services Agency (for example, in the case of the EU Social Fund), and so on.

Again one must stress how the relationship between all these bodies is in a state of flux. Indeed, one can anticipate far more uncertainty and shifts in power within the EU than will occur in the more settled scene at Westminster. A simple example will suffice. With the entry into force of the Maastricht Treaty more power is moving to the Commission and, especially, the European Parliament. Such changes are, of course, significant. They mean that the closest watch must be kept on the EU in years to come.

A second vital principle to grasp in dealing with the Union is that EU law is a legal order with characteristics of its own. The English legal tradition laces great emphasis on the literal meaning of statutes. As A. P. Herbert once remarked, 'If Parliament does not mean what it says, it should say so.' But Union law is different. Each of the nine official languages is of equal validity, even if the meaning is subtly different in each language, and the intention of the legislators is important.

Union legislation takes four main forms;

1. *Recommendations*　There have no direct legal effect but are intended to guide national legislation.
2. *Regulations*　These are directly binding once published in the Union *Official Journal*. So are decisions on such matters as fines.
3. *Directives*　These are binding as to 'the results to be achieved' but Council Directives have to be enacted by national procedures within a time limit. Legal rights can be created even if a particular country fails to meet the deadline.

4. *Decisions*   These are like directives but apply to only some countries or companies, not Union wide.

CONSULTATION AND COMPROMISE

A final main element in this complex political scene is the large number of Union documents produced. These are of varying status and require the most discriminating monitoring. In an average year some 7000 pieces of draft or final legislation emerge.

To follow the trail of proposed Union law through all the relevant documents can be a tricky task. Any proposal usually starts life in the Commission as a situation paper. At this stage the Commission will consult interested parties, but with a marked preference for lobbies organized at a Union rather than a purely national level. Hence the plethora of lobbying groups by trade associations in Brussels.

The Commission will then publish its draft proposal, which goes to Parliament and Council. Parliament refers it to a specialist standing committee, which appoint one of its number as a *rapporteur*. Other interested committees may appoint draftsmen of opinions. These appointments are made on a political basis (there are currently eight political groups), but the task of the *rapporteur* is to represent the views of the committee as a whole. The committee will report to a plenary session of Parliament, which will vote on both the draft Commission proposal with any amendments and the Committee report. Meanwhile, the Council of Ministers will have considered the proposal in working groups and COREPER (Committee of Permanent Representatives – National Ambassadors to the European Union). Attempts will be made to reconcile the Parliament's and Council's views, the Commission acting as honest broker and guardian of the treaties – the outcome of this process is known as a Common Position.

Once adopted, the law is published in the *Official Journal*. If it is a directive, however, it must now be enacted in the 12 member states, where its track can best be followed through the Commission's ASMODEE data base.

It will be seen from the above very necessary description of processes how the emphasis is on consultation and compromise. This contrasts, often very sharply, with procedures in the UK Parliament

Threat to Duty-free

The way in which the British Airports Authority (BAA plc) approached the threat made to a substantial part of its income in the early 1980s provides a good illustration of the various forces at work within the Union.

The BAA exists primarily to run airports but a large part of its annual profit in fact arises from commercial activity, notably its duty-free airport shops. It was, therefore, properly alarmed to learn that the whole principle of duty-free allowances for EU travellers was at risk as a result of a judgment in the European Court of Justice. This arose when a German supermarket chain challenged the legality of sale of tax-free dairy products aboard craft that sailed on day trips deliberately outside territorial waters – the so-called Baltic Butterboats. Procedural law required that the case be referred to the European Court, as duty-free allowances are governed by EU law, and it duly declared in July 1981 that the Butterboats were in contravention of regulations.

It was here that the BAA became concerned. It knew the Commission had introduced legislation in 1980 to abolish duty-free allowances. To several senior officials such sales to people travelling within the Union were a straight contradiction of the idea of a common market. The Commission proposal was rejected at the time by member states well aware of the popularity of duty-free goods. But if this principle were now revived in the light of the Court's Butterboat verdict, it could well rule unfavourably for BAA. A further difficulty lay in the refusal of Germany to accept the Butterboats ruling. Elections were due there, and it was considered unwise to remove cheap butter from the poor while retaining cheap duty-free goods for more wealthy air travellers.

The lobbying task was, therefore, twofold. First, the aim was to make it widely known that duty-free allowances were at risk. The Commission was making reassuring statements on this which were known to be deceptive. Second, there was a need to press for legislation to remove any existing ambiguity over duty-free allowances and in effect, to protect them forever.

Publicity was quickly achieved. This was a strong news story, and there were important interests other than BAA prepared to weigh in. A Brussels press conference for European media was followed by national briefings, all aimed at alerting member governments to the potential loss of income and unpopularity.

The Commissioner concerned was approached and proved sympathetic. Members of the European Parliament were also fully briefed, the emphasis here being on the certain anger among the electorate when MEPs stood in the forthcoming elections if European travellers had lost a privilege that other travellers retained. And in Britain the government was persuaded to intervene in the Court in the Commission's case against Germany. Member states can make such an intervention where they have a direct interest. Other countries also intervened in this way, but Germany presented a special problem. Here it was necessary to provide the government with arguments discouraging the existing stance on cheap butter. A survey was therefore commissioned to show exactly which social groups used airport duty-free facilities. They proved to be far more broadly based than many had imagined, and so the less wealthy would be hit by proposed legislation as well.

All these moves served to highlight arguments against restrictive legislation across the Union. Questions were asked in the European Parliament; letters poured into the Commission from a range of interests; the media had a field day. Despite this, resistance did not collapse overnight. We were repeatedly told that proposed moves were in the direction of fiscal harmonization, and the duty-free allowance was an obstacle to this happy Euro-objective. But in early 1983, a year after saying that legislation to support duty-free allowances was impossible, the Commission approved a draft directive that could provide a foundation for exactly this. The pressure had, in effect, caused a major rethink, followed by tactical withdrawal.

The issue was revived with the entry into force of the Single European Act. To have duty-free allowances within a single market seemed to many a nonsense. The Commission therefore published a list of some 300 legislative measures which would be necessary for the completion of the single market, and this included the abolition of duty-free allowances.

A lobby group called the Duty Free Confederation was formed and fought the battle on the basis of the damage which would be done to airports', shipping companies', and airlines' profits and jobs. As a result they were able to negotiate a derogation, or stay of execution, until 1999.

The problem, however, will not go away, and the battle will no doubt be joined again as 1999 approaches. There is a strong argument that the proposed abolition of duty-free sales on ships in international waters is a breach of an international shipping convention. Watch this space.

Although a lengthy and continuing case history, the duty-free issue does illustrate how campaigns within the Union need to be conducted at a number of levels and one must be aware precisely of the powers of all bodies concerned. This applies to all lobbying, of course, but within the EU the formula is especially complex, and accordingly calls for wider knowledge of institutions as well as greater skill in timing. The need for a Brussels base, or consultants in that fair city, is now an essential for the lobbyists wherever they may be centred in Europe.

FIGHT AND PUBLICIZE

Two particular lessons also emerge from the duty-free saga. First, do not be daunted by statements from officials that 'of course there will be a change'.

Whatever the theory, in practice one can always fight and delay. Witness the Japanese success in resisting decades of action against the mass sale of their goods abroad, while the land of the Rising Sun remains protected against similar foreign competition.

Second, never neglect the media. I shall return to this theme, but over the abolition of duty-free allowances – a topic affecting millions – the clamour aroused in press and on radio was a very significant factor in changing minds.

Broadly, the lessons of EU activity are similar to those applying in Britain. They are, in brief:

1. Maintain a strict watch on impending legislation. The Commission publishes annual programmes, and each incoming president of the Council (it changes every six months, revolving around the member states in turn) makes a statement of intent. There are also long-term programmes in the form of white and green papers. Early warning means greater influence and freedom to move.
2. Make use of Members of the European Parliament, who can obtain any Union documents; put questions to Council and the Commission and get answers to them; amend legislation; be a focus for contacts; and influence not just one but 12 governments. It is not, of course, necessarily the case that UK members will be the best contacts for particular UK campaigns but at least they will direct you to parliamentary colleagues who can better assist. If the cause is acceptable, the country matters less than you might imagine.
3. Keep in close touch with UKREP (the UK embassy to the European Unions). It is far better to lobby the UK government early rather than rely on a British veto at the end. It might well not be forthcoming or effective.
4. Use Union law. If you think you are being hit by unfair competition, then complain to the Commission. Clearly, such steps call for specialist advice.
5. Even if you are not in an assisted area, ways still exist of winning EU finance. This applies to the fields of high technology, training, and education in particular.

As with UK lobbying, it pays to build bridges in advance. There are officials and politicians within the Union who are delighted to talk with genuine business groups or particular interests – indeed, most bureaucrats positively welcome such approaches, which sadly is not as common in Whitehall at levels which are far higher than their counterparts elsewhere.

LOBBYING THE TOWN HALL

Local authorities are almost entirely neglected by many commercial concerns, thus demonstrating a strange set of priorities. Of course, British local government is a waning force. Recent years have seen a significant, and saddening, diminution of their authority to the benefit of a Whitehall which scarcely has a record for more efficient administration. Yet local government accounts for more than a quarter of all public expenditure in the UK and employs well over 2 million people. It also is responsible for decisions closely affecting business, the majority of which remain small.

Statute law controls British local government very tightly. It works to Acts of Parliament, with few general powers to move as it chooses, in contrast to the practice in most other EU countries or North America. Yet there are still wide areas of action, and flexibility of decision can be shown to those who approach town halls correctly.

A first need is to establish which particular department of a local authority is concerned with your requirement. Powers differ widely between the various units but there is always an officer in authority, and invariably he or she will be helpful to an early approach. The word early is again important. Often companies will proceed to a detailed stage of planning and preparation – for example, the site of a new plant – without even making contact with the council whose approval at several levels is ultimately essential. There is then considerable annoyance at the changes the council subsequently insists on making. Thus a letter to the head of the department in question (a telephone call having told one who it will be) should outline the nature of any request ahead of any meeting to discuss it.

The levers of real power in any council usually rest with a few individuals. In some authorities they are senior officers – the chief executive is concerned in most matters of a commercial nature at some stage, as well as the directors of finance and planning. In others, elected councillors hold the whip hand, usually chairs of major committees selected from the ruling party. The movement towards, in effect, semi-paid councillors has accelerated in recent years. Usually decisions are made between a few leading councillors and the senior officers, but, with more than 400 councils to consider, there can be no strict pattern to follow. Again, therefore, we fall back on reconnaissance. Your first contacts should guide you but a little background work, not neglecting the local press, is well advised.

The majority of local authorities are keen to assist business development in their areas. Invariably a council will have some form of development plan by which it is guided. A sensible company will study this and frame any request to meet its objectives. As negotiations proceed the key people can quickly be identified. If councillors, they will appreciate as much as MPs and peers being treated with the respect properly due to those giving their time and effort, often on a voluntary basis. And they are keen publicly to be associated with any success just as much as your national politician. Officers are equally concerned to produce positive results. The more senior the officer, the more likely you will be to meet with willingness to give support rather than nitpicking objection. This is a generalization, clearly, because some low-level officers in town halls are magnificent; but others are not.

Frequently local newspapers, and also to a growing extent local radio, can be most helpful. If they fall in behind your campaign, it can be a great stimulus to both councillors and officers. A band-wagon can begin to roll, carrying any proposal along and speeding the various processes. Councillors from the area most concerned will wish to be involved if the project is, for instance, a new plant or extension to existing works. They may well be modest back-benchers but their advice and voices could assist if delays emerge. Rest assured also that they will rarely shield their faces from the local photographer or fail to speak to any available microphone.

USING THE MEDIA

Mention of local press brings us logically to the whole area of media support in government affairs activity. This is frequently neglected by lobbyists, who often enjoy legal backgrounds and therefore concentrate upon constitutional aspects of the task. What they sometimes forget is that politicians and civil servants are influenced by the media as much as the rest of us. They read – admittedly not always in detail or in depth – the daily press, some serious weeklies, and the Sundays in particular. And of course they watch television, or listen to the radio. So journalists – press, radio or TV – should be friends of the lobbyist as much as any civil servant or politician.

Again the point is illustrated by details of a recent campaign. This was conducted on behalf of Airbus Industries, the European aviation consortium, which needed to get national funds committed in order to move ahead with a development programme matching American competition in the coming decades. There were obvious political allies for the campaign – those with component factories in their constituencies where the job factor loomed large. There was also one serious opponent: a Prime Minister who, supported by her Treasury, was deeply sceptical about whether investment in aircraft manufacture would ever yield a sensible return. In this doubt she was supported by some heavyweight aviation correspondents whose knowledge of past events in the industry was considerable and whose attitude towards Airbus did not have the grassroots motivation of our politicians.

To convert the serious media to the Airbus cause was, therefore, a primary objective. The usual public relations methods were employed – one-to-one senior briefings; visits to Airbus headquarters (fortunately, well placed in gastronomically attractive, sunny France); factual surveys to demonstrate a healthy commercial trend. Over a period of months key journalists began to amend their hostile line. The political allies, much encouraged, worked on the Prime Minister. Eventually she was won over as well.

Media are, in fact, an immense ally in the lobbying process. At Westminster and Brussels there are hundreds of journalists and broadcasters casting around for stories. These must have a political thrust, but then that is nearly always so with public affairs activity. And they must involve politicians in person, which is usually the case anyway. The degree of political attention it is possible to attract to any campaign if there is radio, press, and especially television interest will be surprising even to the cynical. Of course, the aim is to gain favourable comment, and no politician will speak against personal or party convictions. Equally, the promise of a camera whirring away on Abingdon Gardens, against a backdrop of the Great Palace, will bring MPs rapidly out of Committee or Chamber; and, once they have declared themselves publicly for a cause, their help can properly be sought in other ways. The ability to gain publicity for politicians is, as I have previously stressed, one of the best cards in any campaign pack.

This lesson – the promotion of others before oneself – is a key to the effective lobbyist craft. Many concerns are capable of massive self-deception in their campaigns, and can be encouraged in it by less worthy practitioners. Mentions in the Chamber; early day motions; adjournment debates; successful drinks parties in Westminster – all leave one with a warm feeling of achievement without, in the event, gaining real ground. Politicians and civil servants, who after all can be confronted daily with requests from a dozen interests, are adept at the sympathetic answer that has no substance.

Given a sensible corporate plan for pushing any particular interest, the next steps are good timing and persuasive arguments. Stamina comes into it, too, as our case histories have illustrated. If one can demonstrate pressure will be sustained until victory, or a sensible compromise is reached, then opponents will often be more inclined to settle than to fight. But the greatest attribute of them all is modesty. Let others wear the garland of laurels. It matters not at all, provided your point is proved and the campaign won.

Bibliography

N. Ellis, *Parliamentary Lobbying*, Heinemann.

J. Grant (ed.), *The Commercial Lobbyists*, Aberdeen University Press.

B. Patterson, MEP, *Lobbying: an introduction to political communication in Europe*, Government Policy Consultants, Brussels.

M. Smith, *Lobbying: an introduction to political communication in the UK*, Government Policy Consultants, London.

E. and E. Wittenberg, *How to Win in Washington*, Blackwell.

8 International Corporate Relations

Bill Byrnes

CORPORATE RELATIONS IN A CHANGING WORLD

The world in which we live and work has changed. It has become truly international. Investments, technology, products, skills and ideas cross boundaries with increasing ease. The issues which exercise the minds of governments, businessmen and women and campaigners are world issues. The international marketplace is no longer the preserve of the multinational. Its influence reaches companies of every size, anywhere in the world. Citizens throughout the world share concern for the environment, health and the consequences of development.

At the same time, cultures, institutions, economic development and standards of living continue to reflect different histories and social values. We continue to live in a world of nation states. Today, business and corporate relations are conducted in a world of division and diversity, bound together by economics and communications, and attempting to grapple with issues which affect us all. The implications for corporate relations are profound, now and in the future. To see why, and to respond effectively, we need to understand the changes taking place and the directions in which they lead.

A TRULY INTERNATIONAL WORLD

Once upon a time, to be an 'International Company' was really quite distinguished. To be a 'Multinational', with its hint of power and mystery, was even more exclusive. Nowadays, to be anybody in business society, it is essential to be 'Global'. Everywhere in the media, the City and academia we encounter global corporations, with global reach, selling global brands, in global markets, in a world shrunk to a global village. We do not encounter these things so often in real life, and many of the people managing so-called global enterprises find it hard to recognise themselves. They are, however, in no doubt about the dramatic changes which have taken place in the world around them, or about the equally dramatic changes they themselves have made in the way they run their companies.

To get beyond the hyperbole, and to try to understand these changes, it is helpful to divide them into three

- Changes in the world economy
- Changes in international governance
- Changes in the world's citizens, their outlooks, their concerns, and the influences acting upon them.

Changes in the World Economy

The economic changes are perhaps the most obvious:

- Great reductions in transport costs; containers, mechanical handling, roll-on-roll-off, motorways, airfreight.
- The impact of information technology on logistics, management information, customs clearance and supply chain management.
- Continuing economies of scale, leading to international sourcing and production.
- Reductions in tariff and non-tariff barriers to trade.

Business has adapted by becoming more international in its reach and methods of management

- More truly international companies; more international trade by companies of every size.
- International brands, responding to international lifestyle changes.
- Efficient national retail networks, sourcing internationally and giving international access to companies of every size and location.
- International services in fields like finance, insurance, property and advertising.

Changes in International Governance

The internationalisation of how we govern our social and political affairs is perhaps less obvious. But any reader of the serious press must notice the increasing amount of law which is international or stems from international treaties or agreements. Even where there are no GATT or Single Market treaties the regulations of one country increasingly influence those of their neighbours. What the US Food and Drugs Agency decides on pharmaceuticals or food safety will influence regulators throughout the world. Technical standards have to be acceptable internationally if goods are to be exported. And where there are no regulations, there are often codes of conduct from official bodies like the United Nations and OECD, or business organizations like the ICC.

Businesses everywhere are affected. What they can do to defend their interests will depend upon their size and geographical reach. For some it will involve corporate offices in Brussels, Tokyo and Washington. For a smaller company it may require active participation in Trade Associations, and lobbying national governments. But, today, companies must defend their interests internationally or accept the consequences. The challenges are international. The response must be effective internationally.

Changing Citizens and Consumers

Behind the regulations and codes of conduct lie the concerns, outlooks and attitudes of increasingly educated, well informed citizens and customers, influenced by increasingly sophisticated pressure groups and deluged with information by a media whose international scale and speed of coverage is almost breathtaking.

The changing concerns of citizens around the world are the most fundamental changes of all. They are certainly the most crucial for corporate relations. Technology makes things possible but, in open societies, consumers and voters decide how it is used. Even the largest companies compete to understand and respond to consumers' needs and aspirations. Politicians sometimes try to lead but, more and more in the modern world, only in directions sanctioned by voters.

If there were ever any doubt about the leading role of the citizen, it could hardly survive the most cursory examination of the way in which issues like the environment, animal rights, or packaging have come to centre stage, for both companies and governments.

THE IMPLICATIONS FOR CORPORATE RELATIONS

The consequences for companies wishing to communicate, and influence decisions, are fairly clear

- More and more of the key issues are international – racial and sexual equality, product and consumer safety, animal rights, biotechnology, packaging, oppressive regimes, irregular or uncertain payments, international investment, sourcing and factory rationalisation, the welfare of local communities and so on.

- The decision-making and opinion-forming centres are, more and more, either international or located outside home countries.
- Business partners are more likely to come from outside the home country and, themselves, to operate internationally.
- The publics to which a company must appeal are, increasingly, outside the home country, and are influenced by pressure groups in those countries, some of which have international affiliations.
- The work of Trade Associations and business groupings in which companies participate is increasingly international in scope.

If this is the world in which corporate relations are to be conducted, how do we respond to it and exercise influence effectively? Fortunately, the basics of corporate communications and public relations still apply. The task is to apply well known principles in a new, more complex, world.

Reputation, Character and Trust

The starting point is reputation. If reputation is important at home, it is absolutely crucial abroad. Reputation contributes to many things, but the most important of these is trust. Trust is above all essential when uncertainty is present, when participants know each other less, and when different outlooks, histories and cultures are involved. The more international the context, the more likely we are to find such uncertainty and lack of knowledge.

A corporate relations function will spend much of its time dealing directly, under pressure, with concrete, current issues. The extent to which it succeeds will depend a lot on the soundness of the case, the identity of interests between the parties, and the skill with which the case is made. But it will also depend, to a great degree, on the reputation of the company and the quality of the relationships which it has developed around the world. Understanding why this is so gives us some insight into international corporate relations.

If potential business partners, officials, or ministers have to choose whether to ally or co-operate with your company, they will need to know who they are dealing with. They will always start with some impression of you. It may not be very factual or concrete. It is likely to concern your standing in the industry; whether you are generally seen as responsible, dependable and prudent; if you are thought to be innovative or conservative; and so on. These words are all words which we use to describe people, words which suggest character or personality. It is significant that we talk about companies in the way we talk about people.

If Chief Executives or Officials do their homework, they can learn a lot more. They can check out our published accounts, our brands, facilities and technology. They can read brokers' reports, check our press cuttings and take out references.

If they do all this, they will certainly end up with more facts. But much of what they learn from our track record and the people they talk to will still be in terms of our prudence, trustworthiness, co-operativeness, decisiveness, and all those other words which add up to our character. The more far reaching the relationship, and the more they will be tying their reputation to ours, the larger the part these things will play in the decision, because the success of the undertaking will depend upon how we conduct ourselves in future situations which are inevitably uncertain, hypothetical and hard to define.

Such modern business methods as quality management, outsourcing, strategic alliances and supply chain management place increasing emphasis on human relationships, especially in an international context, where there are differences in culture, customs and history. They reflect today's economic and technical imperatives, and will be a continuing trend. A large part of the task of corporate relations in this context, therefore, is about building reputation, and promoting that reputation through long term human relationships.

Appearance and Reality

If that is the task, how is it to be done? Once again, the starting point is obvious – almost embarrassingly so. Reputation is not created in a vacuum. It rests upon the facts. Good or bad communications can put a better or worse face on the facts. And the best of products needs effective marketing. But, for any reasonable sized company to sustain a real gap between appearance and reality, over any significant period, is an unmanageable proposition – if only because the credibility gap will be most apparent to the employees who are required to uphold it.

More positively, facts, like fate, keep happening. We create our track record every day. If there are things of which we are not too proud, we can change. Our corporate relations function should be able to make this a positive story, and a strengthening of our reputation.

Corporate Profiles and Corporate Positioning

All this is very obvious if we are talking about damaging local environments, making dubious payments to officials or blanching the books –

though even these can be performed in varying shades, from Persil white to battleship grey.

Things become more technical when we try to define the specific public profile, image or personality which we want for our business, even more so when we attempt to position ourselves against the profiles of our international competitors, and the various stereotypes in the minds of our target audiences.

Simply to be seen as sound, honest folk is worth a great deal. But though valuable, it is not memorable. In the international sphere, in particular, we are competing for attention with innumerable voices seeking the same ear. If we are to stand out and be remembered, there has to be something to remember us by.

And, of course, we are aiming higher than memorability. We need to be seen in ways which serve our specific business needs. This means sacrifice and consistency. We cannot profess to all virtues, or to be all things to all men. In logic, enterprise is consistent with prudence, creativity with conservatism, caution with agility, and aggression with co-operation. But in the real world we must make choices. We must at least decide where we want the stress to lie.

Some of the characteristics which we will want to stress will relate to business attributes – financial strength, skilled management, advanced technology. Some will be social and human – safety standards, environmental sensitivity, openness, honesty.

The mix has to hold together, to be consistent. But we should aim higher than consistency. We are trying to build something which will fix itself in the mind, as a coherent, living whole, a picture of a certain sort of business, a character, a personality. In marketing terms we are not putting together a formulation or a product specification. We are designing a brand, and a brand that will succeed in the international markets, appeal to people from different backgrounds, and stress those features which are central to their relationships with us.

The task seems formidable, but it is unavoidable. Whatever happens, we will have a public profile. Our only decision is whether we attempt to manage it ourselves, or have others do it for us.

THE INTERNATIONAL CORPORATE PROFILE

Everything which has been said about the corporate profile applies both nationally and internationally. Designing in those parts which are specifically international starts with identifying those Corporate Issues, Business Objectives and Target Audiences which are essentially international.

The strategic external issues are likely to be few in number. Most lists would contain things like

- The environment, with special emphases, depending on our products, on processes and locations.
- Foreign investment, taxation, tariffs and discriminatory legislation.
- Operations in the third world, or under oppressive and undemocratic regimes.
- Pending legislation likely to affect us internationally on such things as permitted ingredients, packaging or disclosure.
- The need for international strategic business alliances.
- The consequences of international rationalisation and factory closures.
- Opportunities for new ventures in Eastern Europe, China or other emerging markets.

The list, or the priorities will, of course, change over time.

Implementing the International Profile

We identity issues, objectives and audiences so that we can take effective, systematic, action. Essentially, this is of two sorts

- The creation of the reputation and relationships which will advance our objectives with our target audiences.
- Direct action on specific current issues, like pending legislation.

Having got a clear view of the profile we need, we have taken the first of the classical three steps

- Decide how you want to be seen
- Find out how you are seen
- Take action to bring the two in line

For an international business, researching the existing profile can be a complex, expensive task. It will require a careful research design, and rigorous concentration on essential features – features relevant to vital corporate interests in key locations. It is unlikely that even the largest companies would have sufficient in-house resources to design and conduct the work – quite apart from achieving the degree of objectivity required.

When it is complete, the result of the exercise is likely to be some changes in the way we conduct our business, or at least clarification of our policies and assumptions. It will almost certainly involve a planned, long term programme to change or enhance the perception of our company amongst key audiences.

Defining Corporate Policies

We will want to move from identification to action as soon as possible. It is useful to divide this process into two steps

- Deciding where we stand on the key issues
- Deciding the action we are going to take.

The first is the process of policy making. An international company will need policies on a range of public issues, if only to answer legitimate questions from the public, pressure groups or official bodies; and to establish itself as a responsible company which recognises public concerns, is prepared to address them, and is open about itself.

The same work will also enable the company to put its managers in a position to respond with confidence to the questions which they will certainly face in business and private life.

The communications tools which issue from this process may differ greatly between companies. They will include pamphlets, policy papers and position statements, aimed at different audiences, and with different shelf lives. The important thing is to see that they address the issues which their audiences wish to be addressed, and which are directly relevant to the company's operations. Together, they should form a coherent publications portfolio, and fit logically into a communications strategy. Staff publications should be part of this portfolio. Documents intended for the outside world are read by employees. Employee publications reach the outside world.

The special requirements of an international programme derive from the different cultural, social and linguistic backgrounds of their target audiences, and from the greater difficulty in ensuring that messages reach those audiences, inside and outside the company. For an international business which is also decentralised, the task is even more demanding.

DEALING DIRECTLY WITH THE OUTSIDE WORLD

In a way, policy-making is easy. It must address the concerns of the outside world, but the decisions are in our own hands. When we try to change public opinion, find common ground with pressure groups, or influence the course of legislation, we play a part, but our audiences are independent agents and they make up their own minds. The sharp end of corporate relations is achieving concrete objectives in the outside world. This might involve achieving a compromise with an influential pressure group on recommendations for labelling, reporting or rejuvenation of processes. It might mean reversing damaging legislative proposals in Washington, Brussels, or Manila. It might be done by direct contact, or through Trade and Employer Associations.

In all cases we will be concerned with formal procedures, factual evidence, and logical, or illogical, argument. But in all cases, there will also be a strong informal human element. Behind the public positions there is often distrust, emotionally charged perceptions, and often just plain ignorance. Between reputable companies, serious politicians and responsible pressure groups, simple human contact can go a long way to reduce prejudices, and to reveal many, if not most, of the participants as decent people able to find common ground. Contacts can develop into relationships. They may be close or arm's-length, but they are all channels for rational discourse and understanding.

Opening the Factory Gate

Industry and commerce often attract distrust. Perhaps, if we stay so much behind our office doors and factory walls, this is not surprising. But we do have one enormous advantage. We can be useful, indeed invaluable, to any minister, official, or campaigner attempting to work in our world.

Civil servants are asked to make recommendations on topics ranging from the control of laboratory experiments, through to the regulations controlling the development of rural sites, to ingredients labelling, or vehicle weights and speeds. Even when they have technical qualifications, their access to activities in the real world is limited. They do not really like to make proposals which prove impractical. Ministers do not like to sponsor legislation which sounds effective but founders on the complexities of the real world. Sincere campaigners wish to achieve real progress. They know that much of this depends on what companies are genuinely able to achieve at acceptable costs. They too need contacts, information and access to achieve their ends.

Business can let the political world see what happens on the ground. It can show the problems and the possibilities. It can make experts available. If this is done honestly and responsibly, relationships and trust can be built up. When these relationships exist, proposals can be discussed before deals have been done inside the ministry, or positions taken publicly – when flexibility still exists. This is sometimes called 'becoming part of the process'. It takes time, effort and sincerity to achieve. In human relationships, with one notable exception, nothing can be achieved overnight. But, when good relationships are achieved, they are effective and beneficial to the company and society.

Going the Extra Mile

Internationally, companies encounter different governments, with different constituencies and differing priorities. In the third world, for example, there is often an urgent need to build up skilled management and professional cadres and to stimulate the development of indigenous businesses. The greatest contribution which an international company can make will always be through the professional training it gives to its own employees, its products, purchases and the technology it introduces. But it is possible to go a little further. Making people and resources available for the development of local small business, education, or increasing skills in local communities is a means both of giving valuable practical help and of showing oneself to be a good citizen, an asset to the host country.

IDENTIFYING AND REACHING TARGET AUDIENCES

Corporate communications is a complex process which costs money and absorbs scarce management time, especially when performed internationally. Selectivity is therefore essential

- Selection of the issues is the first step
- Definition of achievable objectives is the second
- Identifying and reaching the target audiences is the third.

Targeting audiences is the key to selectivity and cost effectiveness. The steps fall out fairly logically

- Identify the audiences which really affect your key objectives
- Identify the audiences' interests and agendas
- Define what it is you want from each of them
- Formulate a strategy and programme of action
- Create an organization capable of implementing those programmes

The audiences will differ for different companies. They will include audiences relevant to immediate objectives like influencing current legislation, and audiences relevant to longer term objectives, like recruitment, or establishing the corporate reputation.

For most international companies the list will include

- Key officials, in the home country, important overseas countries and supranational organizations
- Politicians in key locations, usually with lower priority than the permanent officials, though this varies from place to place
- Academia, internationally, both for recruitment and research collaboration
- Pressure groups in relevant areas
- Business peer groups who influence your reputation and are potential partners
- Employees who, when well informed and well treated, can be ambassadors, but badly treated or ignored may become a fifth column

The objectives for each will differ, as will the best means of reaching them. Variety and complexity apart, they do not differ essentially between national and international audiences. There are, however two points of particular relevance internationally.

Governments, Home and Abroad

There are few, if any, really stateless companies. Any who do become stateless will doubtless gain advantages. But there will also be losses. In the eyes of the German or British governments, German or British companies are part of the family. All governments seek foreign investment, but no sensible government can afford to ignore the needs of its national business sector. From the company point of view there is only one government – or two if you have dual nationality – to whom you can talk as a member of the family. It pays to be sure that, whatever your international ambitions, you remain a family member in good standing.

What are the implications of this for operations outside the home country? While politicians depend on local votes, and must look to local interests, there is a vast difference between foreign companies who are well known as friends and allies, and those who are simply anonymous, or suspected of exploiting the people and economies of their host countries. Their reception when they have cases to present will be very different.

It is not always easy to become a welcome friend and ally, but at least the steps required are fairly clear

- The government must be made aware of your contribution to output, investment and employment
- They must be convinced of your probity and standards of behaviour
- They should find you willing to be helpful, and supportive of the needs of the community
- They must know that their nationals are well treated and have real prospects of promotion

This will not happen on its own. It will require good communications, and investment in contacts and relationships.

Working actively with local companies in Trade Associations and other business groups, and mobilizing the interest and commitment of your own employees, are effective ways of becoming part of a society, not a foreign base within it. Your suppliers also have an interest in your success, as do the Senators and local communities in the places where you have sites. But their involvement on your side is not automatic. Nor can it be turned on like a tap.

Public Relations in Overseas Countries

For the most part, conducting public relations in an overseas country is no different from doing so in the home country. Programmes and structure must, of course be adapted to the institutions, facilities and preoccupations of the society concerned.

The formula 'policy central, execution local' is useful but inadequate. Clearly, the company's fundamental policies and principles must apply everywhere, and nationals must be trained and empowered to play a leading part in public affairs in their home countries. But many important decisions and strategies will relate to issues and situations which are peculiar to each country. And it will often be necessary to raise the level of representation by deploying the company's senior international executives in high level local contacts.

Because you are not, fully, a family member, work in and through local associations abroad is especially valuable. As always with such groups getting good results means putting in resource and effort over a period of time.

There will be the usual differences in facilities between first and third world countries, and differences in approach between Western and Eastern countries. The mix of what one can do oneself, with partners or through local agencies will vary from place to place. The balance between local and central input for any function is a nice judgement in any international business. The corporate relations function is no different.

International Investor Relations

Financial public relations is a specialized field. For companies with major shareholders in many countries, it is clearly a more complex process. The investors, stock exchanges, and analysists in Tokyo, New York, London or Amsterdam do not always have identical perceptions of companies, or look for the same things from them. They are specialized audiences, and need to be understood and treated accordingly.

One thing which the markets do have in common is that they are not just influenced by financial results and quantified data. Share prices depend on assessment of earnings in the future, not the past. The future is not just an extrapolation of historic cash flows. The investor and analyst have an interest in soft data, as well as hard. They must form a view of the qualitative aspects of the business, of prospects, management skills, creativity and attitudes. They are also, for the most part, human beings who read newspapers and will, quite rightly, be influenced by reputation as well as profit attributable.

Corporate relations and investor relations are part of one process, and the more international the business is, the more important are the qualitative messages likely to be. Some companies locate their investor relations in their financial department. Others place it in corporate relations. Some do both in different countries. There are good arguments on both sides. What is essential is a coordinated approach and consistent messages. Closeness to media management is particularly important. During contested acquisitions it can be critical to success.

The Media

Much communication with target audiences is, and should be, direct. Much is indirect, through the media. The media is, at the same time, highly international and surprisingly national. News travels at an astonishing rate. It is not at all unusual for Chief Executives first to learn of events vitally affecting their business from the morning paper or the TV news.

Nevertheless, almost all newspapers and TV stations are national organizations, addressing a national audience. Of course an *International Herald Tribune* or a *Financial Times* will have a significant international readership, and C.N.N. broadcasts internationally. But, for the foreseeable future, dealing with the media internationally will be largely a question of dealing with a wide range of national publications and broadcasting stations, in a great many national markets.

The management of media relations also has its special skills and specialist practitioners. This has its risks. Because it is seen as a specialist intermediary, it is easy to overstate the differences between dealing with the media and dealing with other audiences. In particular, it is easy to put too much emphasis on the individual interview, release or report, reflecting the immediacy and focus of the media itself.

The fact that the media has its own agenda and decides what it will print or broadcast according to its own values, makes it more important than ever to develop a longer term media strategy. An international media strategy will feature a set of consistent messages, directed towards particular channels, underpinned by long term media relationships, and focused on the international issues which most concern the company.

ORGANISING FOR INTERNATIONAL CORPORATE AFFAIRS

There was a time when even companies whose operations were unquestionably international could conduct their overseas activities successfully without any specific, professional corporate relations function. Adhering to local law and custom, with local management and selected partners, agents and representatives making the necessary local contacts and relationships worked very well.

Although the world is now more complex, with local operations much more a part of international strategies, and the international corporation itself much more the focus of local politicians and pressure groups, the heart of any corporate relations activity is still line management. It is they who make things happen on the ground. They are the public face of corporation in their territories. The question is not how to replace their public role, but how to support it, with training, communications materials, clear policies and specialist professional services.

In organizing professional support, the decision between what should be located in the centre and what in each country is unavoidable. There is no simple answer. Much will depend on how decentralized the company is itself, and in what way. For any large company, however, there is an overwhelming case for a strong central function as part of the total structure.

- The key strategies and policies must be decided by the Chief Executive and the Board. For really critical issues, they will often manage the process themselves.
- The outside world looks to the corporate centre for policies and holds it ultimately responsible for conformity. Essentials cannot be delegated.
- Most key issues will involve or be driven by Head Office professional staff in fields like law, finance, or safety. They need easy access to corporate relations professionals.
- A number of highly qualified senior staff will be needed to achieve the results required by large complex companies. It is simply impractical to spread these scarce resources widely.

No matter how good the central department, it is inconceivable that it could meet all the needs of product divisions, geographical regions and subsidiary companies throughout the world. What is required in each of these places will depend critically on the organisation and control structures of the business, and the key external issues with which it has to deal.

While it is difficult to generalize, companies are likely to find it easier to decide what is needed in each of these places than to orchestrate the result into a consistent international whole. This is a key role for the central corporate relations function.

External issues wax and wane. It will rarely be economic for a company to maintain the level of internal resources required to cope at all times. They are also varied. It is difficult, and usually uneconomic to retain the complete range of skills of the highest quality. Most, if not all, companies are best advised to make use of outside resources for at least some of their needs.

There are various options on the market and various ways of using them. The problem for a diverse international business is to use outside resources to meet needs in many parts of the world while retaining coherence, consistency and quality standards. There are agencies which offer, virtually, international services. There are others who operate through alliances and federations. None are equally good in all places and for all functions.

Any choice is likely to involve trade-offs between local and specific topic strength and the ease of dealing with fewer more comprehensive suppliers. That problem is not confined to corporate relations. Whatever the solution, it will only succeed if the relationships are right and the agencies allowed to become part of the family. Good corporate relations cannot be bought off the shelf.

The best structure will, inevitably, differ from business to business, depending on the company's own organization, management style and geographical spread. The choices which companies have to make, however, are often quite similar

- Which responsibilities should be located in the home country, and which in each overseas territory?
- What should be the rules and procedures operating between the Head Office and the overseas countries, to ensure consistency of message and direction?
- Which issues need to be managed internationally, and which can be delegated to local management?
- What are the most effective roles, especially in overseas countries, for public relations and other specialists?
- Which institutions require specific company representatives, for instance, Washington and Brussels offices?
- What use should be made of external consultants and agencies, and how should the home country arrangements be harmonised with local arrangements overseas?
- How much use should be made of national and international trade, employer and business groupings?

The list is not comprehensive, but when a company starts answering these questions the others will raise their heads of their own accord.

CONCLUSION

We have covered a lot of ground, very little of which has been purely international. International corporate affairs is the application of best corporate affairs practice in an international context. The beginning of wisdom is to understand that context, define objectives within it, and organize accordingly.

Bibliography

D. M. MacDowell (trans), *Against Meidias*, (*Demosthenes*), Clarendon.
J. Ober, 'What Democracy Meant to the Athenians', *History Today*, 44(1).
Sir Michael Perry, *Global Brands and Advertising*, Unilever plc.
G. Segal, *World Affairs Companion*, Simon & Schuster.

9 Corporate Advertising

Angus Maitland

Corporate advertising is perhaps the most controversial element in the mix of communications techniques available to a company. Its controversial nature arises from its high cost, the intangible nature of its results and, equally importantly, from a mixture of fear and misunderstanding among the most senior company executives. It does not deliver the direct and measurable impact on market share that a marketing campaign might be expected to achieve and this makes it difficult to justify. All this is reflected in the low and spasmodic expenditure on corporate advertising in the United Kingdom.

Why fear? Corporate advertising is not simply a sub-sector of advertising. It is the face and voice of a corporation. It is a highly public communications technique, and its sponsor cannot hide behind the editor's name as can be done in the results of a corporate press relations campaign. Its use demonstrates a clear and unequivocal commitment to the message contained in the advertisement and, in a rapidly changing corporate environment, such commitment takes courage.

Why misunderstanding? One can only speculate that the misunderstanding stems partly from poor management training and partly from the business culture of the United Kingdom. UK executives in general seem to be afraid of the media and, perhaps in consequence, affect a degree of contempt for it. There are signs that this is changing. A most visible indication has been the recent desperate attempts of companies fighting off take-over bids to make up, in a matter of weeks, for years of non-existent image projection. It is disappointing that it seems to have taken the ultimate corporate threat to focus the mind of UK management on corporate advertising.

THE RATIONALE

What can corporate advertising achieve, and in what circumstances should it be used? Both questions cannot be answered unequivocally, but a combination of research and experience has provided the basis for much greater understanding.

Perhaps the best known study on the effectiveness of corporate advertising was commissioned in 1977 by *Time Magazine* from the US research consultancy, Yankelovich Skelly and White Inc. A study of Corporate Advertising Effectiveness was able, through a delightfully simple technique of pairing corporate and non-corporate advertisers, to demonstrate, using 700 personal interviews with 'upscale business executives', that corporate advertisers enjoyed a higher awareness, a greater familiarity and a better image than non-corporate advertisers. For reasons of cost and less kindly, commercial motivation, studies such as this have been the province of major media with an interest in developing corporate advertising business. A second Yankelovich study for *Time Magazine* in 1979, investigated questions such as the difference between the effect of corporate and product advertising on corporate image. Different approaches to the question of effectiveness have been taken; for instance, the 1984 Erdos and Morgan Inc. study for Barrons analysed the findings from a mail sample of over 3000 respondents from a variety of publics on their views of the effectiveness of corporate advertising. None, however, has quite matched the elegant simplicity of the original Yankelovich design.

By 1993, Yankelovich, Skelly & White (now known as Yankelovich Partners) had conducted three further studies of note; two for a US corporate advertising agency and one for *Fortune Magazine*. The advertising studies undertaken in 1986 and 1988 concerned themselves with the impact of corporate reputation on audience behaviour.

The first of these studies, based on over 1000 personal interviews with high net worth individuals, company executives, research directors from brokerage firms and investment institutions and fund managers from the top 100 investment institutions in the US. This study drew a distinction between perceptions of the attributes possessed by companies with good reputations and the attributes accorded by these respondents to actual companies which were highly rated. The most salient of the differences concerned the role of communications in establishing good corporate reputations. When the audience rated companies in the abstract the attribute 'good communications' did not appear in the top 10 attributes. However, when actual companies were rated, 'good communications' was a key differentiating attribute for companies with good reputations.

The second study took place in 1988 and was based on almost 1300 telephone interviews amongst a sample similar to the first study. Respondents were asked to evaluate 45 companies on 18 favourable attributes and the findings showed that companies with a high overall reputation generally scored above the mean on communicating well. The correlation between the two was particularly close amongst high net worth individuals and corporate executives.

The *Fortune* study, a mail survey, was undertaken amongst a sample of 5000 randomly selected top and middle management *Fortune* subscribers. There is inevitably a degree of bias in that it surveyed those who chose to respond; it did achieve a good overall response rate of 40%. The study identified four components of what is called corporate equity: awareness of and familiarity with a company; overall impression of the company; perceptions of the company (assessed using 15 corporate attributes); and behaviour in support of the company (covering product support, employee recommendation, crisis support, joint venture recommendations and propensity to purchase stock). This study concluded that, firstly, top ranked companies, in terms of corporate equity, were found to have significantly higher price/earnings ratios than lower ranked companies; and secondly, it confirmed the findings of the initial Yankelovich study - that the more knowledgable a target audience is about a company, the more favourable its attitudes are towards that company.

An examination of the history of corporate advertising in the United Kingdom might suggest that corporations' experience of it has been mixed. Few have pursued the technique with consistency. ICI did so in the 1960s and 1970s, and theirs was the first serious TV campaign. It was intended to increase consumers' familiarity with the company and make the public aware of the ways in which ICI research and products benefited the nation. ICI was able to demonstrate a steady upward movement across a range of attitudinal measurements, and the investment the company has made in corporate advertising has been credited with the relatively high reputation the company generally enjoyed prior to its break up in 1993, both externally and among its own workforce.

There is evidence to suggest that corporate advertising needs a fairly lengthy time period to run if it is to be successful. Shell called a halt to all advertising, except that for lubricants, after the oil crisis of 1973/4. Soon the company's advertising agency, Ogilvy and Mather, began to notice small but significant downward movements in the attitudinal measurements in their tracking studies conducted among the general public. Although Shell had some reservations about corporate advertising at that stage, a short but heavy corporate campaign was mounted in the autumn of 1975. The results, measuring 1976 over 1975, showed a dramatic increase on nearly all the favourable measures. By then Esso, BP and Texaco were running corporate advertising campaigns, but they were outperformed by Shell – despite the fact that its campaign lasted only two months. It seems that Shell was able to tap the goodwill built up in investment in corporate advertising over decades. During the next decade and into the 1990s, Shell's approach to corporate advertising became more sporadic, initiated and controlled by the relevant subsidiaries.

The long-term nature of corporate advertising, and the need to consider its effectiveness in the context of other communications techniques, is well illustrated by the best known corporate advertising campaign in the United Kingdom, the £16 million BT 'Power Behind the Button' campaign. This is an example of the creative synergy that can be derived from a close working relationship between agency and client, in this case Dorland and BT's Director of Corporate Relations. Theory would suggest that the enormous success of the BT flotation, in terms of the sheer size of the issue and the number of private shareholders who subscribed, would be preceded by significant attitudinal shifts. This assumption has been encouraged by the media and is encapsulated in Newman's book (1986) on the subject in the phrase, 'the corporate campaign was the bedrock for shifting image and perceptions as well as attracting interest in British Telecom (now British Telecommunications or BT) the company.

Evidence that this is somewhat oversimplified is contained in the book itself. The corporate advertising campaign was launched in November 1983 and ended in August 1984. It was followed by a £10.5 million offer advertising campaign from August 1984 to November 1984. Table 9.1 shows the percentage point changes in six attitudinal tracking measurements between November 1983, August 1984, and November 1984.

Rather than a wholesale shift in image, the evidence suggests that the central objective of the corporate advertising campaign – the emphasis on BT technology – was achieved dramatically when the campaign ended; the measure 'use up-to-date technology' had

Table 9.1   Attitudinal tracking measurements

	Nov. '83 %	Aug. '84 %	Nov. '84 %
'Spend a lot on research and development'	28	41	33
'Provide a good service to their customers'	58	56	53
'Very profitable'	57	61	57
'Use up-to-date technology'	46	61	54
'Charge too much for their services'	51	49	51
'I like their advertising'	16	30	24

Source: BT/MORI.

increased by 15 percentage points. However, by the time flotation occurred over two months later, it had decayed by 7 percentage points. Other attitudinal measurements of a non-technological nature moved imperceptibly or declined; and still others, not shown in Newman's book, such as 'respond quickly to the needs of businesses' and 'give good value for money', also declined. What the retold BT saga often forgets, perhaps inevitably because it is not good copy, is the years of effort and investment that BT laid down long before the year preceding privatization, through an intelligent and creative corporate communications programme which gave the company a robust rating across a comprehensive range of attitudinal measurements. *That* was the bedrock on which the successful privatization was built. As Newman herself says in her book, 'British Telecom's image strengths in the Autumn of 1983 were considerable'.

By the time the 'power behind the button' campaign had ended, BT had succeeded in developing a very strong monolithic brand and, perhaps as a reaction to the company's domination of the UK market (at that time it enjoyed a market share of around 97%), there was a proliferation of sub-brands such as Merlin and Inphone, National Networks and Local Communications Services. In the early years, after privatization, when competition was developing, this help dilute any feeling of market domination. However, it also led to confusion, partly resulting from advertising and PR programmes run for these sub-brands.

Consequently, in 1986, the company decided to rationalise, once again, into a single brand and it reduced the number of advertising agencies serving it to four. The validity of addressing audiences by needs was recognised and three campaigns began, covering personal communications, business communications and specialist customers. A new slogan – 'it's you we answer to' – was developed and linked all of these campaigns. The new approach was launched with the corporate campaign 'thunderbirds' which focused on network modernization. That was followed by 'say you, say me' showing the ways in which the telephone cropped up in everyday personal and business life.

By November 1987, the much acclaimed Maureen Lipman campaign began, using the 'it's you we answer to' strapline as a continuing acknowledgement of BT's accountability to the customer The advertising programme sowed the seeds for a massive culture change at BT which was known as 'Project Sovereign' and which was coupled with a corporate identity change.

In May of 1992, BT launched 'putting the customer first', involving the personal appearance of the Chairman to promote BT's version of the customer charter. In 1993, a new campaign featuring the eminent astro-physicist, Stephen Hawking, communicated BT's status as a world leader in communications, to persuade people to look afresh at BT as a company operating on a global basis and to demonstrate the power and saliency of communication as a world force. The target audience was opinion formers, BT shareholders, customers and the general public. The results were very positive with between 75% and 85% of the 'personal audience' and 71–77% of the business audience agreeing with the objective BT had set itself.

A number of important conclusions can be derived from the above about corporate advertising.

1. It is an expensive technique, but it works.
2. It can build image strengths, but they will decline if it is not sustained. However, having advertised, rebuilding can be achieved rapidly.
3. It may not achieve image objectives that are outside the content of the message.
4. There can be no significant gap between the corporate message and the customer's perception of service and product.

CORPORATE ADVERTISING OBJECTIVES

Corporate advertising is only one technique among many which can be successful in image building. The argument for planned corporate commu-nications is clear and widely accepted: all companies have an image – what Kotler (1976) calls 'the simplified impressions persons hold of an other-wise complex entity' – and the rationale for corporate communications is that this process can assist in matching image and reality.

If it is accepted that a real corporate need exists, then the next decision layer concerns the selection of techniques. The process is highly complex and poorly understood. It helps to separate the longer-term objectives of corporate communications. Oversimplifying, these are:

- To ensure that a company's activities are properly understood.
- To derive the behavioural benefits that greater knowledge and understanding can give.
- To shape the behaviour of staff, customers, consumers and others to the benefit of the company.

The ability of communications to shape behaviour has been demonstrated consistently in the study of psychology; and, since the early work of

Hovland and others (1953) on communication and persuasion, the communications industry has a vast amount of data at its disposal covering a wide spectrum of issues, from the tendency towards consistency in attitude change to the specifics of credibility of source.

Technique selection depends on the nature of a company's publics and the nature of the issues that need to be addressed. One example is the attitudinal changes that led to a re-rating of the shares of the BOC Group on the London Stock Exchange in the autumn of 1982 (Maitland, 1983), achieved mainly by personal contact with chemical sector analysts – a total audience of no more than 50, and a result that substantially increased the market capitalization of the company. There have been many successful re-ratings since then using personal contact techniques, but few have been as well researched and documented as that of the BOC Group.

The whole area of corporate communications demands rigorous planning. Companies must be clear as to the objectives they are pursuing and realistic as to what can be achieved. Planning implies a number of logical stages in the process. These are:

1. *Understanding the publics*   Clearly, those noted above vary in number, sophistication, understanding, and perception. Desk and field research are necessary to understand audience profile, knowledge, and attitudes.
2. *Defining objectives*   Companies must decide on priorities, and these can be encapsulated in a statement of objectives.
3. *Selecting techniques*   The size and sophistication of the audience will help determine the techniques used to communicate.
4. *Developing the programme*   This includes programme planning, budgeting, agency selection, and campaign research and development.

Unless the process of communication is developed on the basis of audience understanding and coherent objectives, the results can be damaging, as demonstrated by BAA's (formerly the British Airports Authority) experience in 1986.

In 1983 the new Director of public Affairs of the BAA was faced with an unusual problem. The market research agency carrying out tracking studies for the BAA concluded that the more it communicated, the more it decreased its research ratings, and that these would improve if it did nothing! However, doing nothing was not an acceptable option at that time, with decisions on major controversial issues such as the development of Stansted Airport being imminent. It was essential to establish the reputation of the BAA in order to ensure credibility for its arguments.

A research-based analysis was initiated. The key target market of politicians and opinion-formers was identified and carefully analysed to establish strengths and weaknesses. A detailed communications strategy was prepared, including advertising, videos, letters, and press releases; also a new industry magazine, *Airport*, was launched for free distribution at major airports. The previous advertising campaign was carefully researched and was found to be ineffective and possibly counter-productive.

A new advertising agency was hired to develop a new campaign, communicating in a positive way the facts about BAA. The first advertisement was a simple quiz designed to involve the target audience and to communicate seven key facts, notably that the business was a successful world leader in its field and did not cost the taxpayer a penny. Further advertisements followed, with a similar approach.

After two years the result was dramatic. Favourability had actually doubled, and the decision to develop Stansted was approved by Parliament. Even more important was the influence on the local community: a major research programme demonstrated that people living in areas near the airport swung from 3:1 in favour of airport development (January 1985) to 5:1 in favour (January 1986).

Early in 1992, British Gas recruited BAA's Director of Public Affairs as their new Director of Corporate Affairs and he was faced with a task which had remarkable parallels to that faced at BAA. At that time, British Gas was running a major corporate advertising campaign which was, perversely, driving down the company's attitude ratings. The Director found that opinion formers, by a ratio of 3:1, reacted negatively to the campaign. His first and easiest decision was to terminate the campaign immediately.

A clear strategy was then developed to build on the significant strength of British Gas customer satisfaction. 89 per cent of the public were satisfied with the overall level of value and service provided but this message was not appreciated by opinion formers. Additionally, the company was at odds with its regulator and the frequent public clashes which had taken place were harming the company's image.

A major programme of personal contact with opinion formers was initiated and quantitative and qualitative research was carried out on a continuous basis over the next two years. A clear statement of the company's vision and values was published and distributed to all staff as well as customers and shareholders. This not only provided an aspiration for staff but also provided a list of criteria by which the top management's performance could be judged.

Qualitative research undertaken later in 1992 demonstrated that whereas favourability towards the company was improving significantly, the company's position on key issues was not getting across effectively, By this time, the company was involved in a lengthy twelve month review by the Monopolies and Mergers Commission (MMC), and considerable care had to be exercised in order to avoid prejudicing the company's case by publicising details of its evidence. The use of corporate advertising now became imperative. A clear brief was prepared, pinpointing precisely the key targets and key messages with the overall objective of communicating the company's vision of being a world class energy company and the leading international gas business. Legas Delaney was selected for the task and the campaign was launched through an unusual radio advertising and sponsorship package on Classic FM. The programme 'Classical Gas', familiar music on unfamiliar instruments, was used to communicate the importance of British Gas's international expansion, in terms of bringing benefits back to Britain.

The campaign proved to be overwhelmingly effective and was extended to television and full page colour press advertisements. A simple creative device was used showing the world with flames emerging from those countries where the company operated, thus linking neatly with the previous product campaign which used British Gas's flame symbol. The message was clear – British Gas's overall expansion was good for Britain, good for business and good for the economy. The campaign concluded with the quotation 'world class begins at home', in order to reassure the UK consumer.

Levels of favourability and support for the key arguments being put forward by British Gas reached an unprecedentedly high level by August 1992, the same month that the MMC published its recommendations. The multiple breakup option advocated so strongly by the regulator was rejected and the regulator himself was forced to abandon it.

It is important to stress that British Gas's corporate communications strategy was not restricted to advertising. In particular, great emphasis was placed on turning round British Gas's image with key opinion forming journalists and, as a result of this and a sustained press relations campaign focusing on British Gas's strategy and fundamental strengths, the quality of press coverage on the company improved considerably and had a major impact in shaping opinion during one of the most critical years in the company's history.

In 1986, Hanson PLC, one of Britain's leading corporations, recognized that, despite that position, it suffered from a low profile amongst the general public and where the company was known its image was often distorted. The size and scope of Hanson's operations was very little understood and, in particular, its successful management of some major UK and US manufacturing companies was hardly appreciated at all.

The company believed that by increasing understanding of these facts, Hanson would benefit in a number of ways, including increasingly loyalty amongst shareholders, reassuring the staff of potential acquisition targets and fostering pride and commitment amongst the company's own employees. Lowe Howard-Spink was commissioned to create a television campaign to improve public perceptions and to provide, in an entertaining manner, the facts about Hanson's joint UK and US operations. The first commercial launched the line 'Hanson. A company from over here that's also doing well over there'.

The performance of the campaign was regularly monitored among samples of around a thousand drawn to represent the target audiences. Although the survey included measurements of advertising impact and communications, the key criterion of success was judged to be the extent by which the campaign raised appreciation of Hanson's success on both sides of the Atlantic. By the end of the campaign, well over half of the adult population knew that Hanson operated in both the UK and US with around 25% being spontaneously aware of Hanson in this context.

Having touched on a number of United Kingdom case studies, and before examining the process in details, it is useful to bear in mind the terms of reference which corporate advertising can cover. The Publishers' Information Bureau in the USA described these well, along the following lines:

1. To educate, inform, or impress the public with regard to a company's policies, objectives and standards.
2. To build favourable opinion about a company by stressing its management ability, skills, technology and so on; and to offset negative attitudes.
3. To build up the investment qualities of a company.
4. To sell the company as a good employer.

As Garbett (1981) points out, the huge scope of these terms of reference has undoubtedly contributed to the difficulty in naming the functions.

UNDERSTANDING THE AUDIENCE

It has been suggested by King (1978–9) that in advertising it is audience responses that matter; a simple and unarguable proposition, but one that is all too often ignored.

Drucker (1954) identifies marketing as 'the whole business seen from the point of view of its final result, that is, from the customer's point of view'. Drucker noted at the time that in Europe 'there is still almost no understanding that marketing is the specific business function'. Corporate advertising must also be viewed from the audience's standpoint. And, like marketing in the 1950s, there is still no widespread appreciation in European industry in the 1990s of the need for response-oriented corporate advertising developed on the basis of desired audience responses.

It might be argued that it is difficult to establish audience response until corporate advertising has run for some time – perhaps two years – and that by any measure it is an expensive way to experiment. But this ignores the remarkable progress that has been made in behavioural research over the last 40 years. Indeed, the existence of a sophisticated behavioural research industry is often widely ignored by business, even when major budgets are being deployed.

A European research study conducted in 1982 (Maitland, 1983) concluded that around 80 per cent of international bank advertising was largely ineffective. The study, among the chief executives and the chief financial officers of Europe's largest companies, assessed spontaneous and prompted awareness of international bank advertising programmes, and spontaneous and prompted responses to the advertisements when these were used as stimuli. The fact that this section of advertising is one of the largest international categories can only underline the lack of communications professionalism in some of our largest financial institutions. A follow-up study (Maitland, 1983) showed that few international banks had used advertising research.

Typically, benchmark and concept testing advertising absorbs around 5 per cent of a corporate communications budget. A small proportion of an investment which is professionally deployed can save the other 95 per cent being wasted. It does, however, involve skill and effort to conduct such research: perhaps that is why, more often than not, it is ignored.

The value which can be derived from primary attitude research is heavily influenced by the investment which is made in preparatory research (McTavish and Maitland in their *Industrial Marketing*, in Macmillan Studies in Marketing Management (1980)). Much work can be done in understanding audiences before the formal research process is initiated. This is particularly important in preparation for sampling. For instance, while consumer populations tend towards normal distribution and are therefore suited to random sampling techniques, more specialized corporate audiences, such as Westminster, Whitehall, and the City, need to be studied and understood in detail before they are sampled; and this understanding must be present when the findings of a survey are analysed.

THE ROLE OF CORPORATE ADVERTISING RESEARCH

There are two areas that research needs to cover, and these form the crucial links in the advertising planning process. The first, concept testing, is concerned with ensuring – as far as this is possible – that the planned advertising campaign is eliciting the desired responses from the target audiences. The second, benchmark and tracking research, is designed to provide data on knowledge and attitudes, and involves a continuing process of monitoring.

Following a careful study of the target audiences, a communications programme should start with a benchmark study, designed to quantify knowledge, opinions, and attitudes, prior to any investment being made. The decision to employ corporate advertising is unlikely to be taken before such research is complete. A benchmark study fulfils two functions:

1. It sets a baseline for awareness and attitudes, against which the progress of the campaign can be monitored.
2. It identifies areas of lack of understanding and misperception among audiences, thus providing the hard data for the corporate advertising brief.

While this approach is conventional and widely used, there is some evidence that, by itself, it may be insufficient. Without entering into the quantitative versus qualitative research debate, it can be stated that the need to understand often complex behavioural responses may not be met satisfactorily by the 'cafeteria' technique, which involves respondents being confronted with a range of statements dreamed up by the research sponsor and the research company. This technique is aimed at defining the image of a company thought its association by the respondent, with some or all of the statements. There is little doubt that this can lead to oversimplification of highly complex behavioural issues, and great care is needed in interpretation. Parallel qualitative work using focus groups is a wise precaution and can usually add significant insight.

Analysis of research findings against the background of communications objectives provides the material for the creative brief and the guidance necessary to develop effective advertising strategy. There is no 'correct' way to create good advertising. However, the use of proposition and concept testing as a key element in the developmental process can help to ensure that corporate advertising is reaching its audiences in a relevant and effective way. Research techniques are, to some extent, determined by the nature of the audience; where small groups can be recruited and researched, the focus group technique, using concept boards, will probably be most appropriate. The objective of this research is to determine the most effective way in which advertising can produce the responses sought by the advertising from the audience.

It is at the concept-testing stage that research interpretation is most important. By its nature, qualitative research depends much more than quantitative research on the interpretation of the message; and, if corporate image questions are being studied rather than brand preference, then the quality of interpretation becomes crucial. The advertiser should keep two simple behavioural 'laws' in mind: first, research executives tend towards a positive conclusion (it is extremely difficult to report to a client that no conclusion can be drawn from the research), and second, creative executives tend towards absolute belief in their own ideas. The choice of supplier in both areas is a decision fundamental to successful corporate advertising. While there is no substitute for conducting primary research into the experiences of other advertisers, initial guidance can be given by organizations such as the Advertising Agency Register at 62 Shaftesbury Avenue, London W1 and the Market Research Society, at 15 Belgrave Square, London SW1.

DEVELOPING A CORPORATE ADVERTISING PROGRAMME

Assuming that a potential corporate advertiser has been through the benchmark research stage and has clear and coherent communications objectives, then it is time to think about budgeting, briefing, and agency selection.

Budgeting is the quantitative expression of a plan and it is, of course, concerned with the future (Maitland (1982)). It is based on management's definition of corporate objectives and is a process where greater accountability is necessary. Budgeting for corporate advertising may seem a long way from corporate objectives, but corporate advertising must be a direct reflection of these objectives. Too often, advertising budgets are arrived at by a process that can only be described as serendipity. Some form of task-related method is by far the most satisfactory, and here the existence of quantitative baseline measurements is clearly helpful.

Judgement is required in estimating the amount of exposure to advertising that is likely to yield attitudinal change. The media research and planning function, described below, will then recommend the most cost-efficient means of achieving this level of exposure.

Armed with a brief and a budget, the next task is to select an agency. This in itself is a complex and demanding process. Sufficient information can be gathered quickly in order to draw up an appropriate list, and the typical procedure is then as follows:

1. Receive a 'credentials' presentation from each agency to establish its record, resource, client base, and so on.

2. Draw up a short list.
3. Brief the short-list companies.
4. Receive a written and verbal presentation.

The huge investment in time required to brief an agency fully should be a sufficient incentive to any company to undertake selection with great care.

Earlier in this chapter the internal audience was considered. Corporate advertising is, or should be, a profound corporate statement and, as such, it should be a management priority to communicate its purpose to employees. Management should keep employees informed throughout the advertising cycle; and indeed, if employees are a key audience, they need to be included in the research process.

Different companies are organized in different ways to handle a corporate advertising campaign, but this should never disguise the need for sensible integration of communications techniques. It is crucial that management and relevant executives are aware of all communications activities, and there must be some form of central control. If this is not the case, elements of a company's communications and marketing programme can work against each other, often to the serious detriment of the company's image. While to some extent a company's marketing programme must be given by market needs, all those concerned must be aware of marketing communications programmes, at the very least. Most advertising agencies now employ planners, and application of the planning cycle to a company's overall communication programme is a worthwhile discipline.

While there is tacit acceptance in all parts of the advertising industry of the central importance of creativity, there is a growing awareness of the need for better direction of the creative function: the quest for creativity that works. While the sensitive measurements of brand market share can quickly kill creative consumer advertising or make it the hero of the hour, a greater element of faith is required in the creative process in corporate advertising. Brand preferences change quickly, but deeply entrenched attitudes change very much more slowly. Corporate advertising's job is to change attitudes. The role of creativity is threefold:

1. To ensure that the attention of the listeners, viewers or readers is caught.
2. To ensure that the audience's interest is sustained.
3. To ensure that the message informs and persuades effectively.

This is no small task and needs some patience, skill and a great deal of hard work. A subjective creative medium is being used to translate corporate policy into a digestible popular message, and the fact that readers or viewers who don't know the company must recognize some kind of benefit puts enormous pressure on the creative function.

The end result of the research and creative process is good advertising and, while value can be added to it by judicious media selection to ensure the right kind of editorial environment, it must be able to stand up on its own. According to Ogilvy (Garbett, 1981) it can achieve this in three ways:

- By being 'plain spoken, candid, adult, intelligent and specific'.
- By penetrating 'the filter of indifference with which most people regard corporations'.
- It should be the quiet graphics and speak the language of editors – not ad men.

Good advertising gives the creative communicator scope to merchandise it in many ways, and so add value to the technique. Many of the most compelling merchandising campaigns have been born in an atmosphere of some desperation in bid-related advertising, for instance, Imperial Group's 'Famous brands growing famously' which failed in the end, and APV's 'Nobody know our business better' which, in its success, created a watershed in mergers and acquisitions development in the United Kingdom.

REACHING THE AUDIENCE

Media research data present the corporate advertiser with a huge challenge. Most of the data have been gathered and paid for by those with the greater direct commercial interest in the findings that are shown by the data. It must not be concluded that such data are misleading, but caution and judgement are urged in their use – a sensible process with any information.

There are several important readership studies, published by Research Services Limited, London available to the media planner covering UK and European corporate audiences.

1. *The European Business Readership Survey*, published every 2 years (last published in 1993) and based on an unweighted sample of over 10 000 senior executives in European companies with more that 250 employees.
2. *The BMRC Businessman Survey*, again published every 2 years (and again last published in 1993) and based on an unweighted sample of over 2700 businessmen and women with managerial responsibilities in UK companies.

3. *The Pan-European Survey*, published every 3 years, (last published in 1992) with an unweighted sample of over 7700. In this case the universe is executives living in high status areas in Europe.
4. *Institutional Financial Managers in Europe*, published every 3 years (last published in 1993), living in high status areas in Europe with an unweighted sample of over 1100 senior financial managers in European companies with turnover in excess of US$150 million.
5. *European Finance and Investment Specialists*, published infrequently with an unweighted sample of over 1300 investment and money managers in Europe. It was last published in 1987 and will again be published in 1994.
6. *Chief Executives in Europe*, published infrequently, with a sample of over 700 chief executive officers in Europe's 2000 largest companies. It was last published in 1990 and will be published again in 1994.

Each of the surveys includes information on readership habits by country or region, company size and type, and respondent responsibility. These criteria can be taken in isolation or cross-referenced using computerized techniques which take into account readership duplication between titles to determine actual coverage of specific target audiences.

There are a number of other secondary sources that are inhibited by lack of access to computer analysis, but are useful in examining readership of small groups (Mori, 1982 & 1985).

It is unlikely that the screening criteria for such surveys will be sufficiently rigorous or comprehensive to match exactly the audience for a corporate advertising campaign. For instance, where corporate advertising is being used primarily as a marketing weapon, audience definition may be highly specific.

Of course it is dangerous to equate readership of a medium with readership of the advertising contained in it. Some attempts have been made to fill this gap with reading and noting studies, particularly by individual publishers. For instance, *International Management* runs an 'ad-evaluation' programme designed to assess the impact of each advertisement on a representative panel of readers. However, it is increasingly the responsibility of the advertising organization to ensure that its advertising is having the desired effect on the target audience, through well established market and attitude research techniques.

Media departments are becoming increasingly sophisticated, and their responsibilities to ensure maximum cost effectiveness are also growing. Generally the media planner will work from the same brief as the creative department – now increasingly developed by account planners – and he or she will be responsible for recommending the optimum level of coverage within the agreed budget. The likely coverage delivered by various media mixes can be evaluated using the sources referred to above. The average frequency of seeing an advertisement can also be calculated using these sources. Timing is also an important media consideration and the 'drip' versus 'burst' debate is likely to continue into the foreseeable future. Great effort also goes into advertisement positioning, based on theories concerning reader behaviour and the value or otherwise of juxtaposing an advertisement with relevant articles.

Positioning is a prime consideration in the media buying function. The buyer's job is to place advertisements at the best possible rate in the most powerful and visible positions, and to balance rate against position.

Television Versus Press

Most of the above discussion has used press media for reference as, certainly in the United Kingdom, the press has been the most frequently used medium for corporate advertising. However, the high-budget corporate programmes, designed to influence public opinion, have of course used television.

The choice of advertising medium depends on the message, the audience and, to some extent, budget, although task-oriented budgeting is becoming more usual. Press campaigns have been used traditionally to reach senior decision-makers and will probably continue to be used for corporate campaigns aimed at such elite groups, who tend to be 'light' television viewers (i.e. those who do not watch a great deal). One advantage of press advertising over television is that more detailed information can be presented. And, although the press does not have the impact of television, the use of colour in magazines and newspapers has added a further dimension to press advertising.

Television undoubtedly has an increasingly important role to play in corporate advertising. It is by nature a mass medium and is extremely effective in rapidly building awareness, as demonstrated in earlier references to TV campaigns in this chapter. In addition to those mentioned, BP has also used television to great effect, as demonstrated by the results of its research published in *Viewpoint*.

The use of Channel 4 programmes, in addition to other ITV programmes such as 'News at Ten', makes it possible to target more precisely the advertising aimed at 'light' viewers, for example those in AB groups. This is a relatively cost-effective and sophisticated method of TV buying, and many advertisers still seek mass audiences, although the demand for such upmarket airtime is now increasing.

A MARKETING DIMENSION

It has long been realized that corporate advertising can result in real marketing benefits. BT's corporate campaigns have been credited with a significant call stimulation impact, and Guinness's bid advertising with a short-term increase in the consumption of its stout product called Guinness.

This relationship between familiarity, favourability, and increased purchase is not surprising in behavioural terms, but it is often ignored in the planning and development of a corporate campaign. It is particularly relevant in the industrial market where buyers are less susceptible to sales promotion (Maitland, 1983).

MONITORING THE PROGRAMME

Earlier in this chapter the role of benchmark and tracking research was discussed. Monitoring a corporate advertising programme is not simply a cast of replicating the benchmark study and examining changes across a range of factual and attitudinal dimensions.

Corporate advertising is not the only formal way in which a company communicates with its audience and indeed every action is a form of communication. Also, of course, the best planned advertising campaigns can be destroyed by exogenous factors.

Clearly, therefore, it is important to ensure that the monitoring factor has much wider terms of reference than those implied in the tracking research procedure. It must be able to evaluate the impact of a variety of factors on a company's image and reputation and to comment intelligently on the relationship between the behaviour of a company and its communications. When these become out of tune, the seeds of long-term damage, which can often be quite serious, are planted. The monitoring function must be the guardian of corporate advertising in the sense that the latter must carry the truth and not attractive fiction.

THE FUTURE

As our world grows in complexity – while becoming much more accessible to people through improvements in the ease of travel and the efficiency of communication – the need for corporate communications in general, and corporate advertising in particular, must grow.

With change becoming even more rapid, and corporate and financial institutions becoming bigger and more international, progress can be assured only by widespread understanding and appreciation of companies' activities, objectives and general behaviour in a wide social, political, economic and ethical sense.

Communications techniques and technology must continue to improve to meet this need. To achieve this, more talented people must be attracted into the field of corporate advertising, particularly in the creative and planning disciplines, and a greater sense of reality must develop within those major corporations whose activities increasingly affect our everyday lives. Also more creative use must be made of the media options that are at present being improved and added to by technology.

There is now an enormous range of advertising opportunities to reach both mass and specialist audiences in cost-effective ways. The benefits of corporate advertising are clear. All that is needed is the vision to use it to its maximum effect.

Bibliography

P. Drucker, *The Practice of Management,* Harper.

E. Garbett, *Corporate Advertising: The What, the Why and the How,* McGraw-Hill.

C. I. Hovland, I. L. Jarvis and H. H. Kelley, *Communication and Persuasion,* Yale University Press.

S. King, 'Public response: the key to corporate advertising', *Advertising Writer.*

P. Kotler, *Marketing Management,* 3rd edn, Prentice-Hall.

A. J. Maitland, 'To see ourselves as others see us', *The BOC Group Management Magazine.*

A. J. Maitland, 'The marketing problems facing international banks and the role and effectiveness of international bank advertising', paper presented to the Conference on Financial Communications in a World Recession, April 1983.

A. J. Maitland, 'Great accountability in marketing budgets', *The Accountant,* February 1982.

R. McTavish and A. Maitland, *Industrial Marketing,* Macmillan.

Mori, readership surveys of MPs, financial journalists and 'captains of industry'.

K. Newman, *The Selling of British Telecom,* Holt, Rinehart & Winston.

Viewpoint, 21.

10 Sponsorship

David Wragg

For many years, sponsorship has occupied an increasingly important role in many marketing and public relations strategies. Nevertheless, there is nothing new about sponsorship as such. Many major household names have been involved in sponsorship for a long time, with Johnnie Walker whisky, for example, having sponsored golf tournaments since the early years of the present century.

There are, of course, those who will argue that the history of sponsorship goes back much further, and no doubt there were some suitable Victorian examples. Those who point to the support which the wealthy provided for struggling artists and composers during the eighteenth and nineteenth centuries, however, are confusing sponsorship with patronage. The distinction needs to be made since the sponsor expects a tangible return for the money and effort expended on an activity or an event, while the patron is less concerned about a return, and may be perfectly sanguine over the prospects of success.

One of the many difficulties which practitioners have with sponsorship is that the term is used so widely, and often by people who do not understand its true meaning. This is surprising in an industry which, according to a European Union committee on culture and media, provides £2800 million of support annually for sport and art throughout the twelve member states. These figures are considerable, and can almost certainly be regarded as inaccurate. The industry works on estimates partly because people do not fully understand what sponsorship is, and partly because many sponsorship deals do not reveal the figures. The figures are further distorted by the need to spend a considerable sum over and above the agreed cost of the sponsorship itself so that the activity can be fully supported and full value obtained.

Being precise about the true definition of sponsorship is not mere pedantry, it is important to understand what it is so that the value of sponsorship to business can be fully appreciated. It is important to appreciate whether or not your company is engaged in sponsorship or patronage so that the related activities can be planned and budgeted. Examination of the definitions will at once show why the differences are so important.

Sponsorship can usually be described as the support of an activity or an event which would not otherwise be self-financing through the usual commercial criteria. The sponsors should have definite objectives which the sponsorship will fulfil, such as engendering goodwill and influencing potential customers, and ensuring a higher profile for their name or the name of a particular product or brand. The more obvious and high profile examples include the funding by business of major sporting events or performances by opera or ballet companies, or the mounting of a major exhibition of the visual arts. Yet, sponsorship is far more widespread than these examples, as we will see later.

Sponsorship is an agreement between the organisers of an event or activity on the one hand, and commerce on the other, and in exchange for financial support, the sponsor or sponsors will expect their criteria to be met in full. Commercial concerns commit funds to sponsorship for a definite return, not for the sake of it.

On occasion, companies find themselves sponsoring an activity which might be commercially viable. This is not because the activity, or those engaged in it, need additional money, although that might explain why the sponsorship is available, but because the sponsor needs the profile which the sponsorship bestows.

The best sponsorships are those which are remembered by the target audience long after the sponsorship itself has ended.

Patronage may seem like an old-fashioned term for sponsorship, but today one can use the term for any sponsorship which lacks commercial motives and which is far more altruistic in its motivation. It differs from charitable donations inasmuch as the activity or event being supported is unlikely to be one which can be regarded as charitable.

Charitable donations are a contribution, usually by a company, or some other commercial concern, to an activity which is not commercial, but which will help the community or members of that community, and which does not have the objective of providing a commercial return for the donor. It is possible for there to be major public relations benefits, but many donors will take the view that these are less important than the donation itself. Major medical charities and those which aid those elements of society which are deprived in some way, are often popular and usually sure of at least a small token donation, but companies will also give money for projects to do with the nation's heritage, and, not all claimants have to be registered as a charity to be sure of a donation.

Although in some countries, including the United Kingdom, many artistic organizations have charitable status, for all practical purposes, major artistic events and activities can be regarded as sponsorship cases. In PR and marketing terms, charities are those organizations which meet a specific need amongst the less fortunate members of society, or other similar objectives, such as animal welfare, environmental and educational concerns, for example. Political parties are not generally regarded as being charitable concerns! Corporate support for charities amounts to more than £165 million annually in the UK alone.

Of course, there is one other difference between sponsorship and charitable donations which will be relevant to those who are organizing the larger event with a higher combined income from ticket sales and sponsorship. It is this: in the UK, and in many other countries, sponsorship deals are subject to tax along with any other major business transaction, which in the UK means a potential liability to value added tax, and elsewhere to similar taxes, while charitable donations are not taxed. It is, of course, wrong to redefine a sponsorship as a charitable donation to evade VAT since such action is likely to bring both the sponsors and the organizers into conflict with the tax authorities.

Corporate hospitality is an opportunity for a company to entertain important customers, distributors or agents, or other useful people, such as suppliers, journalists or investors. Good examples of this are to be seen in the elaborate entertainment facilities for business guests at major sporting events, or in the provision of theatre, opera, concert or ballet tickets to important contacts, often with special arrangements made for pre-performance and interval drinks, and with a lavish supper party afterwards. Art exhibitions will often include a private preview for the sponsor's guests, with suitable refreshments, of course!

One should not regard the provision of facilities or the loan of equipment as being sponsorship. If a sports star is always seen using one manufacturer's equipment, that is product promotion and not sponsorship, even though the free supply of equipment has obvious financial benefits for the star in question. Using a prominent personality in advertising campaigns instead of an actor is not sponsorship either.

SPONSORSHIP TODAY

Amongst the changes which have been taking place in the sponsorship market in recent years has been the growing interest amongst charities in what is sometimes described as 'social sponsorship'. This implies that companies are sponsoring worthwhile causes, with charities persuading them to devote part of their marketing budget to charitable endeavours. Some government departments have been encouraging charity organizers to believe that there are large sums available for charitable work. The problem is that companies may have to consider either devoting additional funds to charities or cutting back on sponsorship. Some charity organizers believe that they can offer companies marketing opportunities, but one has to be particularly careful in assessing these. One shoe polish manufacturer sponsored the Scouts in 'Job Week', providing cleaning materials so that scouts could act as shoe shine boys, enabling the Scout's Association to raise funds and at the same time publicize the shoe polish. It worked, but one has to accept that the activity was relatively low key, and of limited duration and benefit. Such obviously mutually beneficial opportunities are not always immediately obvious.

Another change has been the tendency to use sponsorship to avoid restrictions on advertising. The ban on television advertising of tobacco products in the United Kingdom has led the manufacturers to provide large sums for televised sporting events likely to be watched by the tobacco manufacturers' target audience. Motor sport has been a prime beneficiary, but the sums involved have not been disclosed, although one claim is that tobacco sponsorship accounts for no more than 20 per cent of all sponsorship devoted to this particular sport. Most recently in the United Kingdom, sponsorship of independent radio and television programmes has been permitted, enabling potential sponsors in the UK to enjoy similar benefits to their counterparts in other countries, including the United States. There are still a number of restrictions to ensure the continued independence of the programme makers, especially in news and documentary programming. The main restriction is that the sponsor's business must not be connected with the topics handled by the programme. As an example of the way in which this works, tour operators, hire car companies and airlines or travel agents would not be allowed to sponsor a travel or holiday programme, but a major credit card company, Barclaycard, can do so. Since many people will use a credit card to pay for their holiday or to cover expenditure whilst on holiday, the benefit to the sponsor is clear.

There are few restrictions on the sponsorship of printed matter, although one has to question the wisdom of doing so. Newspaper and magazine publishers who seek sponsorship, often for special supplements, are blurring the distinction between advertising and sponsorship. There are other problems for both parties. The publisher might be perceived as having abandoned editorial independence. The sponsor can also be perceived as having an undue influence. In the case of one financial supplement to a Sunday newspaper, any praise of the sponsoring bank could have been seem as having been influenced by the sponsorship in the eyes of the reader, while any condemnation of a rival bank could be viewed in the same way.

WHY SPONSOR?

Businesses sponsor because they expect a definite return for the expenditure. The decision to support a particular project or activity might be influenced by community relations motives, but this does not detract from the activity being defined as sponsorship. Indeed, a major benefit of sponsorship is to improve the image of the organization, and community or social sponsorship, which might favourably influence the attitudes of customers, the media and politicians, and even appease pressure groups, has its attractions.

Of course, sponsorship is part of what is sometimes described as the 'marketing mix', and has to compete with other activities, such as advertising or public relations when plans are being prepared. Nevertheless, often sponsorship cannot be ignored when strategies are being examined. This is especially true for the tobacco manufacturers, seeking to by-pass bans on television advertising of tobacco products, but it can also be true too for other types of business as well. Well-established products sometimes find editorial coverage difficult to obtain, and sponsorship of a major event is one means of lifting the company name or the brand back onto the editorial pages, enjoying the benefits of an editorial mention when the reader may well have skipped over the advertising.

Sponsorship is not necessarily a question of a 'hard' sell, and instead the process is more persuasive. This also applies to the community involvement of many companies.

Charitable donations are another form of support, and indeed there are relatively few which do not make charitable donations. Companies do this because they feel that they have a duty to put something back into the community, and an interest in the welfare of that community. Just as individuals donate to charities because they believe it is part of good citizenship, companies do so because they wish to be viewed as good corporate citizens.

Many companies today are moving beyond simple donations towards corporate community involvement. According to Neil Shaw, chairman of the sugar refiners, Tate & Lyle, it can also confer a competitive advantage:

'In today's world, price is very important. But if the price is competitive, other things about the firm, such as service, the way it responds to a complaint, and so on – everything to do with the way it is perceived, will swing things its way. Corporate community involvement has certainly helped us sell, and buyers are confident that they are dealing with a first class company – because of the type of people they deal with.'

In summary, there are several reasons why an organization will sponsor:

- The need to raise awareness of the organization or its products.
- The opportunity to use sponsorship, especially if televised, to circumvent bans on television advertising of tobacco products.
- Image-building, through association with worthy sponsorships, including the arts, or associating the organization with a geographical area through sponsoring a national event or team.
- Opportunities for corporate hospitality so that customers, investors, or distributors can be entertained.

Many sponsorship opportunities allow a combination of two or more of these reasons. Indeed, one should expect a worthwhile sponsorship to provide a range of benefits.

DEFINING OBJECTIVES

Even so, before even seeking a worthwhile sponsorship, it helps to be clear about the objectives for the sponsorship. In particular, you should have:

- Specific image-building, community relations or marketing objectives in mind.
- Taken a decision over whether the parent company or holding company, if there is one, an operating division or subsidiary, a product or a brand is to be promoted through the sponsorship.
- Analyzed the potential sponsorship so that you are confident that the right audience, or audiences, will be reached.
- Made sure that there will be no risk of conflict with corporate objectives and no chance of embarrassment – appreciating that certain activities might be controversial, have a risk factor due to safety or other considerations, and might not be appropriate in image terms.
- The complete picture regarding the costs, as well as the benefits.
- Ascertained that the activity being sponsored is being run by people who are capable and reliable organizers, and ideally both able and

willing to obtain publicity within their specialized media and with specialized journalists in the general media, since often these will be different from the usual media contacts known to the sponsor's PR department.

- Ensured that your organization is the sole sponsor. Sponsorship should never be shared with another sponsor, since this creates confusion and divided loyalties amongst those being sponsored, and effectively reduces media coverage as journalists, short on time, space and patience, cannot be expected to mention every sponsor.
- Whenever possible and appropriate, ensured that your organization's name as sponsor is being linked with that of the event, and even if this is not possible, all publicity material should mention the sponsor.
- In addition to the cost of the sponsorship, sufficient funds will be available to incorporate the sponsorship into advertising and to product promotional items and entertainment possibilities relevant to the sponsorship. As a rule of thumb, most organizations expect to spend as much again on supporting the sponsorship as they will on the basic sponsorship.
- Considered added value before agreeing to the sponsorship. For example, will sportsmen or famous entertainers be prepared to meet your guests at a social occasion after a game or a performance? This adds considerably to the sense of occasion for the guests.
- Examined the sponsorship for opportunities to involve employees (good for morale) or customers, such as offering reduced rate tickets or competitions centred around the sponsored activity.
- Planned for research to ascertain name or brand awareness amongst the target audience before and after the sponsorship – unless it is an ad hoc event.
- Avoided teams, and even more so, individuals, who might be involved in controversy or even suffer illness, death or injury, preventing them from fulfilling the sponsorship. If you are supporting your company's home town team, then all well and good, but always remember that teams and individuals can lose as well as win, and some companies do not like being associated with failure.
- Been concentrating on those sponsorship opportunities which can be maintained for two or more years, so that the benefit of being associated with a particular activity is enhanced by repeat exposure, just as advertising often goes unnoticed at first and needs repeat exposure. On the other hand, you should not allow your organization to persist with the same sponsorship for so long that the sponsor's name becomes taken for granted and merges into the background.

If you should decide that a particular sponsorship has run its course and cannot provide further benefits, that it is simply not cost-effective, do remember that a good sponsor will always give adequate notice, a year or so, of the intention to discontinue the sponsorship, allowing the organizers time to find a fresh sponsor.

WHAT TO SPONSOR

Suitable opportunities for sponsorship include:

- Sporting events: Always highly popular with sponsors, and more likely than the arts or heritage projects to offer naming possibilities.
- Artistic events: Usually lower profile than the popular sporting events, but often likely to appeal to a particular type of customer or distributor, and more likely to appeal to husband and wife than many sporting events. An added advantage is that most occur during the evening, which can make it easier for guests to attend.
- Local amenities: These can do much to foster local goodwill, but the benefits can be eroded over the years, even if the name of the sponsor can be incorporated into the name of the building, etc. Unfortunately, many amenities can sometimes suffer over the years, and either a continuing commitment is needed, or one will have to be assured that the building will not become shabby.
- Broadcast programmes: Sponsorship of these is a recent innovation in the UK, but can be effective for mass market consumer goods. Minority interest programmes on the arts or finance, for example, can sometimes be a cost-effective sponsorship for the manufacturers or suppliers of prestige goods or financial services.
- Restoration projects: These can include preserved railways, canals and so on, but these seldom offer a high enough profile for the costs involved.
- Books: Low cost, but often low profile, unless they support marketing objectives. This is one reason why banks sometimes sponsor books intended for the smaller business, and building societies sponsor books on family finance or setting up home.
- Activities for young people, such as letter-writing contests.
- Conferences, although these have a limited benefit for the sponsors.
- Exhibitions, fairs or shows – providing that the sponsor's name is mentioned on publicity material as the main sponsor. It is often more cost-effective to sponsor an event at an exhibition or show than to sponsor the entire show.

The question is, of course, just which is the right sponsorship opportunity for your organization? Many organizations will maintain more than one major sponsorship. There are several reasons for this. One is that they recognize that their customers, or any other target audience, will not always be interested in just one subject. It makes sense, for example, if funds permit, to sponsor one of the arts as well as a major sport. If sufficient money is available, a major community sponsorship could also be an option.

Another reason for splitting the sponsorship activity is that many events are seasonal, and more than a single sponsorship can ensure continuous exposure throughout the year. One can also have sponsorship programmes which are renewable at different times, so that you do not have the task of deciding whether or not to renew, or to replace, all of your main sponsorships during the same year.

Not all organizations are able to afford a substantial sponsorship budget, and it is better to handle just one sponsorship well, and obtain all of the benefits just mentioned, than to spread the money and other resources too thinly. Small, and seemingly inexpensive sponsorships are all too often low profile, and frequently shared. It is not unusual for local branch managers of a large number of major retailers all to provide a small sum towards supporting a minor sporting event or an amateur dramatic production. Sometimes this is necessary in the interests of customer relations, but it is not sponsorship, but patronage, a gesture of goodwill rather than a costed and planned commercial decision.

If funds permit, then your sponsorship can always be extended, providing increased corporate hospitality opportunities, or adding more of the same. For example, if you are sponsoring an orchestra, additional concerts can be added to their programme or the production of a compact disc or other recording can be sponsored. Another popular means of extending a sponsorship is to add something for children or for those with disabilities. Taking the orchestra example, concerts for schoolchildren, or meeting the cost of cheaper concessionary tickets for the elderly or handicapped could be useful. Sponsors of a major sport could provide a schools league, or offer to underwrite the cost of providing coaching – perhaps a 'master class' – for promising school children.

It is important that the sponsorship matches both the organization and the target audience. One building society sponsored shows and competitions for the breeders of a particular breed of cattle, simply because these were the hobby of the then chairman. Yet the building society had no business interests related to farming or cattle breeding, and the majority of customers, whether savers or borrowers, had little knowledge and even less interest in the subject.

It is no coincidence that companies producing products for motorists sponsor motor sport. Banks do not sponsor activities which will influence young people, and their parents, such as concerts and school drama competitions, simply by chance, but because they will be influencing young people both when they come to select a bank account, and when they leave school or university and enter the job market.

Many sponsors look for ways of involving employees and their families, including providing reduced rate tickets, or in the case of the performing arts, free tickets for dress rehearsals. These are all small benefits which can boost morale and aid team spirit. It is sometimes possible to involve customers, even though they do not warrant fullscale corporate hospitality, again through offering discounts or using competitions centred around the sponsorship.

The importers in the UK for Volkswagen, the German car manufacturer, sponsor a number of activities, including school crossing wardens, based on their concern for the environment and the advertising slogan 'If only everything in life was as reliable as a Volkswagen'. Support for heritage projects is also an important aspect of this – and the fact that most visitors to many historic sites are motorists!

A clear cut policy on sponsorship, with one or more significant sponsorships with the right profile for the cost and for the nature of your organization's business, will also make it easier to resist offers of ad hoc sponsorships. There may be occasions when such sponsorship opportunities are too good to refuse, but all too often the notice is too short for the full benefits to be obtained. Worse still, all too often there is also the suspicion that you are being asked to support something which has already been rejected, at least once, and which is treating you and your company as a last resort.

One can also target sponsorship. A company which is undertaking a major music sponsorship might also add a private concert on the eve of publication of its financial results for investment analysts and financial journalists, for example. Alternatively, such important audiences can be invited to the company's box at a major sporting event.

Compatibility with the business and with the audience are the key criteria in selecting a sponsorship. An affluent audience, middle-aged and above, will not be favourably influenced by football or pop music, but could be favourably impressed by support for tennis or horse racing, or support for the theatre, classical music, opera or ballet, or for the visual arts.

Racing, with connotations of gambling, might not be the best sponsorship for a financial institution, while sports with a high risk element could also conflict with businesses which need to take safety seriously.

Some activities are also difficult to project into the popular imagination. The Whitbread Round-the-World Yacht Race has achieved a high profile for its principal sponsor, but the sponsors of the individual yachts have had to change the names of the vessels to reflect their company names, and even so, success will depend on whether or not the target audience is interested in yachting. Many sponsors steer clear of yachting because so much of it takes place out of sight.

It is important that the message is linked with the sponsored activity, whether it be stability, concern for the environment, for youth, or even pace and excitement. With sponsorship, the medium might not necessarily be the message, but it can slant it and affect the tone of the message considerably.

Patience can also be important. The right sponsorship opportunity might arise at the right time, but it may be that the right opportunity will have to be sought. This also means that it might be necessary to await the ending of an existing sponsorship deal, or alternatively, that a sponsorship opportunity might have to be created. It is possible to create a new sponsorship, but in some areas, there are signs that resistance is growing, especially in sport, where some organizers feel that too many new events have been created in recent years to meet the needs of sponsors.

It is important to review the sponsorship opportunities which either exist or which will become available within the foreseeable future. If necessary, sponsorship consultants can assist on this, and so too can many of the organizations which exist to promote business sponsorship of the arts and of sport. These can, as advisers and even as brokers, bring together prospective sponsors and those seeking sponsorship.

NEGOTIATING A SPONSORSHIP

Whilst many organizers are very professional and well attuned to the needs of sponsors, and recognize the importance of meeting these, others are not aware of the needs of business. It is no exaggeration that there are still those who believe that their activity or event will be sponsored because it is a nice thing to do. Even worse, there are those who believe that they have a right to support from industry and commerce.

When dealing with an approach for sponsorship from the organizer of an event or an activity, you should expect them to provide you with the following information:

● The name of their organization and its activity, if that isn't obvious.
● What is being sought in terms of sponsorship, and this means not only what the sponsorship will cover, but also whether general sponsorship is

required or support for a specific item of expenditure or a particular event.

- Whether a single package is being offered, or a menu of items from which sponsors can choose.
- Any other sponsors currently providing support, and the nature of their support.
- The costs of the sponsorship.
- The audience or following of the event or activity.
- The period of the sponsorship.
- The media interest in the sponsorship.
- Whether the name of the event will be changed to reflect the sponsor's involvement.
- The costs of any additional items.
- Entertainment possibilities.
- Whether those involved, such as sportsmen or actors, will be available for publicity purposes.
- The possibility of the sponsor using the sponsorship in advertising.
- Whether the sponsor will be given advertising and marketing opportunities, such as space in programmes or around football grounds, and mailing lists of supporters.
- The help which you can give to the sponsor in obtaining media coverage.
- The success of the event in previous years.
- The involvement of previous sponsor, if any, and if so, the reason for changing sponsors.

Ideally, the event should allow the sponsor ample opportunities for a mention of the sponsorship, especially if the business is the only or the major sponsor. The best opportunities are those which allow the sponsor's name to be included in the title of the event, but this is not always possible. It is important sometimes to allow additional funds so that the sponsorship can be advertised, and this is especially so if the opportunity does not exist for the sponsor's name to be incorporated into that of the event or occasion. Sometimes the sponsor can also gain goodwill, and increase the chance of a kindly editorial mention, if the sponsor can provide assistance for the media at those events of interest to them, so that, for example, the sponsor provides facilities and entertainment for art critics to see a preview of an art exhibition or a dress rehearsal of a play, or ensures that there are sufficient desks, typewriters and telephones, and coffee, in the press room at the sporting event. Some journalists object to mentioning the name of a sponsor, but many will compromise. Never expect a mention in every sentence – but one mention in a report on a sporting fixture, or the statutory two mentions in a broadcast, is neither unreasonable nor unrealistic.

Beware of shared sponsorship, since this does little for any of the companies involved, unless, of course, all one wants is an entertainment facility in return for the money! Nevertheless, this isn't really sponsorship as defined earlier and often corporate entertainment facilities can be obtained for far less cost than a sponsorship.

Sometimes, shared sponsorship occurs by accident, as when two rugby teams, sponsored by different businesses, come together for a game. This is often unavoidable, especially in international sporting events when the different national bodies will have made their own independent sponsorship arrangements.

It is important to have a sponsorship agreement which sets out what both parties expect from the sponsorship, and which states which aspects of the sponsorship will be handled by the sponsor and which by the organizers. The costs involved and the sponsor's responsibilities must be defined, including any provision for dealing with inflation. It is not unfair to insist that rival organizations are not allowed to advertise or otherwise be represented at the event, providing that the organizers have the power to guarantee this, and the sponsor is prepared to pay a premium for it.

Inevitably, sponsors should not only seek to obtain good value from their sponsorships, they should also expect to pay for the better managed and higher profile events. If television coverage of a sponsorship is important to your company, then it is not unreasonable for the agreement to specify this. If it is an option which will enhance the sponsorship, but which is not of itself crucial in making the decision to sponsor, offer an incentive clause: paying x amount for the sponsorship, with an extra y amount if television coverage is obtained. This still applies even if the sponsor, rather than the organizers, has to negotiate with the broadcasters to ensure that the event is televised.

MAXIMIZING THE BENEFITS

Sponsorships don't just work by themselves, no matter how conscientious and efficient the organizers. A great deal of work has to be done by the sponsor. As a general rule, one must expect to spend as much on supporting and developing a sponsorship as you would spend on the sponsorship itself. It is possible to spend less, but a substantial number of supporting activities can add value to the sponsorship and raise its profile.

Typical of these additional items are:

- *Advertising* Many sponsorships need to be advertised, and while the organizers will publicize the event or activity itself, the simple fact of the sponsorship is often worth advertising to the followers of the event. Many sponsors can use the advertising to increase business from the followers. One building society used its national bowls sponsorship to seek additional business from club secretaries managing the funds of local bowls clubs, even though this was not the primary objective of the sponsorship.
- *Branding* Increasingly, major sponsorships are being branded, bringing the sponsor and the event together. Whilst such brands might appear to be a luxury, they provide a distinctive logo which can be used in the sponsor's own advertising material, reminding prospective customers of the sponsorship.
- *Hospitality* Corporate hospitality or entertainment costs are usually over and above the cost of the sponsorship itself.
- *Promotional items* The golf umbrellas and other paraphernalia of sponsorship also help to ensure that the sponsorship becomes more enduring and more visible.
- *Media relations* True, editorial space costs nothing, but getting there can be expensive. The benefits were mentioned earlier, as was the fact that often your existing consultancy or in-house PR function might lack the resources to handle the sponsorship. The cost of PR consultants, and of organizing press offices and even providing a results service may need to be taken into account. You may also want to organize media events, such as using the sportsmen or performers in branch openings, and all of these can add to the costs.

In common with so much else in public relations, it is the attention to detail and good planning which makes so much sponsorship effective. Good creative ideas, rather than simply imitating competitors, will also help. It is important to take a broad view, using advertising and media relations to reach the target audience, and involving customers and employees whenever possible.

FURTHER INFORMATION AND ADVICE

Arts Council of Great Britain, 14 Great Peter Street, London SW1P 3NQ
Tel: 071-333 0100

Association for Business Sponsorship of the Arts, ABSA, Nutmeg House, 60 Gainsford Street, London SE1 2NY Tel: 071-378 8143

European Committee for Business Arts and Culture, CREC, Nutmeg House, 60 Gainsford Street, London SE1 2NY Tel: 071-378 8143

Institute of Sports Sponsorship, Francis House, Francis Street, London SW1P 1DE Tel: 071-828 8771

The Sponsorship Advisory Service, c/o The Sports Council, 16 Upper Woburn Place, London WC1H 0QP Tel: 071-388 1277

The Sponsorship Advisory Service for Scotland, c/o The Scottish Sports Council, Caledonian House, South Gyle, Edinburgh, EH12 9DQ Tel: 031-317 7200

The Sponsorship Association, 16 Partridge Close, Chesham, Bucks, HP5 3LH Tel: 0494 775710

European Sponsorship Consultants Association, ESCA, 16 Partridge Close, Chesham, Bucks, HP5 3LH Tel: 0494 791760

The Directory of Social Change, Radius Works, Back Lane, London NW3 1HL Tel: 071-435 8171

Business in the Community, 8 Stratton Street, London W1X 5FD Tel: 071-629 1600

The Council for Industry and Higher Education, 100 Park Village East, London NW1 3SR Tel: 071-387 2171

National Council for Voluntary Organisations, 26 Bedford Square, London WC1B 3HU Tel: 071-636 4066

Scottish Council for Voluntary Organisations, 18/19 Claremont Crescent, Edinburgh EH7 4QD Tel: 031-556 3882

Bibliography

Charity Forum News, 54 Church Street, Tisbury, Salisbury SP3 6NH.
Hollis Sponsorship & Donations Yearbook, Hollis Directories, Contact House, Sunbury-on-Thames TW16 5HG.
Sponsorship News, PO Box 66, Wokingham RG11 4RQ.
Sponsorship Yearbook, Hobsons Publishing plc, Bateman Street, Cambridge CB2 1LZ.
D. Wragg, *Effective Sponsorship*, Kogan Page.

11 Media Relations

Roger Haywood

CREATING GOODWILL AND UNDERSTANDING THROUGH EFFECTIVE NEWS COVERAGE

When organizations consider the many publics upon whom they depend for success, they often overlook one of the most important: the media. Sometimes this omission is not accidental. The argument runs that the media are a *channel* of communication, enabling the organization to reach the desired audiences. However, at the same time the media constitute one of the most important audiences; they should receive a treatment that is as considered and professional as for any other group.

If your organization treats the media simply as 'messengers', then it is unlikely to develop the most effective programme of media communications. News and comment on the organization may be superficial and spasmodic. Those stories that do appear may also be tackled on a one-by-one basis, rather than as further chapters in an unfolding story; this deeper coverage is more likely to result when the journalists concerned are kept fully briefed and understand the policies of the organization.

(There is an incidental but important factor that supports this more imaginative approach towards the media; journalists are not commenting on the organization *only* when they are writing stories or broadcasting – they are projecting a perspective every time they discuss the actions and policies of the organization with the many key opinion-leaders with whom they regularly mix. Surely it helps to keep such influential figures well-informed and imbued with positive attitudes?)

Even talking about 'the media' can be a danger for some less experienced levels of management. This convenient word covers an enormous range of publications, from national daily newspapers through to publications operating at a regional, local, or even parish level; trade, technical, and professional journals from the popular to the esoteric; special-interest publications ranging from women's magazines with circulations in the millions to little handbooks designed for small groups of buffs. And, of course, there are the broadcast media with an equally wide spread of local, national, and even international programmes. It is for these reasons that the expression 'press relations' should be avoided and 'media relations' used instead. (Similarly, few company statements are likely to be 'press' releases; most will be news releases.)

Above all, remember that whatever the variation in style of publication, the people creating them are journalists, individuals with professional skills; and it is towards these people that the most effective media relations campaign must be directed.

UNDERSTANDING HOW THE MEDIA WORK

The news aspects of the media are run by journalists – usually! Certainly, all important decisions about what news appears in print or is broadcast are taken by journalists. Even at the highest levels of management, the journalistic viewpoint tends to be the most important.

The summary of this journalistic viewpoint is, *What will interest my readers, listeners, or viewers?* If you understand and remember this simple fact, you will have mastered the most important step in understanding how the media work. Every time you write a news release, draft an article, supervise an editorial photo session, set up a media interview, or discuss an angle with a journalist, remember to put yourself in his or her shoes. What will interest their *audience?* What will be acceptable to their editor, who is (or should be) the most perceptive focus of the readers' interests?

Journalists need material that is relevant, topical, accurate, fast, comprehensive, substantiated, concise, unbiased, and, ideally, exclusive – or, at the very least, with a special angle. Furthermore, they require this material in vast quantities and in a non-stop regular flow.

Some of the realities of effective media relations can be learned only through experience at the sharp end – working with journalists. Most of the guidance points in this chapter are drawn from personal experience (covered in more detail in *All About Public Relations* – see Bibliography). Aspiring public relations practitioners should also study the concise notes on news releases, press conferences, organizing special events, and so on that are published by the Institute of Public Relations as practice papers and by the Public Relations Consultants Association as guidance papers.

LEARNING TO APPRECIATE WHAT IS NEWS

The public relations adviser must be critically objective in the preparation and issue of news material. Central to any effective media relations campaign must be a hard core of news. Many journalists believe that a news sense is a rare quality. In truth, it is based largely on common sense. Bad news is *not* the only news; but it is only the *exceptional* story, good or bad, that will make news.

And it is perfectly legitimate to *create* news. If it is new, has never been done before, is interesting and relevant ... it is news. The first woman chairman of a public company is news. The first export order for an unexpected household product (such as hair curlers) to China is news. A 16-year-old apprentice being invited to open a new high-technology laboratory is news. The winner of a travel scholarship who has never been abroad is news. The invitation of careers teachers to the launch of a new product is news. Public relations practitioners should use this 'new is news' factor to create improved coverage.

Obviously, what is news in an engineering publication may not be news in the parish magazine, and what is news for a local radio station may not be right for national television news.

EARNING THE RESPECT OF JOURNALISTS FOR YOUR ORGANIZATION

Practitioners who are efficient and businesslike will demonstrate to any journalist that they reflect the quality of their organization. Those who are friendly, available, constructive, helpful, and co-operative will probably be pleasant people to deal with – and therefore might come higher up on the list of contacts that every journalist keeps for comment. Why should journalists work with people they don't like and who will not help them, when there is someone who will provide equally good copy but is more understanding?

Journalists rate candour as a key quality in an executive responsible for public relations, and prefer to deal with public relations people whom they know personally.

The principle is simple. Effective practitioners start by building their own reputation with journalists, and from this will spring the good work undertaken on behalf of their organization.

A recent survey of some Washington correspondents confirmed that there was virtually unanimous support for the fact that a news conference should be held to handle a major news announcement only where questions were essential. Some two-thirds of the respondents felt that news conferences were abused as a communications technique yet virtually all claimed to read press releases.

COMBINING ACTIVITY TO CREATE A CAMPAIGN

Different elements may often be combined to create a balanced media relations campaign. Indeed, sustaining effective media relations entails not just
the occasional (or even regular) flow of news, but the development of a
relationship between the organization and the media that is honest, direct,
and two-way. A particular objective (for example, better customer awareness) may be tackled by creating a campaign of media relations activity;
when such campaigns are undertaken continuously and in parallel to meet
broad objectives, the activity comes under the category of a media relations
programme. (In other words, a *campaign* has a beginning, a middle, and an
end to meet an identified objective, while a *programme* is the continuous
sum of such components.)

News Releases

News releases should be issued only to those journals that have a direct
interest in the material. Do not scatter stories to all. Always provide a contact name and telephone number. Be certain that the telephone is properly
manned, if necessary 24 hours a day, 365 days a year.

It takes many years of training and experience to be able to present
information in the concise and direct style necessary for news releases to
be used by editors. A basic writing ability is essential; but, with care and
practice, an average writer can develop into a good news writer. Certain
guidelines that may be helpful:

1. Always ask who, what, why, where, and when, and be sure that these
   questions are answered in every news story. Train yourself to eliminate
   just as vigorously as you add. If material does not answer one of these
   questions, what is it doing in your story?
2. Develop your writing skill. Draft, redraft, edit, polish, and perfect the
   copy. Read publications and understand what makes news and how it
   is put together. Analyse the writing skills of good journalists:
   understand the good; criticize the bad.
3. Write stories to suit the publication. If, for practical reasons, your story
   has to go to a wider range of media, always draft it in the style to suit
   the most popular of these. Better still, produce different stories for
   different types of news outlet.
4. Always keep the copy tight, concise, and factual. Never fudge an issue
   or create a misleading impression. Substantiate any claims. Separate
   fact from belief by putting the latter into quotes. ('Research chief, Dr

John Smith, confirmed the vehicle exceeded 200 mph. "We believe it's the fastest in the world", said ...', etc.)

5. Write the story from the point of view of the journalist. Although it is a statement from your organization, it should be presented so that it can be used directly in the publication with the minimum of editing. Comment, observation, or speculation should be included in a story only in quotes or footnotes.

6. Get the main news point into the first paragraph and preferably the first sentence. Organize the paragraphs so that the most newsworthy are at the top. This will allow the journalist to edit from the bottom; the paragraphs you can most easily afford to lose, therefore, should be the ones towards the end of the story.

7. Keep sentences short, use positive and not negative statements, use active verbs, avoid inverted clauses, and cut out any subjective material or superlatives. Keep separate points in separate sentences. Break each collection of points into separate paragraphs.

8. Put the copy into modern journalistic style. Eliminate any old-fashioned phrases, formal or pompous language, jargon peculiar to the industry, and cliches or colloquialisms that are not accepted as standard current English (or the appropriate language).

9. When you have written your story, check through to make sure that it meets all these criteria. In particular, be certain that the news is at the *beginning*. Often, draft news releases can afford to have paragraph one taken out!

10. Go through your copy again: tighten, edit, improve, check all spellings and punctuation. Get someone else to read it before it goes for release, asking them to criticize and query. Avoid becoming sensitive about your own copy; learn to be self-critical. Push yourself to the highest standard possible.

Interviews

Within your organization there are some fascinating and authoritative people. Present them to selected media for interview. Prepare briefing notes; arrange a convenient time and place for the interview; provide travel arrangements, and lunch or other facilities that would be hospitable, but no more. Before the meeting takes place, brief the person interviewed and, separately, the journalist. Train your interview subject in media techniques. Help your interviewee with any tricky questions that may be asked. By all means, attend the interview to effect the introduction, pour the coffee, or whatever; but do not take part unless the interview is going off the rails. In the worst case, remember that you *can* stop an interview, but you cannot ask a journalist to forget what has already been said. Trust journalists and get them to trust you. Say as little off the record as possible; however, never lie or hide the truth. If the timing of a question or discussion is not convenient, then explain why you cannot help, and offer to give an early story as soon as it is possible.

Editor Meetings

Make sure that you regularly meet the editors of key publications for your industry. They should know you well enough to be able to talk to you at any time they wish. Make sure that your meetings with them cover some items of substance and are not merely social occasions. Research a strong news story for each such meeting, then follow up. Arrange for key editors to meet relevant senior personnel within your organization as necessary (see 'Interviews' above).

Articles

Many publications carry authoritative articles. Make sure you are monitoring all publications relevant to your industry. Recognize opportunities for articles. If you see a news story that is contrary to your company's views, suggest an article as a follow-up. If you see a trend in the industry of which others may not be aware, suggest an article to cover it. If one of your management colleagues introduces a new technique in his area, suggest an article to describe it.

Always agree with the editor on the deadline, length, and style. And always meet the deadline. Clarify with the editor whether this article is to be published as a by-lined piece from the company or as if it had been prepared by an independent journalist.

Edit drafts or background notes into acceptable journalistic style. Listen to all views but never allow yourself to be overruled by any manager who has less public relations experience. Take responsibility for final approval of all copy issued by your organization. Explain early to all managers preparing drafts that you will be editing their copy. If any executive is unreliable in delivering on time, suggest that the main thoughts are put onto tape; alternatively, ask to interview the executive.

Features

Many publications carry regular features covering particular subjects that will be of interest to readers. For example, home magazines may regularly look at bathrooms; industry journalists may regularly look at marketing or exports. These often provide opportunities for contributions – perhaps by-lined by an executive of your company. Suggest a facility visit to your organization for the publication's editor. Alternatively, arrange an interview with a senior executive or provide company background notes.

To identify opportunities, ask relevant publications for their editorial features lists. Calender those features that come up regularly at the same time each year. Write regularly to the features editor with new ideas. Make sure you do this well in advance.

Letters

Publications like to receive authoritative letters on topics of interest to their readership. Be sure your company writes where relevant. Agree on a corporate policy. Encourage regional personnel to write letters to the appropriate media. Help them in their initial drafts. Ensure that any response to a published item is very fast; some letters can actually be sent by telex or telephone, or be hand-delivered. Look for opportunities to open a debate, as well as contributing to an existing discussion.

Press Office

You must have a press or information office to deal with media enquiries. There should be enough telephone lines to deal with the expected level of calls, including emergency situations. Be sure that there is a proper procedure for dealing with telephone press enquiries. Press officers must know to whom to turn for information. Every call must be answered immediately. If the information is not available, then the call must be returned within the time promised. Journalists respect public relations people who meet deadlines. Do not offer to call back if you know the information will not be available. Say so; explain why. Do not be tempted to present information that you cannot give. Do not allow your colleagues to hold back information that is already openly available. Avoid unnecessary secrecy.

Be sure that the press office has up-to-date photographs of all the senior management, together with short, current biographical details. Only use effective photographs, and hold a range of situations – formal photographs, action shots, and so on. Build up a complete library of news photos in black and white, in colour negative, and colour transparency. Include, for example, all manufacturing processes, products, export activities, factory locations, the fieldwork of your society/charity, and other relevant items.

Make sure that all current statistical and financial information relating to the organization is readily available. Build up a library of company information and standard articles that can be sent in the post, immediately on request. It is helpful if the press office is equipped with telex and facsimile transmission. A subscription to one of the commercial news distribution services and a London messenger service is also invaluable.

Read every newspaper and trade publication relevant to the industry. Senior executives must be advised of any relevant references. Follow up any news opportunities that result from this media monitoring. Make sure that there is a telephone number available 24 hours a day, 365 days a year. Also ensure that all public relations personnel have the telephone number of every key publication and the home numbers of senior executives.

MAKING MEDIA CONFERENCES EFFECTIVE

An ill-planned or unnecessary media conference can spoil your potential for future events. If you waste journalists' time, do not present the right information, or are not well organized, you may well receive poor coverage from your event. Even worse, you will find it difficult to get journalists to report future activities or attend other events.

Different rules apply to media receptions and to media conferences. A media reception is usually arranged to provide an opportunity for executives and media to meet, perhaps to provide background, often as a social or semi-social gathering at an event that the media are already attending – say, an electronics manufacturer's reception at a business fair. A media conference, on the other hand, is a news event, where new information is to be presented and *discussed* by the media.

Be very objective when considering a possible media or news conference. The first question to be asked is whether the conference is really necessary. If the information could be better handled by issuing a news story, arranging an interview, or placing an article, then it is probably not necessary to hold a news conference. Remember that a weak press conference may attract the media – but only once.

Some companies feel that they should hold an event because it is about time they met the press or because they want to introduce a senior executive, or even because there are sufficient funds in the budget to allow such an event. Unless there is hard news, resist this temptation; perhaps instead you could hold a suitable reception when the opportunity arises – say, at your next national exhibition.

There are a number of factors that would make a media conference advisable:

1. *The strength of the news* It is essential that there is a strong, urgent news angle. A review of company progress or an update on the market is unlikely to be strong enough. Ask yourself if the journalists you propose inviting will be as enthusiastic about attending when they know the story.
2. *The need to discuss angles* If the implications of the news require discussion, then a media conference might provide the ideal opportunity. If the news needs to be interpreted in different ways by different publications or by the broadcast media, it can be sensible to call the journalists together to give them the opportunity to ask questions.
3. *The human relations side* Some new developments have a human relations aspect, and this can be difficult to put over in a printed news story. If you have a good news story *and* a magnificent boffin or a powerful new marketing director, then a media conference might be welcomed by your industry journalists wishing to establish contact with these executives.
4. *The complexity of the story* On occasions, the sheer complexity of the news makes it difficult to put over in the printed form, in which case journalists will appreciate the question-and-answer nature of a conference. This might apply in high-technology sectors, or with a new campaign launched by an environmental group, or a major change in a company's overseas investment programme.
5. *The courtesy factor* Some announcements are of such importance to specific industry sectors that the relevant specialized journalists would expect to hear these at first hand. If there are only a few publications concerned, this might be better done as a personal briefing with the editors concerned, possibly over a working lunch.

Location

Judge whether the interest centring on your organization's location, say, is stronger than the convenience and possibly better attendance of an event in the capital or regional capital. If it is a completely new process, test facility, or production development, an historic building renovation or a conservation project, then a site visit may be appropriate. If it is a product launch, a production expansion, or an appeal announcement, it may be better held in the city.

Journalists on national newspapers or consumer publications are most unlikely to spend a day visiting a remote facility unless it is of the utmost significance. One persuasive method of getting heavyweight journalists from behind their desks is to give them the opportunity to meet the top people they cannot normally reach.

Equally, the pressures on the limited time of trade journalists must be considered. They may justify an excursion if the story is strong enough, or if they will see processes or meet people important in their industry.

Venue

In-plant, on-site, or hotel? Again, the decision depends on what is to be seen. Often a press conference will be timed to run over lunch; therefore, catering facilities will be important, which will probably give a conference venue or hotel the edge.

Often, a convenient hotel room is all that is required. But sometimes an imaginative and relevant alternative can be located. Effective media conferences have been held in universities, hospitals, training ships, historic castles, and even in aircraft.

An essential point is to check carefully any possible venue, personally. Make sure that the standards are acceptable. Novelty will not excuse poor facilities, inconvenient location, or bad catering.

Timing

Do not run an event longer than necessary. Complete the business briskly. Journalists under pressure will be able to get their story quickly and leave; those who want to probe further will be able to stay on. Many successful press conferences are held late morning or late afternoons; this enables them to run on to refreshments, buffet, or even lunch or dinner, as appropriate.

Try to allow a few minutes for latecomers at the start of your conference, for example by arranging the start to run over coffee or drinks.

Hospitality

Treat attending journalists as important business guests – in other words, as appropriate to the occasion. If the event is to run over lunchtime, a buffet is normally preferable to a formal sit-down lunch (although a formal lunch might be best for a handful of senior financial journalists meeting the chairman). Hospitality should be good, though not lavish. There's an old editor's saying that still holds true – 'What counts is news, not booze'.

Programme

Try to plan to complete the business *before* the less formal hospitality part. Lunch before the business should be avoided, even when travel times may mean delayed lunch.

A typical programme for a city centre event might be:

11.30   Arrival, sign in, media packs, and coffee
11.45   Introduction by a senior director
11.55   Product demonstration or facility visit
12.15   Questions and answers
12.30   Drinks and lunch

Any travel, assembly, and meeting times would be longer for, say, a media conference on site.

Receptions

One of the public relations team should receive your guests, check them in (against the list of acceptances), hand out any press information, and introduce them to the senior director hosting the event. The public relations reception official needs to be have the necessary cloakroom facilities, plus telephone, typewriter, train times, and other information journalists might require.

Badges are more acceptable these days, though some journalists still object. Certainly your own staff should carry their names and positions in large, clear lettering on their badges. Avoid guest badges that can tear delicate materials or adhesive ones that will mark suede and leather.

Invitations

Draw up a press list and send your invitations out between three and six weeks in advance. The date must be checked to ensure that it does not clash with any competing or major public event.

Printed invitations are sometimes useful to set a theme, but they are not essential. A personal letter with reply-paid card is probably best. Be sure you give enough detail to enable journalists to judge whether they wish to attend. Draw up the acceptance list and ring round nearer the date to check any non-respondents. Confirm any substitutes or replacements.

Content

Try to put life, style, activity, and pace into the event. Avoid unnecessary gimmicks. Always demonstrate a product or system where you can. Keep it smooth-flowing and professional. Use film, video, tape, slides, charts, and models as relevant and necessary. Ensure that you use only articulate and well-informed speakers. Keep the number presenting to a minimum. Make the presentation positive and direct but *not* a sales pitch. Avoid panels of worthies. Train and rehearse your speakers. Brief all other participants particularly on handling the media and dealing with questions. Agree on answers in all difficult areas.

Press Packs

Printed information relevant to the story should be collated into a suitable media pack. A specially printed folder may be relevant if your organization will be holding many such events. A standard folder is acceptable provided it is attractive: it is the contents that count.

The folder will contain the news story and main news picture. Other items might include copies of speeches, background industry statistics, personality pictures and biographies, and an organization profile. Do not overload with unnecessary material. Include no standard items; all copy should be prepared particularly for this event. Certainly think carefully before including publicity items such as sales leaflets.

Follow-up

On the day of the event, mail the information pack to those journalists who were interested but did not attend. Note any special requests from attendees and process these – requests for pictures or facility visits, for example. Issue appropriate thanks. Collate all costs and check against original budget. Hold a debriefing session with the responsible executives to analyse good and bad points. Record these to influence future projects.

Media conferences can achieve very dramatic results. From my own experience, a media conference enabled one office equipment manufacturer to sell the whole of his first year's production, a small provincial company to significantly cut staff turnover, a manufacturer to improve relations with factory neighbours, and a construction company to secure better financial backing from the City.

To make a press conference work, however, you must help your organization to define exactly what it is you intend it to achieve and to ensure that these are realistic aims. Your immediate market at a press conference is the journalists who attend; their primary responsibility is to their readers, listeners, or viewers.

If what your organization has is of relevance and of interest to the public served by the media, you will have an effective conference. If not ... you should not have called one!

USING THE SPECIAL NEEDS OF THE BROADCASTERS

The ability of radio and television to reach an audience can be appreciated from the cost of their advertising! Advertisers spend this sort of money because of the audience delivered, the attention achieved and, most important, the results obtained. Yet both radio and television are available media for good editorial ideas; too few of these come through public relations channels.

Programme Requirements

Local radio stations are always looking for local news. National radio programmes like 'You and Yours' and 'The Food Programme' regularly use commercial news items. Television programmes such as 'Panorama' and 'Tomorrow's World' also use commercial news items, presented in the right way.

Local and national radio and TV can reach millions. Programme makers are all in the ideas business. The sheer volume of radio and television currently being broadcast in the United Kingdom means that there is a massive demand for good material. The same is true across much of Europe, the United States, Canada, and in many other industrialized countries of the world, where an estimated 90 per cent of public information is now received through broadcasting.

In Britain, the annual, *Who's Who in Broadcasting*, will help identify the people who put together such programmes. A news release may be acceptable to put a factual news story in front of the news editor, but a personal approach is nearly always best.

Radio and television are immediate media. Stories will not last. Timing is critical. New stories need to be presented quickly to editors. Facilities for interview, location recording, studio guests, and so on must be provided immediately they are required. Deadlines are tight and, with electronic news gathering, are getting tighter. Live material from remote locations can now be slotted directly into news bulletins. Some associations and unions are establishing their own studios so they can offer TV stations an instant spokesman on key news topics. Some of these links are by satellite so they can transmit across the nation and, eventually, across the world.

But timing is important in another sense. The presentation has to be crisp, immaculate, and professional. Radio and television audiences have the ability to switch off or change channels instantly. As a result, broadcasters are constantly working to keep a high level of immediate interest in their output.

Effective public relations advisers will be creating broadcast news opportunities. But they need to know how to handle a radio or television journalist when approached to provide information or facilities. Check what programme it is for. Will it be live or taped? Will the contribution be edited? Who else will be appearing? Who will conduct the interview or discussion? What topics or questions will be covered? Will there be an opportunity to see/hear the final programme before transmission? Will there be a live debate to counter any misunderstanding or damaging assertions from other participants?

Training

There are many excellent training courses available to help you or your colleagues present your organization's case in the best possible way. Make sure that all senior executives who may be required to broadcast are trained in the techniques. Decide whether you, as public relations adviser, are going to act as spokesperson or as behind-the-scenes negotiator.

Radio Interviews

These tend to be less aggressive than those on television. This does not necessarily make them easier, however. Listeners tend to have other things to concentrate on – driving the car or digging the garden. The power of the spokesperson's personality has to come over positively. Gestures (or pretty face) will not help. The speaker has to project his or her interest into the words and voice. This is a skill that *can* be developed.

Ironically, although the speaker cannot be seen on radio, the studio situation can be surprisingly confusing. Often there is only a short informal build-up to radio interviews. The interview subject can be sitting down one moment and then seconds later going out live.

Always take advantage of any rehearsal opportunity. Run through the points, checking tricky questions. But remember that the interviewer reserves the right to ask *anything* he or she likes. This might include subjects that have not been discussed in the briefing session. If the interview is taped, the interviewee can refuse to answer; the silence will have to be edited out.

Television Interviews

On television, attention is focused on the (often) small studio area where the guest and the interviewer will be sitting. Therefore, it is easier to concentrate on the subject in hand. However, while a surge of adrenalin helps some people to sharpen their performance, others can be stunned into mumbling incoherence.

There is no substitute for experience. Watch television and see how it works. See how people deal with questions. Tape as many interviews as possible and rehearse your own answers to the questions. Learn to identify the effective techniques, the irritating habits.

News and Feature Programmes

Become acquainted with the different types of programme presented. News items are highly condensed; feature items might be slightly more in-depth; while full-length investigative-type programmes can often be hostile.

Barratt, the house developer, saw the timber frame building system destroyed and millions knocked off their share price as a result of a single investigative programme.

British Airways' 'dirty tricks' campaign, claimed illicit payments to footballers, water companies' problems with marine pollution – all were first exposed by television, and to enormous effect.

A developer working on an imaginative new shopping centre in a provincial university town provided facilities for a television company, but was later horrified to find that the finished film used footage of attractive existing shops (implying they would have to close) which were not even in the development area, and avoided any shots of the derelict, characterless properties that were due to close.

Special-Interest Programmes

Both radio and television present special-interest programmes. These tend to be less aggressive because the broadcasters are working in the same industry week after week. The programmes are dependent on the degree of cooperation they get from people who work in the special-interest sectors, such as gardening, antiques, motoring, or leisure.

This does not stop such broadcasters from being hard hitting, but it does ensure that they are reasonably accurate and fair in any criticism. Be sure that you know what the broadcaster is aiming at before you or one of your executives agrees to co-operate. Insist on knowing how your contribution is to be used, and in what context.

Location Interviews

There are a number of ways in which interviews can be organized. With major news events, a participant may be stopped in the street and a camera or microphone thrust at him or her. Be sure your spokesman is not caught out by such situations. If the organization has been in negotiation over a proposed plant closure, consider the possibility of an interviewer standing on the steps of the offices when your personnel director comes out. Think beforehand about what is to be said. If this is limited by the negotiations, construct something that will still give the broadcasters a piece of useful television or tape. However, remember that *you* are in charge: it is quite acceptable for you or your spokesman to politely excuse yourselves and break away after making a short statement.

Telephone Interviews

On occasions, your organization will be asked to give a telephone interview. This should be resisted if possible. The quality will be bad, and you have no control over the editing and the usage of the material. Furthermore, the viewer or listener may get the impression that it was not important enough for your company representative to go to the studio.

An executive in a studio interview may well have a down-the-line interview (talking to a studio monitor) but will have to look as though he or she is having a real-life conversation with the interviewer. The best advice is to ignore the electronics and talk to just one real person. The same principle applies on down-the-line radio interviews, where that 'real' person may be a microphone in front of the studio guest.

Panel Discussions

Advanced preparation here, as always, is helpful. Consider the points you would like your executive to get over. It is not always a good idea to be the first person into a discussion; equally, the discussion should not be allowed to go too far before your spokesman starts to make points. Make sure your organization's views are put over effectively but not over-extensively.

You or your spokesman should be quite prepared to put normal politeness quietly to one side. Do not allow yourself to be brow-beaten by the chairman, but answer the question in the way you would like. Do not try to be too clever by turning the question into the one that you would have liked to have been asked – this can only be done by very professional interviewees.

Syndicated Radio Interviews

In the UK, there are now many organizations that will produce an interview on tape, syndicated to local stations. The above basic principles still apply. However, as your organization is paying for the service, you will receive more help in the preparation. Remember that the final radio tape has to stand up to broadcast standards or it will not get used. The syndicating companies will not allow the interview to become soft; they want – and you want – good usable material.

Studio Interviews

Face-to-face interviews are invaluable because your speaker is not competing for attention, though he or she is competing for the time. If the interview is live, then the amount of time available will be known beforehand, and there is likely to have been more discussion beforehand about the areas to be covered. If the interview is to be filmed and edited, its length might depend on the amount of interest that the speaker is able to generate. Never agree to a five-minute interview that will be cut down to 30 seconds on-screen.

Consider carefully the points you or your spokesman want to put over. You may need to identify the questions that are to be asked in order to weave these into your answers.

Always treat interviewers as professionals trying to do a professional job. Their only major advantage is that they will have more experience. Do not try to challenge them on their own area of professionalism; but remember that they are extremely unlikely to know as much about the sector under discussion as you or your spokesman.

Never bluff. Handle naive questions politely. If the interviewer is asking a simple question, it is because the viewers or listeners would like to ask the same simple question. There are many ways of presenting the truth, but avoid misrepresentations.

Listen carefully to the stance that the interviewer is taking. Quite often he or she is representing the public at large. This is perfectly fair; you need to judge whether he or she has got a better measure of public feeling than you yourself.

Some Broadcast Tips

Put adequate preparation into what you or your spokesman is to say. Do not rely on being a spontaneous speaker. Concentrate on the good news and avoid temptations to justify yourself. Do not allow the interviewer to get on top of the situation. Keep your cool; concentrate on the essentials. Do not be diverted. Learn to convert technicalities into simple lay language. Do not say anything on-air or off-air that you might regret later. Prepare for yourself or your executive a brief of the main points you wish to cover.

Do not, under any circumstances, drink before the interview. Wear clothes appropriate to the situation. Avoid annoying mannerisms. Concentrate on what *you* want to say, not on what *they* want to say. Think of interesting ways of illustrating your points. Keep it enthusiastic. Avoid jargon. Talk through the interviewer to the audience. Do not allow yourself to be interrupted. Correct any inaccuracies in the questions.

Look honest, sound honest, and be honest – then you and your organization might be believed.

HOW TO WORK WELL WITH JOURNALISTS: A CHECK-LIST

1. Make your story factual, and never write anything that would embarrass a journalist if it appeared in print and were challenged.
2. Use the most effective way of getting the copy in front of the journalist. This may well dictate whether it should be a conference, a news release, or a telephone call.
3. Write in the style that you would like to see used when the material is published, resisting superlatives and assertions.
4. Respect the journalists' independence and never expect favours or special treatment.
5. Respect the journalists' professionalism and expect them to respect yours.
6. Get to know the journalists with whom you are most likely to be in regular contact and learn what makes them tick.
7. Never allow your non-public relations colleagues to dictate what should go into a news story unless you are convinced that it is right.
8. On everything that you are researching or writing, constantly look for the fresh news angle.
9. Never knock the competition, either in the written or the spoken word – if journalists want to know what they are up to they will have to ask them directly.
10. Handle the bad news as positively and confidently as you do the good.
11. Avoid embargoes if at all possible and use them only where they are strictly necessary.
12. If there is the slightest possibility that an incident could create bad news, have the courage to release this before the enquiries begin.
13. Have a contingency plan for dealing with the problems that can be reasonably expected – and public relations machinery for dealing with those that cannot be expected!

14. Prepare standby statements on issues and incidents where journalists may require comment, and be sure that these are issued to all personnel who may need to talk to the media.

15. Be certain that all news stories are also issued internally and to professional advisors (such as the organization's advertising agency, accountants, marketing consultants, and so on).

16. Treat any aggressive or unsympathetic journalist calmly and evenly – you will never win an argument with a journalist.

17. Do not allow yourself to be bullied by the media, and remember that you represent not their interests but the organization that is paying your salary – *they* will never forget it!

18. Try to tailor as many stories as possible to individual publications or key commentators on your industry.

19. Do not allow any of your non-public relations colleagues who are not properly trained to talk directly to the media without your close involvement.

20. Regularly check your news by discussing your PR angles with colleagues from other organizations or non-competitive companies.

21. If you find that you cannot give journalists the complete story, always explain why this is so and when you will be able to fully up-date.

22. Always keep every promise to the media – not just the big one ('I'll let you have an exclusive on this when the acquisition is finalised'), but also the small ones ('I'll ring you back in five minutes').

23. Look for good picture angles to support the written word – particularly when dealing with television.

24. Never assume that a journalist understands the background; always find this out by asking the right questions.

BUILDING BROAD COMPANY CREDIBILITY ON STRONG MEDIA RELATIONS

Obviously, media relations will be only part of a broader public relations programme. However, this element will often be one of the most effective ways to reach the audiences upon whom the organization depends.

Certainly there is much research that shows the credibility of messages that reach the public through the editorial media in comparison with, for example, advertising, where the reader (or listener or viewer) balances the information against the fact that it is a bought message.

Even some of the most sophisticated public relations campaigns will be built on a base of good media relations. Certainly there can be no general public relations practitioner who can claim to be effective unless he or she is a master in media relations.

Bibliography

S. Blank, *Introduction to Public Relations*, Modino.
F. Jenkins, *Public Relations*, 4th edn, Pitman.
W. Howarth, *The Practice of Public Relations*, 3rd edn, Butterworth Heinemann.
H. and P. Lloyd, *Teach Yourself Public Relations*, Hodder & Stoughton.
N. Stone, *How to Manage Public Relations*, McGraw-Hill.

12 Communications Research

Christopher West

THE CONTRIBUTION OF RESEARCH

Surprisingly, in this age of communication, the business world is still populated by some poor communicators; individuals and companies who feel that staff, customers, owners, and others who can influence the fortunes of the organization, can be left in partial or complete ignorance of corporate objectives, strategies, needs, and methods without any ill effects. However, the days of successful autocratic management have passed, along with the 50-hour working week and child labour. Successful companies are distinguished by frequent and intense communication between managers, and, for complete success, this practice is extended to all groups that are involved in the operations of the company. It must be recognized, however, that it is one thing for a small group informally to understand one another's requirements and motives and quite another for this to be achieved among much larger groups, where a formal communications strategy is required.

No strategy can be planned without information, and good communication, like good marketing, will be achieved only if communicators understand the real needs of their target audiences. Many corporate executives feel that they obtain such information automatically, either from their own contacts and experience or through the corporate grapevine. This may be true to an extent, but experience indicates that it is rare for an executive to be made party to the whole truth or the unvarnished truth, especially when dealing with subordinates or others with positions to defend. Strategies based on half-truths or folklore are unlikely to be well conceived. The need for action, the objectives of the communications campaign, the methods by which the campaign should be conducted, and the specific messages that are likely to produce the desired result can be decided only by reference to factual and unbiased information on the current awareness, perceptions, and requirements of the audiences that the corporation wishes to reach.

Sometimes the requirement is obvious. A new company knows that it has to work hard to gain awareness of its existence and objectives. A company entering a take-over battle knows that it has to fight to persuade shareholders to support the present management. A period of intense labour

195

difficulties must be followed by a period of bridge-building with the workforce. But more often than not, the need for a communications strategy is far from obvious, and, even when it is apparent, recent data that will determine the type of campaign and the most appropriate and effective communication channels are rarely available to management.

A national building society with a London head office, regional offices, and hundreds of branches used a company newsletter as a means of passing on information on corporate developments, changes in policy, and personnel and social news. The intention was not only to create a family feeling but also to ensure that staff were sufficiently knowledgeable to answer questions from outsiders. The system appeared to management to work well, but when probed by research, this proved to be a false impression. The newsletter was seen as an instrument for distributing official propaganda, designed to conceal the truth rather than enlighten the staff. Issues of major concern were carefully left out of the newsletter. In response, an unofficial newsletter had been started and was widely circulated. This covered the real issues and had gained considerable credibility, but it was totally outside the control of management. The dangers were obvious and real. The research also showed that the communication needs varied considerably by grade of staff. Those in responsible positions required more detailed information to be communicated in personal briefings. The more junior staff also required personal contact with their managers not only on matters directly affecting them but also to obtain information on the general progress of the company. Written communications were seen as a means of providing supporting information, but not as the main method of communicating. A video of a statement by the chairman or managing director smacked too much of 'Big Brother' and was generally counter-productive. Not surprisingly, these findings stimulated the company to concentrate on the oral flow of information down the management chain and to attempt to re-establish the credibility of official written communications. The cynic would say that the research showed only what any half-competent manager knows already, namely, that people must be made to feel that they matter in an organization. It is nevertheless amazing how often this simple fact is overlooked in corporate communications strategies.

The communications planner must be in a position to answer seven key questions:

1. How effective is the current corporate communications programme?
2. What is the nature and extent of the communications problem?
3. What new or corrective messages need to be transmitted?

4. Who should receive the messages?
5. How can the messages be most effectively (or cost-effectively) transmitted?
6. What is (or has been) the effect of the communications programme?
7. Is there a requirement for further action?

In order to answer each of the above questions, the communications planner requires reliable, objective information drawn from the relevant audiences within and outside the company. Without such information, the strategy will be based on feelings, guesswork, and prejudice. As with all areas of marketing and planning, data to support decision-making can be made available using market research techniques; to ignore this facility is to increase the risk of failure unnecessarily.

Communications Problems

All companies have to communicate effectively with a variety of publics. Their staff, customers, shareholders, and bankers form part of a body of stakeholders who in one way or another, and to varying degrees, can influence performance. Whether a problem exists or not depends on how well the communications task has been performed in the past and on external factors over which the company itself has no direct influence. In a dynamic environment there is bound to be a continuous stream of events that threatens corporate performance unless a correct response is made. In addition, the company's own actions and policies can create images and attitudes that impair performance. Examples abound. Over the years, countless British companies have carefully crafted an image of being poor on delivery and unreliable as regards the service they offer. In reality, their performance may be no worse than their foreign rivals, but it is the image that counts rather than the performance. Mercedes owners are quite used to placing the order for their next car when they take delivery of a new model, to ensure that the car is available when they require it; but who accuses Mercedes of poor delivery lead times?

A communications problem exists if the perceptions of target audiences are at variance with the truth and are detrimental to the performance of the company. At its simplest, the problem can arise from the circulation of inaccurate information. Labour relations are plagued by the circulation of rumours and half-truths masquerading as firm corporate policy. Share prices are a perennial victim to rumoured take-over bids or changes in profit expectations. Misinformation is eagerly latched on to in the absence of an adequate flow of reliable information from authoritative sources, but it soon comes to light when it is fed back to the corporation as supporting evidence for some corrective action. The subtle problems are more difficult to cope with, simply because there is no mechanism by which they automatically come to light. How does the company discover that a lacklustre stock market performance is due to the chairman's lack of charisma and his consequent inability to project enthusiasm for the company and its business? How does it discover that the real reason for lost business is that the accounts department has pressed too hard for payment in the past and the company is therefore perceived as being totally unsympathetic? The answer, in both cases, is research. The real attitudes and perceptions of the company's publics can be probed and explained in considerable depth by the use of research techniques.

Research can go further than just showing the truth of the current situation. Knowing current attitudes and perceptions is only part of what is needed. To formulate a strategy the company must also know what impressions its publics should hold in order to act in the company's best interests. In other words, it needs to have a model of the ideal image profile which it can aim for; pulling the actual image profile as far as possible into line with the ideal image profile then becomes the task of the communications strategy. Obviously, the information that is to be communicated needs to be truthful, and therefore the same research observations may initiate operational changes within the company.

The reasons why unfavourable attitudes and images persist are to some extent of academic interest, but they need to be explored if repetitions of the problems are to be avoided in future. This is particularly true if the cause lies in some inadequacy in the company's communications programme. Companies may create problems by providing too little information or by using the wrong communications methods. Long silences and insufficiently detailed information releases generate vacuums that are liable to be filled by speculation. The frequency, the depth, and the methods of communicating need to relate to the requirements of the audiences, and research can establish what these requirements are.

Determining the Message

In order to define a solution to the identified problem, research can be used to pinpoint the precise messages that will result in a change in attitude. All publics have an ideal image profile, which is conditioned by the business in which the company is operating, the publics' objectives and needs, the company's past performance, and comparisons with other organizations. Most of these requirements can be defined and measured by research.

Attributes such as friendliness, efficiency, concern with customer problems, and reliability are readily recognized by customers and others and are often used to describe organizations. The importance of each attribute in determining whether, for example, customers are willing to do business can be weighted and the actual performance of companies on these factors can be rated. These measurements are vital in determining communications strategies.

To an extent, companies can educate their publics on what they should be looking for, but inevitably they hold their own opinions as well. The messages that should be transmitted in the communications programme are those that are likely to cause the target audiences to abandon beliefs that are unfavourable to the company and adopt new favourable opinions repositioning it either close to the ideal or in an appropriate position relative to competition. As indicated above, the messages must be supported by fact in order to be credible, but when dealing with people facts are much easier to establish than perceptions. A pound of image is worth a ton of performance, but it is harder to establish and more difficult to remove.

Identifying Target Audiences

The target audiences for communications strategies can be defined quite simply in macro terms: employees, shareholders, customers, and media are all easily identifiable groups. However, the communications programme may need to be more narrowly focused on sub-segments of the total audience or on groups that are particularly influential in shaping opinions or affecting performance. Rifle shot strategies aimed at the specific trouble spots or opinion leaders and opinion formers may prove to be far more cost-effective than broadcast approaches covering all members of the groups. Identifying such individuals is a key research task.

Selecting the Optimum Communications Channels

Just as the communications needs of an audience may be far from obvious, so are the methods of communicating effectively. Communications methods and media are well defined, but their role in a specific communications strategy needs to be determined by reference to the requirements of the audiences. There is an ever-present danger that approaches are adopted because *management* finds them acceptable, and what is acceptable to management may be very far from the real requirements of the audience. Only the audience itself can define what is acceptable and appropriate, and there is little doubt that the effectiveness and credibility of the message can be influenced by the means by which it is communicated. The gravity and degree of confidentiality of the message and the size of the target audience should all influence the communications channels. Few employees would wish to hear of their salary review by means of an advertisement, but shareholders do not require a personal meeting with the chairman to be notified of movements in the share price – indeed, were such a meeting to be called, they would fear the worst.

The effectiveness of a communications approach can be influenced by fashion, by the extent to which it has been used previously for similar purposes, by the message itself, and by the extent to which it reaches the target audiences. Judgements on each of these require research-based information. Overworking an approach may blunt its effectiveness, but there is no means of assessing whether it has been overworked other than by reference to the audience at which it is to be aimed. Previous use, or abuse, of a medium may well have undermined its credibility. Staff newsletters may be perceived as too frivolous, too closely allied with a particular segment of management, or simply too dull to be of value as a serious method of communicating future policy. Only research among staff can establish the true position.

APPLICATIONS

There is a tendency to regard research as a one-off exercise designed to fill obvious gaps in knowledge. This assumes that, once acquired, knowledge rarely requires updating or amending. In the corporate environment, it also assumes that the actions of the company do not result in change. Although it is true that some information becomes obsolete only slowly, most situations involving people are highly volatile. Opinions and perceptions do change, and if this is to be tracked, the research process must be continuous.

Communications research is most appropriate at four stages of the programme:

1. To assist in the formulation of the strategy.
2. To test whether the proposed campaign meets the objectives of the communicator.
3. To test the effect of the campaign.
4. To monitor developments following the commencement of the campaign and, if necessary, to initiate a new strategy.

Strategy Formulation

The use of research for strategy formulation is commonly accepted. This is the point at which the communicator's ignorance is most noticeable and where the need for objective data is greatest. Unless the company is already engaged in a monitoring programme, research itself will not highlight the need for a communications strategy. The cycle is most commonly initiated by events, changes in policy, or deterioration in performance.

Basic research to prepare the strategy fills the secondary purpose of establishing a benchmark against which the success of the strategy can be measured. It is just as important to know where you have come from as to know where you are going.

Research to assist in the preparation of a strategy needs to be wide-ranging, covering all aspects of the communications process and all actions that will result in an improvement in the company's situation. This commonly involves research among samples of the target publics themselves.

Pre-Testing of Campaigns

Once a strategy has been devised, complete with target audiences, messages, and media, some form of testing is essential in order to ensure that it will produce the required effect. To launch a campaign without testing its effectiveness risks not only wasting all or part of the campaign budget but also compounding the problem. However well intentioned, a bad campaign may prove worse than no campaign at all. A pre-test is a modest insurance policy.

Post-Testing of Campaign Effectiveness

Success of the campaign can be judged only by measuring the changes in attitudes and perceptions that have resulted from the campaign. This is achieved by means of research carried out after the campaign has been completed.

Tracking Studies

Tracking changes in attitudes among audiences by means of continuous research or periodic surveys is a refinement of the process which is not always necessary but can certainly contribute to the maintenance of a correct profile. Continuous monitoring should be considered during periods of rapid change or when it is essential to have up-to-date information ready to hand, for example during a protracted labour dispute or a contested bid. For the most part, management can be kept adequately informed on attitudes and opinions by means of occasional surveys. If undertaken, these may signal the need for a new or revised communications strategy.

RESEARCH TECHNIQUES

The quality of the information provided by the research programme is a function of the quality of the research techniques used. Research is a highly specialized activity, and it is difficult for the non-researcher to determine how the research should be undertaken, let alone actually do it. Furthermore, it is sometimes difficult to judge the quality of what is being offered by a specialist research supplier, unless there is some means of independently checking the results. Although this may be possible for quantitative market surveys, it is rarely so for qualitative research into opinions and attitudes. The user of communications research is therefore heavily dependent on the supplier of services to ensure that the approach and techniques are appropriate and valid. The purpose of this section is not to provide a detailed review of communications research techniques, but to offer readers sufficient preliminary insight into the mysterious practices of the researcher to enable them to understand what they are being offered.

In general terms, information can be collected from secondary and primary sources and can be acquired by means of a variety of research techniques. Secondary research involves the collection of data that have already been published in reports, the press, and other generally or privately available sources. Secondary data are normally obtained by a literature search. Primary data refer to original data obtained directly from participants in the business, normally by means of sample surveys. The nature of communications is such that primary data are required to solve most problems; secondary data may be available, but the communications problems of companies are generally so specific to their situation at a particular time that specially tailored research is essential to obtain real understanding. Primary data collection involves the use of personal and telephone interviews, group discussions, and special analysis routines in order to capture relevant information from a sample, which is representative of the entire target audience being considered. The types and volume of research techniques to be used depend on the information to be collected and the respondents who will provide it.

In communications research, the most commonly encountered techniques are:

- The communications audit.
- Published data search.
- In-depth personal interviews
- Telephone interviews.
- Mail or internal questionnaires.
- Group discussions.
- Media research.
- Advertising assessment techniques.

The Communications Audit

The communications audit is a means of describing and assessing the tangible and intangible communications resources of a company that are available to the communications planner. The resources comprise the communication skills of the staff, the media available to disseminate information, the value placed on the media by information recipients, and the information base that the company holds on the publics that it needs to reach. The purpose of the audit is to determine whether the company has sufficient resources, whether it is making adequate use of what exists, whether what is done is properly planned and organized, whether there is untapped potential to be exploited, and whether there are gaps in resources that need to be filled. The audit is carried out by means of contacts with key staff responsible for initiating communications and among the recipients of communications both within and outside the company. The latter is needed to assess the levels of communications skills as perceived by the recipients, and on the values attached to the media available to the company.

A typical audit of staff communications could involve the following steps:

1. A critical review of the communications objectives and policies of management.
2. An appraisal of the staff responsible for internal communications.
3. An assessment of the information held on staff attitudes and information needs.
4. An examination of the methods by which information on staff attitudes and information needs is collected.

5. A detailed examination of staff journals, newsletters and other formal methods by which information is distributed to staff, covering content, format, and frequency.
6. A study of the informal communication channels through which staff receive information.
7. An evaluation of the value placed on each communication channel by various grades of staff.
8. An assessment of the credibility of the messages disseminated by each communication channel.

Such an audit would show whether the resources were adequate and the types of changes that should be instituted in order to improve communications. Similar programmes could be undertaken in most other target audiences with refinements reflecting their particular status and structure.

Published Data Sources

Published information can cover a wide range of communications and marketing topics, and, although it is rare for it to relate directly to a corporate communications problem, it may provide useful background. The most widely available data relate to the numbers of individuals and organizations in specified target groups; descriptions of communications programmes undertaken by similar organizations; evaluations of the effectiveness of comparable communications campaigns; the readership of journals; and, in some cases, expenditure by competitors on specific communications programmes. These data are generally available from official sources, private surveys, academic publications, marketing journals, and the marketing and communications trade press. Expenditure data may be deduced from statistics on media advertising.

Although they are of indirect use, it is well worth searching for published data, not only because they will provide answers, but also because they may assist in directing the more expensive field research. Obtaining the share register of a company that is the subject of an acquisition bid is an obvious and essential preliminary to communications aimed at them, but it can also be used as a sample base for shareholder research. Information on how rivals have improved their labour relations may well provide some interesting guidelines for research among the company's own staff.

A significant advantage of published research is that it is generally inexpensive to acquire. A few days in a good business library can pay worthwhile dividends.

Field Research

The most relevant information comes from direct contact with samples of staff and client recipients of the messages being communicated. If a company wishes to know what its publics think, what they would like to think, how they would prefer to receive information, and the types of information they would like to receive, the simplest way to find out is to ask them. It is normally impossible to ask all of them; nor is it essential to do so. A survey carried out among a sample will provide all the information that is required, provided that the sample is representative of the group as a whole.

The major techniques for making contacts with samples of respondents are personal interviews, telephone interviews, questionnaires sent through the post or the internal distribution system, and group discussions. The major difference between the techniques is the method of making contact with the respondents and the length of the contact, but this obviously affects the volume and depth of information that can be obtained. It also affects the cost of the research programme.

Personal interviews

Face-to-face interviews are the workhorse of the research business. They may be totally unstructured, meaning that the direction of questioning is evolved during the interview in the light of the answers given, or they can be partially or fully structured so that predetermined types of information are collected. Their main advantage is that they can probe respondents' attitudes and feelings in depth and can seek explanations as to why respondents feel the way they do. The main disadvantage is that they are time-consuming for both the researcher and the respondent. However, in the more sensitive areas of communications research, that can be a small price to pay in order to ensure that the data are adequate and that the respondents feel that they have made a full contribution to the research programme.

Telephone interviews

The questions asked in face-to-face interviews can also be put by telephone. Telephone interviews techniques cannot be used to obtain in-depth understanding, but they are quite suitable for obtaining structured information. They are particularly useful where time is limited. The telephone has gained ground as a research technique because it is cost effective and enables the researcher to obtain responses from samples of respondents quickly. Its usefulness in this respect has been further enhanced by computerization. CATI (Computer-Aided Telephone Interview) systems display questionnaires to telephone interviewers and also capture the data. Edit checks can be built into the program so that the answers are tested as they are entered. CATI systems will also manage the sample by displaying telephone numbers remaining to be called to interviewers as they become free, and even organizing recalls. Analysis can be almost instantaneous as the survey is completed or at any stage during the interviewing process.

Self-completed questionnaires

Self-completed questionnaires have fallen out of favour for general market research but are retained in communications research, largely because the respondents have some interest in providing a reply and the response rates are therefore sufficiently high to provide valid data. Self-completed questionnaires are particularly suitable for obtaining information from respondents who are travelling frequently or are otherwise difficult to contact during the normal working day. They are also useful when it is necessary for respondents to think at length about the questions before replying.

Group discussions

The depth of understanding provided by a survey can be radically improved by using group discussions as a means of collecting information. This technique interviews groups of respondents simultaneously so that they hear each others' views and provide a reaction to them. Normally, six to eight respondents are brought together, sometimes in specially equipped rooms with recording facilities. The discussions may last several hours and topics are explored in great depth. The added understanding is provided by the interplay between respondents, and the role of the interviewer (or moderator) is to guide the discussion, rather than ask specific questions. However, the cost of recruitment and the need to provide some form of incentive, plus the heavy calls on research time, mean that the technique is very costly and must therefore be used sparingly. Fortunately, the data yield from a single group is considerably more detailed and informative than individual interviews with an equivalent number of respondents. Group discussions therefore play an important role in the types of qualitative research required for communications planning.

Questionnaires and check-lists

The single most important research tool that is common to all four techniques is the questionnaire or check-list. If this is inadequate and omits essential topics, the data yield will be incomplete; if it misleads the respondents, the answers will be wrong. Designing questionnaires is a major research skill and it may well take a number of re-drafts and a pretest before a satisfactory document is finally produced.

Media Research

As the name implies, media research is designed to provide data on all aspects of the media by which information is communicated. For national, local, and trade press it covers the numbers of readers of specific journals, the structure of the readership, and readers' comprehension and retention of the information they have taken in from journals. It can also provide reactions to specific copy and messages. Its uses are wider than corporate communications, but obviously the techniques are of value in assessing the usefulness of channels and the effect that they have on recipients. Media research is largely undertaken by the media themselves for their own planning purposes, but the corporate communicator needs to be aware of its existence since it can be a useful information source.

Advertising Assessment

Advertising research is another specialization that can be directly and indirectly useful to the communicator. It is of direct use if advertisements are to be used as part of the communications mix; it is indirectly useful in that some of the techniques that have been used for advertising may be of value for assessing other methods of communication.

Advertisers have developed an armoury of sophisticated techniques for the pre- and post-testing of their output. These concentrate on identifying the messages that have the greatest impact and recall among their target audiences and therefore are communicating effectively. Corporate communicators have an idea to sell rather than a product, but their requirement is the same: they need to know that they are getting through in the best possible way. Therefore they can borrow some of the advertisers' research technology. Ratings of messages, recall tests, association tests, and recognition tests (such as Starch) are all worth considering when evaluating a corporate communications campaign.

Internal and External Research

Since communications can be either internal or external, the research must also be directed at audiences within and outside the company. This does not have a major effect on the techniques to be used, but it can influence the ways in which they are deployed. Internal audiences are more likely to co-operate but at the same time will be more sensitive, since they stand to gain or lose directly. The fact that research is being undertaken may be perceived as a threat. It may also be used as an opportunity to pass messages back to management. The results are therefore prone to biases which must be recognized in advance and neutralized. Sampling internally may also raise problems. Participation may be seen as a status symbol, and management is sometimes at too much pain to ensure that certain individuals are given a chance to express their views. This process can impair the representativeness of the survey.

Research among external audiences may be dogged by relatively low interest on the part of respondents and a consequent reluctance to co-operate but it is unlikely to encounter more than the normal research biases.

OBTAINING AND USING THE INFORMATION

Once the information required has been specified, the communications planner needs to initiate the research process by which it will be obtained. The major decisions to be taken are:

● Who will obtain the data?
● What resources will be deployed?
● How long will the survey take?
● How much will the survey cost?

Communications planners need to devote as much time to determining how their information is to be collected as to deciding what information is to be sought. It is reasonably evident that the quality of the information will depend on the skills with which the research process is carried out. Badly organized surveys generally produce poor data. There is also a cost implication. Research is rarely inexpensive, and in budget-conscious organizations planning is essential to ensure that surveys are carried out as cost-effectively as possible. In any survey, time, resources, and cost are almost inseparable. Long, complicated surveys requiring high levels of skill cost more than short, simple exercises. As in all services, the main input to a research programme is time, and the more time that is spent, the higher the cost. Costs are sometimes disguised if the research is carried out by internal employees, but they are present nevertheless, and in today's financially driven organizations, research services are more than likely to be cross-charged between departments.

In all types of research involving interviews, the number, type, and length of interview are generally the major determinants of cost and are therefore a common cost yardstick. Because they take longer to complete, personal interviews are generally more expensive than telephone interviews. In corporate research, interviews with senior staff require more skill than interviews with junior staff or members of the public, and are therefore more expensive. At 1994 prices, interviews can cost between tens of pounds each to over £100. Thus, a large sample survey, even if it covers respondents that are easy to locate and uses a short questionnaire, is likely to cost between £5000 and £10 000. Where executive time is required, for example for desk research and analysis, this would be charged at £300–£400 per day. Group discussions currently average £1500 per session. Research bills are unlikely to be low, and so when budgets are limited, as they invariably are, the communications planner must plan the execution of any research exercise carefully in order to ensure that maximum value is extracted.

Internal and Bought-in Resources

Most communications planners will have little choice over whether they use in-house or external resources to collect their data. Relatively few companies employ market research staff, and of those that do, few employ enough to carry out major research surveys. However, it is worth examining briefly the merits of the alternative approaches.

Internal staff are close to the business of the company, are thoroughly familiar with its structure, and generally have collected information about the business on a regular basis. They are well up the learning curve and need minimal preparation before commencing any new survey work. Their major disadvantage, particularly if the research is to be undertaken among staff, is that they are part of the organization that is itself the subject of study; their objectivity is therefore liable to be questioned. For research among external groups this is less of a disadvantage, but even then there is some risk that the information given may be biased by the respondent because it is sought directly by an employee of the company.

The independent view offered by external consultants has value, though a price is paid in terms of the longer learning time that will be required before they can commence. Perhaps more importantly, consultants can provide skills and resources that are required infrequently and are therefore unlikely to exist internally. Communications research is unlikely to be a constant feature of corporate life, and a standing team would hardly be justified unless they had other tasks to fulfil. Some of the research skills are highly specialized and can be fully employed only if the researchers are working for a number of clients. This of course enables them to observe a wide variety of communications problems, and what they lack in industry or company knowledge may be more than offset by their ability to cross-fertilize from similar situations in other environments.

Proposing a Survey

Whichever resources are to be used, there are a number of stages that planners must go through in order to ensure that they get what they want at a price they can afford. These are:

1. To prepare a clear brief describing their requirements.
2. To obtain a proposal from the research team.
3. To select the best approach on the basis of the proposal.

The brief is the most important step. If it is incomplete, the survey will not provide all the data the planner requires. If it is over-elaborate, too much information will be collected and the survey will be unnecessarily expensive. The brief should contain the following information in order that the researcher can make the most appropriate proposal:

- Background on the company and the problems it is experiencing.
- The reasons why information is being sought.
- The uses to which the information will be put, or the topics that need to be addressed in any recommendations arising out of the research.
- Information already held which will form a basis for the new research.
- The geographical scope of the survey.
- The information that is required.
- The publics that should be covered.
- Guidance on the research methods to be used.
- The time available for the survey.

The brief is not intended to provide a complete blueprint for the survey, but only a statement of what the planner requires. It is the researcher's task to convert the brief into a formal proposal or offer. The proposal will use the material contained in the brief to show the precise information that can be collected, the methods that will be used, the time needed and, if relevant, the cost. In making the proposal, the researcher should seek to guide the planner by eliminating objectives that are impractical and suggesting additional approaches or information that can be collected without adding to the overall cost. Once accepted, the proposal not the brief provides the guidelines for the research and is the basis of the contract between planner and researcher.

Where competitive proposals are sought, they also become the basis for the selection of the researcher. The quality of the proposal is a significant indicator of the quality of the organization making the offer, but it is not the only factor to be taken into account. The proposal shows whether the researcher has understood the problem and is capable of making a cost-effective response. However, the planner should also consider other factors that will indicate whether the quality of the project will be adequate. Some of these may be covered in the proposal, but if they are not they should be asked for. They include the previous research experience of the research team, the biographies of the staff that will be working on the project, the physical resources available to the research team (such as computing hardware and specialised software), data bases available to the research company, and any specific research techniques in which the team is particularly skilled. In making the final selection, remember that the lowest quote is not necessarily the best. In research you generally get what you pay for, and wide discrepancies between quotations mean that you are being offered different surveys. Be certain that the quote you accept is going to provide you with the information you require at levels of accuracy that are acceptable.

Running the Survey

Once the survey is commissioned, the planner's task is far from complete. Sitting back and waiting for the researchers to report is inviting problems. It is essential to keep in regular touch with the research team in order to ensure that the survey is progressing on time, that any modifications in approach or data yield suggested by the research are agreed upon in time, and that any early findings are acted upon. The planner should also review and agree the questionnaires that are to be used and should consider the results of any pilot work. Research expertise is not essential to make an intelligent contribution.

Close involvement does not mean subjecting the research team to a constant third degree. They have to have room in which to manoeuvre, and additional meetings are wasteful in time and resources; on the other hand, the results have to be used by the planner, and once the survey is complete it is too late to make good any deficiencies that have arisen during the research process. No research team objects to regular reporting meetings and they will normally cost for them.

Getting Value for Money

The value of the research project will be determined by the actions taken at all stages, from briefing to reporting. Detailed specification of requirements, careful selection of the research team, and close involvement during the survey will all help to ensure that the planner gets value for money; but there are a number of further actions that will improve the ultimate usefulness of the project.

Planners should disclose their requirements to the researchers as soon as possible. By doing so they can make use of any previous experience that the researchers have had and will probably be able to design a better brief.

Relevant information known to the planner should be provided to the research team and not held back as a means of checking the results. There is little point in paying twice for the same information.

The project should be large enough to generate valid and convincing data and no larger. Small samples might be quite adequate in certain circumstances and there is little point in paying for more research than is needed. The researchers' guidance should be sought on what is adequate.

The information yield should not be extended so far that interesting but unactionable data are collected. If the results cannot be acted upon within six months of collection, they are not worth having.

Finally, the information must be used. This sounds obvious, but there are far too many instances of surveys languishing on shelves rather than providing the background for action.

Bibliography

M. Baker, *Research for Marketing*, Macmillan.

R. Birn, P. Hague and P. Vangelder (eds), *A Handbook of Market Research Techniques*, Kogan Page.

P. Chisnall, *Marketing Research*, McGraw-Hill.

S. Crouch, *Marketing Research for Managers*, Heinemann.

P. Hague, *The Industrial Marketing Research Handbook*, Kogan Page.

P. Hague and P. Jackson, *Do Your Own Market Research*, Kogan Page.

J. May, *How to Make Effective Business Presentations*, McGraw-Hill.

M. Moroney, *Facts From Figures*, Penguin.

K. Sutherland, *Researching Business Markets*, Kogan Page.

R. Walker (ed.), *Applied Quantitative Research*, Gower.

R. Worcester and J. Downam (eds), *Consumer Market Research Handbook*, Elsevier.

13 Corporate Social Responsibility: The Case for Active Stakeholder Relationship Management

Sarah Portway

INTRODUCTION

No company operates in a vacuum. Whether privately owned or publicly quoted, every company is dependent on effective relationships with a wide range of groups which have the capacity, individually and collectively, to influence a company's success or to frustrate or even spoil its endeavours.

For the purpose of this chapter, Corporate Social Responsibility (CSR) is defined as the process by which a company manages its relationships with these constituencies. Companies have a choice. They can actively manage such relationships or they can let them develop and mature as the imperatives of the business demand. This chapter argues that active management of a company's behaviour towards these constituencies is becoming increasingly important and will become even more so as the world within which business is conducted becomes more complex and more competitive. Most companies already actively manage some of these interactions, for example with their customers and their employees. The other relationships, which are perhaps less direct in their immediate impact on the business, have tended to receive less direct attention.

This chapter is divided into three sections. The first defines a company's stakeholders and elaborates on the case for active management by a company of these relationships. The second section then looks at one of these relationships in more detail, that is the relationship between a company and the broader community within which it operates and outlines the development of the discipline of Corporate Community Involvement. The third section outlines how a company can apply active stakeholder management principles to its Corporate Community Involvement activities.

The Stakeholder Concept

The relationships mentioned above can most easily be described using the stakeholder concept. Stakeholders are individuals or groups who have a vested interest in a company's operations, who interact with a company in one or more of its activities and on whose co-operation or active involvement a company depends for its continuing business success. In broad terms a company's stakeholders can be defined as:

- *Providers of Capital*   institutional and individual investors on whom the company is dependent for the provision of equity and who depend on the company to provide them with a return on their investment;
- *Customers*   the consumers of a company's goods and services on whom the company depends for revenue and who depend on the company to meet their needs often both immediately and in the long term;
- *Suppliers*   other companies on whom the main company depends for the provision of goods and services (very similar to the customer relationship described above) and who depend on the main company for a continuing revenue stream.
- *Employees*   individuals on whom the company depends for its access to skills, knowledge, commitment and loyalty and who have a dependency on the company's current and future business success to secure their own livelihoods;
- *The Community*   the broader society within which a company conducts its business which has a dependency on the company's continuing business success to generate sufficient wealth and employment to maintain local prosperity and on whom the company depends for it licence to operate. It is important to note that 'the community' is not a homogenous entity. It embodies political organizations, at both national and local levels, as well as the concepts of neighbourhood and communities of interest.

Each of these relationships represents dependencies and expectations, they demand mutual respect and imply responsibilities for both partners. Implicit in the notion of the stakeholder is the concept of interdependency. This does not mean that the relationship should not be demanding and rigorous requiring very high standards. Nor does it mean that conflict will not arise between the expectations of each of the stakeholders. Two examples quickly spring to mind. A shareholder's interest in return on investment may demand improved productivity that necessitates a reduction in the size of the workforce; hardly sitting comfortably with the expectations of employees for continued job security. Likewise the community may wish to demand certain environmental standards which, pushed down the line, will have a very significant effect on a supplier's ability to produce the required goods and services at a price the company is willing to pay. Active management of these relationships will however give companies information about the impact of their business decisions on the various groups with which they are mutually dependent and will allow decisions to be taken about the inevitable trade offs on the basis of knowledge and understanding as opposed to gut feeling or intuition.

ACTIVE MANAGEMENT OF STAKEHOLDER RELATIONSHIPS

Trends in the United Kingdom suggest that there is an increasing focus on managing the stakeholder relationships as part of the general impetus to improve the competitiveness of UK business. The focus on corporate governance stimulated by the Cadbury Committee is evidence of the need to clarify and improve the relationship between the providers of capital and company management. An increasing emphasis on customer care and service to the customer, as demonstrated by customer charters and customer satisfaction programmes, illustrates a growing appreciation of the importance of customer retention to business success. Partnership sourcing through which companies and their suppliers work together, sharing business strategies, transferring skills and technology, and working towards agreed standards of quality, reflects increasing awareness of mutual dependency. The current emphasis on employee empowerment, teamwork and people as assets, as evidenced by kitemarks such as the National Training Awards and Investors in People are recognition of the critical importance of a motivated, capable and continuously improving workforce to compete in today's global marketplace. The growing emphasis on environmental performance within businesses and the need to report on environmental activities through independent audits or adherence to standards such as BS7750 reflect an appreciation of the importance of sustainable development within our community.

These trends are backed up by research which suggests that management of a company's corporate social responsibility is becoming increasingly important. A recent survey of 700 key opinion leaders in the UK[1] asked respondents to list the most important aspects in assessing a company's corporate responsibilities. Active communication with the workforce, paying suppliers on time, staff training, equal employment opportunities, developing better environmental solutions all came ahead of providing a good return on investment for shareholders. In addition eighty one per cent of respondents indicated that a reputation for being socially responsive is becoming a competitive advantage. In another study[2] 117 Captains of Industry interviewed in the summer of 1993 were invited to comment on what they saw to be the most important issues that needed to be addressed by the RSA Inquiry into Tomorrow's Company. Second only to the international competitiveness of UK business came the need for long-term cooperative relationships with stakeholders.

If stakeholder relationship management is to become increasingly important to businesses then as a management practice it needs to be moved away from the periphery right into the core of business planning and management. It is easier to see how this can be achieved in some of the relationships than others – for example many companies would already claim, and rightly so, that the management of the company's relationships with its customers and its employees is at the heart of its business strategy. It is the very process of applying basic business practices to all of these relationships that can help to illustrate their strategic nature and how they can best be managed to the benefit of the business. Managed corporate social responsibilities demand the same rigour to be applied as to any other business process. In other words it is necessary to

1. Set objectives
2. Define strategic directions and levels of investment
3. Identify and implement activities to fulfil the objectives
4. Measure the success of the programmes in meeting the objectives
5. Report to the relevant audiences on progress

Application of these basic business disciplines to the management of CSR provides companies with the necessary tools to decide what levels of resource to allocate to the activity and what impact the programmes it develops have. In this way, what have all too often been seen as the 'soft' elements of business activity can be managed and measured and become more integral to business success.

The 'manage and measure' approach is beginning to emerge in the field of Corporate Community Involvement (CCI) – perhaps one of the 'softest' and most intangible of CSR activities. The remainder of this chapter will look at how CCI can be used as a strategic business tool in managing a company's relationship with the community.

It is important to note at the outset that CCI is just one of the ways a company manages its relationships with the community as a stakeholder. It is important that it should not be seen to be the only one. Inevitably, just about every activity a business undertakes will have an impact on the community within which it operates. How and where a company locates its offices and plants, how it markets and promotes its products and services, how it deals with its waste products, how it transports its employees and its products – the list is enduring – all have an impact on the community. It is this fact that makes the argument for active stakeholder management principles to be applied to every business process so compelling. CCI can however bring the company and the community closer together and so build the relationships that enable the interdependencies to be managed through a constructive and co-operative approach as opposed to one based on confrontation and distrust.

CORPORATE COMMUNITY INVOLVEMENT

The discipline of CCI has developed significantly over the past decade in the UK, but it is not by any means a new practice. Indeed its roots in the UK can be traced back to the family owned businesses such as the Rowntree Company, Pilkington and Cadbury whose basic principles of operation incorporated a paternalistic duty of care for the communities in which they operated. It embodied a recognition that the company itself could not survive unless there was a prosperous community from which to draw its employees and in which to conduct its trade. The local communities within which these companies operated were often wholly dependent on the company, as the major employer, for their continued wellbeing. Here in many ways we see the very epitome of mutual dependency. Although these family companies have now grown or become part of larger and sometimes global organizations, the ethos has remained and indeed has spread to other companies.

With the move away from local companies, residing in local communities and conducting their trade in those local communities, the practice of community involvement has tended to become more diffuse. Informed by a sense of responsibility to put something back into the communities from which companies derived their profits, community involvement initially reflected a more philanthropic approach. The direct link between a company's needs and the community's needs in the philanthropic approach is not so clear. Here the company feels a level of obligation and discharges that obligation through financial contributions, usually to non-profit making organizations which perform important social welfare or cultural activities for the benefit of the community at large. In the UK, obligation has in some circumstances been coupled with fear. It was certainly the case that the number of companies contributing to community activities increased quite considerably in the early eighties as a result of the riots when companies began to see the danger signals for their own business performance of social divisiveness and instability.

Under this model companies establish charitable funds from which to make their financial contributions. Mechanisms for disbursal of funds vary considerably – at one extreme with the Chairman or CEO making decisions on the basis of his or her personal preference, through to the establishment of charity committees which make decisions on behalf of the Board, or to the creation of separate Trusts, administered at arms length from the management of the company, through a Board of Trustees charged with disbursing contributions made to the Trust by the company. In some cases shares in the company are made over to such Trusts, which thereby acquire a second stakeholder interest in the company's success.

The distinguishing feature of the corporate philanthropy model of CCI is that, in general, the company does not expect anything in return for its contribution. The company is fulfilling its responsibility; it is a one way stream.

The one way stream develops into a two way stream with the concept of enlightened self interest. Here companies recognise that they have a responsibility to contribute some of their profits into the communities in which they operate, but they take the view that it is also in the companies' interests so to do. What those interests might be will vary from company to company, or from situation to situation. It may be that a company wishes to deflect potential criticisms that its profits are making a small number of people wealthy, while others remain underprivileged. It may be that it wishes to promote itself as a caring company to the communities in which it operates. It may be that it wishes to reflect concern for its employees by contributing to an activity for which its own workforce has demonstrated concern. The important differential here is that companies not only want to do something, but they also want to be seen to be doing it. Immediately this requires resources from within the company, firstly to decide what it is that the company wants to be seen to be doing and secondly to communicate to the audience the company has decided it wants to tell about its activities.

The increasing number of brochures published by companies giving details of their community activities is a reflection on the extent to which companies have shifted away from the one way stream of corporate philanthropy towards the two way stream of enlightened self interest. To a disinterested observer, some of these may raise in the mind a question as to which side of the equation has assumed greater importance, enlightened giving or self interest. The recent growth in the phenomenon of cause-related marketing, where a company associates a marketing promotion with a charitable cause, has certainly provoked this question to be asked more often, pointing to the need for very careful communication of company activity in this field.

Increasingly therefore some companies in the UK are developing their CCI thinking still further and are adopting a strategic approach to their corporate community involvement which assumes an even greater level of mutual benefit. Here we begin to see a return to the principles of mutual dependency that drove the early family companies to support their local communities, but without the paternalism that marked their approach. Here too we begin to see the concept of managed stakeholder relationships entering the world of corporate community involvement. There are many reasons for these developments, not least the maturation of a field of corporate activity that has become more professional over the years, but there are some key emerging themes that have prompted leading UK companies to adopt a more strategic approach to their CCI activities

1. Recent years have seen a fundamental shift in the UK of the roles of the public, statutory, private and not for profit sectors. Initially sparked by a political ideology driven to wind back the frontiers of the state, this has broken down the barriers between the various sectors and has led to a much greater understanding that no one sector of society can be expected to provide solutions to complex and diverse problems on its own. There is a greater awareness that just as societal problems actually effect every sector of society in one way or another, so their solutions also require joint action.

2. The increasingly global market place in which companies are operating require UK companies to compete with the world's best. This means that the resources we draw on to develop, manufacture, market and sell our products and services have to be of the highest quality. We are therefore increasingly dependent on the infrastructure to provide our competitive edge. The research base, education and training capabilities, the physical infrastructure, the regulatory environment and even general health, welfare and crime levels will help to determine the success or failure of our companies. Companies increasingly see the benefit of investing their own time and resources to contribute to improving the country's capacity to deliver the necessary general environmental conditions to the very highest standards possible.

3. After a decade of individuality in the eighties, trends suggest aspirations for the nineties include a more caring society in which there is a stronger sense of community. Some of the country's most celebrated

successes of the entrepreneurial mood of the 1980s have not survived into the 1990s and some notorious business behaviour has thrown into sharp relief the need for balance in business activity. Businesses are increasingly thinking therefore about their own values and whether they reflect societal values more broadly.

4. The stresses and strains within the fabric of modern society have made people all the more aware of the limited ability of the state to guarantee prosperity. Dramatic social changes – in marriage and divorce, single parenthood, single households, in changing patterns of work (from lifelong employment with one company to multiple careers), in the place of women in society, in attitudes to crime and violence, in the proportion of the elderly in society, in attitudes to once sacred institutions such as the church and the monarchy – have raised awareness that interdependence is an inevitable consequence of and prerequisite for the effective practice of individualism. The rights of an individual and of a company to exist and operate freely in society are inextricably linked with their responsibilities. Freedom is the biggest responsibility as well as the greatest right.

5. The development of organizations whose very reason for being is to increase partnership between business and the community has increased awareness of the business benefits of CCI, has increased the spread of good practice and facilitated networking between corporate affairs professionals within companies. Business in the Community is one example of this type of organization at a national level, but there are many more working on specific issues or programmes at both national and local levels.

CORPORATE COMMUNITY INVOLVEMENT AND ACTIVE STAKEHOLDER MANAGEMENT

In this context companies are looking more closely at their community activities as a tool to enable them to manage their relationships with the broader community strategically. This process involves using the business disciplines referred to earlier.

Setting Objectives

Unless a company has clearly articulated strategic objectives for its CCI programme, the contributions it makes to the broader community will tend to be ad hoc and prone to individual preference or whim. All companies receive many more requests for support from external organizations than they can possibly hope to meet, particularly at a time when public sector funding is under extreme pressure. By developing its own strategy a company can proactively decide what types of activity it wishes to participate in and why; it can then respond much more effectively to requests that are not consistent with its strategic directions. This is no different from deciding what business a company wants to be in and communicating that to customers and potential customers. Just as a customer will not go to a company to buy paint if it knows the company only sells wallpaper, so a community organization involved with supporting older people is unlikely to approach a company that has clearly stated that its major focus for community activities will be on programmes that support young people.

Setting strategic objectives places an onus on senior management to be clear in their own minds about why their company should be involved in community activities and what sort of activities are appropriate for it to participate in. For strategy to be most effective, it needs to be part of the Board Room policy of a company and it needs to have been subject to discussion and examination within the context of the company's overall business strategy. In this way it can be most beneficially linked to the business goals of the company and can be structured to add very real value to the business.

In IBM UK we undertook a wide ranging review of our CCI strategy and programmes in the late 1980s. The review involved consultation and discussion with people within the company and with community leaders and resulted in the adoption by the Board of a new strategy. One of the most symbolic, but nevertheless important, changes that resulted from that review was the change of name of our activities from the CSR programme to the Community Investment programme. We chose the word 'investment' very deliberately because we wanted to achieve two results. First we wanted to convey to people within our business that the community programme was part of the mainstream of our business activity; by viewing it as an investment we were expecting to place the same business disciplines on the activity as we would on our other business activities and we would be reviewing the success of the programme by the extent to which it delivered the returns we had identified. Second, we wanted to convey the message externally that we viewed our community activities as a two way stream, that we wished to participate in activities that were of benefit to us as well as to the recipient of our support and that we would be looking for a return on that investment.

The concept of return on investment for CCI should not be confused with return to the bottom line. The latter implies an expectation of direct financial return for a community involvement. While there may be some circumstances where it is possible to make this connection, (for example in the field of cause related marketing), it is not this imperative that drives IBM's community investment programme. When we speak of a return on our investment we are placing an internal discipline on ourselves to identify, at the outset before we participate in a programme of support, what objectives we are seeking and to put in place a mechanism that will enable us to measure the extent to which we gained the return that we set out to achieve.

IBM set three major objectives for its overall community investment programme

1. To contribute towards a favourable social and economic environment for IBM's business;
2. To be recognised by selected target audiences as a leader in corporate community involvement;
3. To promote the morale and motivation of employees.

These objectives have continued to inform our community investment programme since the late 1980s with very little modification. Each year we review our objectives, our strategic directions and our programme of activity at Board level to ensure that our activities continue to support business goals. In addition these objectives provide the framework from which to determine our strategic directions.

Defining Strategic Directions

To maximise the impact, visibility and benefit of CCI it is necessary for companies to decide what specific areas the company will focus on and what resource (both in level and in kind), the company is prepared to invest. For this process to be of most value to the business there needs to be a mechanism to integrate strategic planning for CCI within the broader strategic planning processes within the company. Most companies undertake some form of environmental scanning or scenario planning as part of their business planning process. The same backdrop provides a very useful starting block for CCI planning and sets the CCI programme at the heart of strategic business activity. CCI can also, however, bring something to the environmental scanning exercise. Through a company's involvement in community activities a wealth of information becomes available to the company about future social issues and concerns. These can be fed into the strategic planning exercise for the business as a whole and can enhance the information available to the company in planning its future business strategies.

One of the key tools we have used in IBM to help us to decide on the strategic directions for our Community Investment Programme has been issue management. This is the process of identifying public policy issues that are of interest to IBM for two reasons; they either create threats to our business activities in terms of imposing limitations on the capacity to conduct our business or they present opportunities for us by stimulating new markets, or creating new needs for our products and services. Issue management is applied across the full range of public policies that may have an impact on our business, from economic, fiscal, trade and industry policies, through to education and training, social and environmental policies. Through the issue management process we define the issue, decide what IBM's objectives should be in our participation in the public policy debate on the issue and develop a course of action that will help us to fulfil the objectives we have set out to meet. Clearly not all of the public policy issues we manage as a business lend themselves to being addressed through the community investment programme, but many do and we therefore use our issue management process as a key input to the process of identifying what strategic directions we should set for our community activities.

Through this exercise we identify what issues are important to the business. But that is only half of the story. The process of management of stakeholder relationships is about mutual dependency. It is therefore important for us to understand what issues are important to our stakeholder 'the community'. To do this, we must listen to the community and understand its issues and concerns. This is in part the responsibility of the 'issue manager' designated with responsibility for managing an issue area within the Corporate Affairs Function. It is his or her responsibility to know the major priorities of government, to understand the views and concerns of interest groups, local communities, opinion leaders and community leaders. He or she undertakes this role through attendance at conferences, research and reading and analysis. But, just as in our marketing and services function we want to make sure we understand our customers needs directly, so we take the same approach with the community. For the past 6 years we have had a Community Advisory Panel which is chaired by the IBM Main Board Director who has responsibility for our Community Investment Programme. Its membership consists of 4 community leaders and 4 senior managers of IBM. It meets quarterly to review the strategic directions of our programme and for the external members to give us insights into emerging issues within the community that we should consider addressing in our community investment programme. Rolling 2 year membership for the external members ensures that we maintain continuity, while refreshing the inputs we receive.

The third input we use to help us to decide on our strategic directions is our employees. Given that one of our objectives for the community investment programme is to promote the morale and motivation of employees, their input is vital. Many IBM employees are active in their local communities, some as part of a company initiated scheme, others purely at their own initiative. Most IBM employees have concerns about issues in the communities in which they live and work. All IBM employees are members of the community! In each location where IBM has a major physical presence, a Location Manager is appointed who has responsibility for IBM's participation in local community affairs. He or she receives support and guidance from the Corporate Affairs Function and is used as the main formal channel through which employee input is gathered. Informal input is however neither discouraged nor slow in coming forward and through our electronic mail communication system we continually receive suggestions from IBM employees about activities we should be pursuing. One of the attributes we strive to achieve in our community investment programme, without diminishing the importance of the issues we address, is the idea that involvement in these activities can be fun – employees who have become involved attest to that; we are dependent on their input to make sure we continue to reflect their interests in the activities we decide to support.

Currently in IBM we have 4 focus areas that comprise our strategic directions:

1. *Education and Training.*   An effective education system is essential to the prosperity of the UK. IBM's business, our customers, our suppliers and society in general all depend on the education system to equip people with the skills and knowledge to make the most of their potential. IBM contributes to the education and training system through supporting employees who are or wish to be school governors, by encouraging partnerships between local IBM offices and local schools, by participating in national policy organizations and by supporting specific programmes which encourage good practice in the use of information technology in education delivery.
2. *Voluntary Sector Empowerment.*   The voluntary sector is increasingly important in society, with ever greater demands being placed upon its services. Voluntary organizations are being required to be more accountable and more efficient in their approach. Business can play a role in 'empowering' the voluntary sector through the transfer of its own skills. IBM participates in this process through the provision of training opportunities to voluntary sector managers, through our secondment pro-

gramme, through short term consultancy programmes and through supporting IBM employees who wish to participate in voluntary activities in their local communities as well as developing specific programmes which support improved use of information technology in the voluntary sector.

3. *Support for People with Disabilities.* There are over 6 million people in the UK with some form of physical disability. The advent of the personal computer has presented many of these with a new opportunity to realise their potential, particularly through education and employment. IBM is one of three partners which established The Computability Centre in 1992. This is a national charity which provides independent advice and information on the use of computers by people with all types of disability.

4. *Environment.* The sustainable use of natural resources is a key issue for businesses and government alike. IBM's environmental policy has been in place for over twenty years and commits us to adopt very high standards, in our own environmental management. Through our Community Investment strategy we seek to complement our internal practices through supporting external activities which promote good environmental practice, which increase environmental awareness in the education system and which push forward the boundaries of current knowledge through scientific research.

Levels of Investment

Currently in the UK the most common method of deciding what level of resource should be directed towards CCI is the guidance used for companies aspiring to become or to remain members of the Per Cent Club, who commit to allocating between 0.5% and 1.0% of net before tax profits to community activities. This is a helpful benchmark, but it does not serve to establish the effectiveness of the way the money has been spent, nor the value for money the company has received. It is in addition of little help to companies who are in a loss making position!

A strategic approach to CCI makes it easier for companies to decide on the level of resource they should direct towards their programme of activity in order to meet their stated objectives. Over the long term, the strategic approach also gives companies the tools with which to measure the impact of the contributions they have made to date.

An actively managed CCI programme also has implications for the type of resource to be directed towards the activities. A programme based on mutuality of benefit requires quite different resources from programmes based on philanthropic motivation. For the latter it is possible for a company to manage its CCI activities through a decision making committee and a cheque processing function. For the former a company requires people resource to develop the strategic directions, capacity to manage the programmes to ensure that the objectives set out are reached, a focus on communication to ensure that the targeted audiences are reached and evaluation tools to measure the impact of the programmes. If this sounds much more labour intensive, that is because the company's expectation on the return for its investment from this approach is that much greater.

In addition the type of resource to be contributed may well be different. The philanthropic approach provides resources to another organization which enables it to undertake its own work. Actively managed CCI can mean working closely with an organization to help to deliver mutual goals; hence the most valuable resource may be people skills to augment the skills of the organization, or it may be equipment, or it may be access to a company's facilities and in house services. The scope of resources available within companies to contribute to CCI activities is often only limited by imagination. The opportunities for a company to add value go far beyond its capacity to write cheques as was clearly demonstrated by the 1993 Joseph Rowntree Trust Report *More than Money – the impact of Corporate Community Involvement on the Voluntary Sector.*

Increasingly in IBM our Community Investment Programme has been devised to provide opportunities for IBM employees to participate in activities, be it through secondments, through volunteering or through short term assignments to undertake community projects. In part this goes back to our objective to promote the morale and motivation of employees, but that is not the only reason. In every piece of research we have undertaken in recent years we have found that when given the option of money, employee skills or our products and services, community organizations that have had some involvement with IBM have told us they found the involvement of IBM employees in their programmes the most valuable contribution they have received. And from our perspective, we believe that there is a growing benefit to be reaped by the company in employee skill development through participation in community programmes.

IDENTIFICATION AND IMPLEMENTATION OF ACTIVITIES

A clear set of general objectives, coupled with strategic directions and knowledge of available resources makes project selection and management a much easier task. It is much easier to sift requests into those that clearly fall outside the company's criteria and those that require further investigation. Within IBM, we have found the issue management approach has once again helped us here. Issue managers over the years have developed considerable knowledge of their area of specialisation and are therefore well equipped to make judgements about requests for support we receive and the organizations that come to us for assistance. But perhaps more importantly, as we have developed a clearer understanding of our own objectives we have found that our approach to project selection has become considerably more proactive. So for example, if we decide on an issue on which we wish to focus and a specific activity we wish to undertake, we are more likely these days to go out and seek a voluntary sector partner that we could work with on this than we are to wait for ideas to come to us.

Partnership is a fundamental principle for our Community Investment Programme. It embodies the concepts of mutual dependency and mutual benefit and has been without doubt one of the major success factors in what we would see to be some of our flagship projects. Identifying community partners brings with it similar challenges and frustrations as finding business partners. Successful partnership demands trust, equality of treatment, honesty, accountability, flexibility and prior agreement on objectives, resources, and responsibilities; but the pay offs far exceed the costs, because it is through partnership that companies can really begin to make a difference and add value to the communities within which they operate. Partnership is such a strong feature of our Community Investment Programme that no major project takes place now unless it is in partnership with an external organization.

It is through partners therefore that we manage and oversee our major projects. This means that we do not need to have a large team of community investment project managers within the company. Issue managers and a small team of community relations professionals manage our relationships with our partners through which our programmes are delivered. Their level of knowledge about the company and our community investment programme objectives enables them to bring IBM's requirements and resources to the partnership. It is our partners that have the credibility, community knowledge and service delivery expertise to be able to implement the programmes. This inevitably means that quite often, part of our financial contribution includes an administration charge for our partner – our experience is that this is a much more cost effective way of running our programme than trying to do it all in-house. Partnership is a two way stream, and there is no doubt at all that we have learned an enormous amount from working with community partners; we have improved our understanding of the communities in which we operate and enhanced our capacity to use our community investment resources in the most efficient and effective way, both for IBM and for the community.

EVALUATION AND MEASUREMENT

Perhaps one of the most difficult management disciplines to apply to CCI is the discipline of evaluation and measurement. Indeed in the absence of clearly articulated objectives and strategic directions it is impossible to do. Yet without evaluation and measurement a company cannot know whether its CCI programme is having any impact at all – what business person would tolerate the absence of such basic tools in a mainstream business activity? If CCI is to become an increasingly important element of stakeholder management, evaluation and measurement are essential.

It is important to be clear on the distinction between evaluation and measurement. Evaluation enables a company to review a programme, to look at its stated objectives, to monitor the impact of the programme on the recipients and to draw conclusions about whether the objectives were met, whether the programme implementation could have been improved and whether the activities actually made a difference. Measurement on the other hand is often a quantitative assessment of what has been achieved which gives some indication of the relative standing of the outcomes of an activity and which may provide data that enables a company to make an assessment of whether it is deriving a return on its investment.

Evaluation and measurement of an individual project is much easier to undertake than evaluation and measurement of the impact of a total programme. It is possible to design a mechanism for evaluating or measuring the impact of a single project. It is often valuable if this can be undertaken by an independent evaluator who is able to take an objective look at the life of the project and draw conclusions that are not shaped by direct involvement in its delivery. Each evaluation can contribute to making the next project better in design or execution. Whether it is possible to build a picture of the overall success of the CCI programme from the evaluation and measurement of individual projects is questionable.

Evaluation and measurement at broad programme level is much less developed. Qualitative and quantitative surveys do exist, that companies subscribe to, which collect and analyse public and opinion leader views about the importance of CCI and the issues that companies should be addressing. These surveys also rate the performance of individual companies in the CCI field. Likewise data is collected by a number of organizations about the levels of resource contributed by individual companies and the strategies that companies pursue. The piece of the jigsaw that appears to be missing is the one which provides a mechanism to evaluate and measure a company's achievement in fulfilling its own strategic objectives and to track the company's performance in a way that can be reported to its community stakeholder. It will only be when this piece is in place that CCI measurement will take its place as a tool in managing stakeholder relationships alongside customer satisfaction programmes and employee opinion surveys.

COMMUNICATION

Effective evaluation and measurement will also make the task of communicating much easier as it will be possible to communicate results and outputs rather than activities. Nevertheless it is quite clear, even before we have got to that point, that strategic CCI implies a desire on behalf of a company to make an impact, to be involved in activities that make a difference and thereby to enhance its relationship with the community as one of its stakeholders. Very little impact can be made if nobody knows what has happened and it is for this reason that effective communication becomes a critical tool in the management of corporate community involvement. However CCI, if all has gone according to plan, is good news and good news does not always receive the attention it deserves!

A recent survey of the media about coverage of CCI found that 92% of those surveyed agreed that 'companies should be prepared to spend more on communicating their community investment programmes', but only 8% of the same sample were extremely interested in receiving information about companies' activities.[3] Even more reason for companies to be focused and realistic in their approach to communicating their CCI programmes.

The first question therefore has to be who is the audience – the second question – what is the message. Only once those two questions have been answered is it possible to decide on the most appropriate vehicle to get the message across. Clearly audiences and messages will vary depending on whether communication relates to the CCI strategy as a whole, to large national programmes or to smaller local projects. Nevertheless the discipline of asking the questions is relevant every time. Other major points for consideration are –

1. Employees are the most cited way that people outside companies hear about community projects; therefore the importance of employee communication can never be underestimated. Employees tend to know more

about their own company's CCI programme if they are personally and actively involved, which points to another very good reason for encouraging employees to participate in CCI activities. Other mechanisms for communicating with employees include – in house journals, electronic bulletin boards and location notice boards. Senior executive leadership is also an important mechanism to communicate to employees. Just one reference by the CEO at an employee meeting to how much he or she values employee involvement in community activities can make all the difference. Whatever action a company takes to inform its employees about its community investment programme, it will never be enough.

2. Local media are generally far more likely to be interested in CCI stories than national media. The likelihood of coverage will be greater if an event provides a photo opportunity and press releases provide all the background material to make writing the article as painless as possible. A press release that focuses on the largesse of the company is unlikely to make a major impact. A release that emphasises the difference the company's contribution is making to the quality of life of the local community is much more likely to be picked up. Companies that take an active interest in the community organizations they support and are seen on site are likely to be remembered more than those that send their cheques in the mail.

3. The national press is less likely to be interested in covering specific company initiatives as in covering new strategic directions or leadership initiatives by company executives.

4. Third party endorsements can be an extremely effective way of gaining coverage of CCI activities. Participation in award schemes is one way to disseminate information about a company's programme. Involvement in innovative programmes which attract the attention of opinion leaders is another. In IBM we discovered that one of the unanticipated, but very positive consequences of establishing our Community Advisory Panel, was that the community leaders who have participated as members of the panel now know considerably more about our programme of activities and have, in their spheres of influence become roving ambassadors for IBM's Community Investment programme.

CONCLUSION

There are growing and compelling reasons why companies need to adopt a proactive approach to management of relationships with their stakeholders. The growing interdependence between a company and its various constituencies demands a strategic approach which can also be a way to improve a company's competitive edge. These relationships are likely to become increasingly important in the more complex global market place businesses will confront in the future. Management of these relationships will not eliminate conflicting pressures between the stakeholders, nor the need for trade offs. What it will do, however, is to provide a clearer understanding of the impact of a company's decision making on the various groups that make up the body of interest in that company's behaviour. It will also make the trade-off process more transparent and objective. Effective stakeholder relationship management will require, however, that companies adopt basic management practices in responding to the needs and aspirations of their stakeholders. While there are signs that companies are beginning to see this need and to adopt practices that enable them to assess and reflect the mutual dependency of the stakeholder relationship, there is still a long way to go, particularly in the fields of measurement and reporting.

As far as Corporate Community Involvement is concerned, this can play an increasingly important role in managing a company's relationship with the community as a stakeholder. There is clearly a two way stream of benefit between a company and the community which can best be applied to the maximum advantage of both parties through the adoption of a strategic approach to CCI. Companies need therefore to view these activities as part of their broader long term business strategic investments, making a positive contribution to the business as a whole. Strategic management of a company's CCI activities is desirable and possible. The opportunity to do so will be significantly improved by developing effective measurement tools.

Notes

1. *Business and Community: A New Partnership for Mutual Benefit*, Opinion Leader Research, October 1993.
2. Research study undertaken by MORI for the RSA and Greenly's Limited 1993.
3. OLR Survey.

Bibliography

S. Carmichael and J. Drummond, *Good Business*, Business Books.
D. Clutterbuck, D. Dearlove and and D. Snow, *Actions Speak Louder Than Words*, Kingfisher and Kogan Page.
D. Logan, *Transnational Giving*, Directory of Social Change.
RSA Tomorrow's Company, *The Role of Business in a Changing World*, Interim Report of the RSA Tomorrow's Company inquiry.

14 The Practice of Corporate Identity

Nicholas Ind

There are a lot of people who have a fairly superficial understanding of corporate identity and the practice of it. They are always talking about 'these people paid a million dollars for a logotype.' The logotype certainly gets a lot of exposure, but in terms of a professionally developed full programme, it is one of the smallest elements.

(Steven Gilliat, Lippincott & Margulies).

What is corporate identity? It can either be the design of a logo, or a million pound (or dollar) programme that involves evaluating corporate communications, determining a branding structure and implementing a cohesive design system that includes all corporate expressions. The problem is that it is both of these. Not surprisingly the concept of corporate identity is confused. The press use the term as an alternative to logo – ICI's roundel would be referred to as its corporate identity. Practitioners define it to suit their ends. Public relations advisors advise on it. Writers squabble over its meaning.

The confusion has largely come about because of the way in which the discipline has evolved. What we might call identity consultants are mostly design consultants. Thirty years ago they would have been designing logos, as well as interiors, products and displays. Then such consultancies as Wolff Olins in the UK and Lippincott & Margulies in the US started to specialise in corporate identity and look at all the various ways a company might express itself visually. Corporate identity became strategic. The idea was that what the company Chairman said ought to echo the presentation of the company through design, advertising and PR. This benefited the client by recognising the interdependence of communications. It benefited consultancies by enhancing their fees. However, not everyone went along with this idea. Some consultancies remained committed to a design led approach, arguing with some plausibility that they were not really qualified to get involved in behavioural science and employee relations. In a 1991 study by identity consultancy Henrion Ludlow & Schmidt and researchers MORI into international attitudes towards corporate identity, Chris Ludlow compared the results to an 1989 study:

What's still remarkable is the extent to which people agree on the importance of corporate identity yet differ in their definition of what it is. It's almost as if corporate identity is something that fills a vacuum. (Hancock, 1992)

DEFINITIONS

There may be little consensus on the meaning of corporate identity and related terms such as corporate image and corporate communications, but the need for definition is clear. The perspective taken here is strategic: of the need for all communications to work together, cohesively, over time. Here the logotype is just 'one of the smallest elements.'

Corporate Identity and Personality

Corporate identity equates to a corporate sense of self – that which makes an organization unique. It is comprised of an organization's history, its beliefs and philosophy, the nature of its technology, its ownership, people, the personality of its leaders, its strategies and its ethical and cultural values. Although these corporate attributes can be communicated through an identity programme, well established 'identities' are hard to change. 'Identity is not something cosmetic: it is the core of an organization's existence.'

Consequently, when a company talks about changing its identity, by which it normally means its logo, it is being either inarticulate or inaccurate. Most identities evolve slowly over time in response to changing strategies and market conditions. Occasionally the process can be accelerated by a corporate trauma, such as privatisation or a take-over. Even then the extent to which vestiges of the old identity remain intact is remarkable.

Not all commentators would agree with the above definition. David Bernstein, for examples sees the signals or visual cues a company sends out as identity and he equates a company's distinctiveness as personality. Similarly, Wally Olins of the UK consultancy, Wolff Olins, describes personality as the 'soul, the persona, the spirit, the culture of the organization manifested in some way.' For Olins visual identity is 'part of the deeper identity of the group, the outward sign of the inward commitment'.

Corporate Image

Corporate image is in the eye of the receiver. An organization may communicate its strategy and achievements in an attempt to create an appropriate image, but it is the reception of that message that is important. Therefore the corporate image is the picture an audience has of an organization 'though the accumulation of all received messages'. Organizations commonly believe that they only communicate when they want to, through such mechanisms as advertising, literature and public relations. In reality an organization communicates all the time, through everything it says and does. For example, the Metropolitan Police's advertising presents a professional image of the force, but for most people their image of the police is derived from media coverage and direct interaction. In the case of the latter this is often anything but professional. The police stations are often shabby and run down, correspondence with the public is poor, and as Wolff Olins, report (1988) on the force notes:

> The Met has traditionally placed little emphasis on external communications... It's not easy to find a police station phone number and it often takes minutes before the phone is answered. And when someone answers they are quite often unhelpful.

This holistic view of corporate image demonstrates why organizations should be wary about making false or inflated claims in advertising or PR. Inevitably you get found out when people experience the organizational reality and find it wanting. A whole variety of audiences from bankers to investors, journalists, government officials, employees, trade unions, suppliers, wholesalers and consumers, need to be communicated with and to have communications backed up by performance over time. Although the message needs to be consistently communicated, organizations also have to recognize that these audiences will often have differing expectations and images. For example, when British Gas announces record profits, this may be very good news to investors, but customers, the regulatory authority and trade unions may see the results as evidence of the company exploiting a privileged position. Therefore decisions have to be made about how to present such messages and the tone may need to be altered to accommodate the interests of the relevant audiences. This is the task of corporate communications.

Corporate Communications

Corporate communications is the process that translates an identity into an image. It involves the obvious methods, such as advertising, PR, as well as buildings, products, and importantly the quality and attitudes of employees. For these to be cohesive the identity needs to be widely understood and accepted. The effect of a lack of consistency is that an organization's audiences will tend to have a confused image.

The Value of Logos

A logo is a symbol, whose value lies in the associations that people attach to it. Those associations are, in turn, built up from experience. If you presented a new corporate graphic to people and asked them what it signified you would probably get a large range of answers, determined largely by cultural background. Present them with a well known symbol, such as the Mercedes Benz badge and they will probably identify the symbol with ideas of quality and strength. A new graphic can suggest a certain corporate style, determine the area of corporate activity, cause certain audiences to re-appraise an organization and indeed act as a catalyst for organizational change, but it cannot be a panacea for more fundamental corporate ills.

WHY COMPANIES UNDERTAKE IDENTITY PROGRAMMES

Companies undertake identity programmes for a whole variety of reasons. However, they tend to come under the umbrella of a perceived image problem – the recognition that how the organization is perceived is not how it would like to be. This dissonance tends to be caused either by environmental factors, such as competitive moves, a change in consumer attitudes or a legal change or by internal factors, such as re-structuring, a merger, a privatisation, or a new strategy. Within the generalised objective of improving or changing an image, the specific catalysts for identity programmes are as follows:

Improving internal communications

Companies rarely communicate internally as well as they think they do. Often barriers exist within organizations that prevent effective communication. People guard their own turf jealously and tend to identify with their own immediate group or division. Within the police force this is particularly prevalent with specialist operatives looking down on uniformed police officers, who in turn look down on civil staff. In one European automotive manufacturer, the company happily accepts what are called chimneys-vertical divisions, which fail to communicate with each other. Yet there are benefits to creating a sense of corporate purpose:

> There are many opportunities available to senior management to define a larger corporate purpose, to stress the importance of inter-relationships, and to discourage parochial behaviour by business unit, group and senior managers. A strong set of firmwide values and a strong corporate identity are vital links in reducing cynicism toward committees, resolving conflicts and so on. (Porter, 1985)

Often communications are not only inhibited across the organization, but also vertically. Strategies need to be communicated downwards and the ideas and creativity of employees need to be channelled upwards. This requires structures, mechanisms and a conducive operating environment: employees have to believe in the value of their contribution.

Heightening awareness

Organizations that fail to articulate who they are and what they do, can often end up with a blurred image. This can be a very real disadvantage when an organization comes up against a better known competitor or needs to raise money on the stock market or wants to influence customers. We all feel more comfortable buying from an organization that we know, and research indicates a close correlation between familiarity and favourability.

Improving the stock price

US companies such as Bausch & Lomb and Sara Lee have undertaken programmes directly aimed at improving their stock performance. While there is no substantive evidence to link the identity programme with the share price, qualitative research has shown that financial audiences do take note of identity programmes, provided they are substantiated by corporate performance.

Communicating new strategies

When companies adopt new strategies they may need to signal their intentions to a variety of audiences. One way to do this is through the adoption of a new logo or name. For example, when the US company Transamerica wanted to signal its move from a broadly based conglomerate to a focused financial services organization, it dropped its well known 'T' symbol and adopted a new logo based on its pyramid shaped building in San Francisco.

Providing the flexibility for growth

An outdated or limiting naming policy can inhibit a company's corporate strategy. For example, when Nissan decided to compete in the luxury car sector, they believed that their existing name was wrong for the market. Rather than just create a sub-brand name, a new organization was created with its own dealerships, around the range name of Infiniti.

Consistency

Over time an organization may acquire a whole variety of subsidiary company and brand names. Without control, the presentation of the company can get confused and contradictory: new logos are developed, different naming policies are adopted and literature acquires a wide variety of forms and styles. In many cases the corporate identity brief is not about creating either a new name or a new logo, but simply instilling discipline and logic back into the company's presentation, so that it is easily understood by all audiences.

Integrating two companies

When two companies come together there are always a number of branding issues to be resolved. Either the company names are simply put together as is often the case with advertising agencies, whose acronyms grow ever longer or sometimes a new name is developed. An example of the latter was the creation of Unisys out of the merger of Burroughs and Sperry Univac. Whichever the solution, all forms of visual presentation will need to be amended creating the opportunity to review the presentation of the company.

Resolving company structures

When a company's business structure has changed from its original base to such an extent that it becomes inappropriate, it creates the need to review the identity. This was the rationale behind the development of a new logo for Western Union, which had traditionally been associated with telegrams and telex services, but in recent years had moved into new sectors, such as electronic mail, which overshadowed the company's traditional areas of business.

THE IDENTITY PROGRAMME

Once an organization has recognized the existence of an image problem, most often it will work with an identity consultancy to find a solution. Occasionally companies opt for a d-i-y approach and occasionally they get their PR consultancies to manage the process for them, but for the majority the preferred working partner is the strategically biased designer. Most of these designers will undertake a research phase that looks at the organization and its environment.

The research programme tends to be qualitative (group discussions and one to one interviews) rather than quantitative. This enables the consultancy to probe, through semi-structured discussions, the real issues about a company's reputation. Although the scope of the research will be determined by the nature of the brief the overall objective is to establish the identity of the organization and compare this with the image of the organization amongst its various audiences. Additionally a consultancy will normally undertake a more subjective study, called the visual audit – an assessment of all the ways and means that the organization communicates. By looking at everything from literature to signage to office interiors it will determine whether the company's communications are consistent, relevant and supportive of the organization's strategy.

The research is not an end in itself. Rather it should help the consultancy and client to understand the views of all its various audiences, pinpoint any likely future implementation problem areas and determine the degree of dissonance between what the company is, or seeks to become and its image. There are three broad scenarios here.

1. The company reality and image are in tune with each other. This would suggest the company has been successful in presenting a clear and accurate picture of itself.
2. The image is significantly better than the reality. This might arise where a company has had such a strong reputation in the past, that the majority of people still believe in it, in spite of evidence to the contrary. This scenario is rare and tends to be confined to infrequently bought goods or services. Eventually, the image catches up with the reality as more and more people experience the product.
3. The reality is better than, or at least different to the image. This is the most common scenario and the result of a failure to communicate effectively. It can lead to people having a confused or outdated picture of an organization. For example, the drinks and food group, Grand Metropolitan plc is still referred to by people outside the small band of financial analysts who follow it, as a hotel owner. Certainly this is where the company's heritage was, but it sold all its hotel interests many years ago.

Whichever scenario exists, companies are often a mixture of operational and communication problems. Although the focus of the identity programme is on communications, the operational factors cannot be ignored as they will inhibit the effective implementation of recommendations.

COMMUNICATIONS STRATEGY

In the brief from client to consultant the communications strategy may already be defined and the task may be focused on a branding issue: what to call a merged company or how to present the company's hierarchy of divisions and subsidiaries. However, when the brief is more comprehensive and the requirement is a complete review of communications, the research programme should lead to the definition of a communications strategy. This strategy should determine the positioning of the company within its competitive environment and how the positioning will be communicated. If dissonance is to be avoided, it must be based on the reality of the company's performance. Also it should be:

Forward looking and based around long term goals

For example, if the organization has an history of acquisitions and divestments, it would be counter-productive to develop a positioning based on a notion of organic growth and stability. The communication strategy must take account of likely strategic developments.

Unique

Mission statements have a tendency to be rather alike and contain platitudes about 'putting the customer first', 'quality' and 'being the best.' However, each organization contains unique attributes (if it looks hard) that will be relevant to its audiences and distinct from the competition. As companies and products tend to become more alike each other – 'there is a natural force reducing product differentiation over time in an industry, (Porter, 1980) it becomes ever more important that companies make the most of their distinctive features.

Single-minded and all-encompassing

In other words, it needs to be easily understood by all internal and external audiences and able to permeate the whole organization.

The communications strategy should determine the role for all communication mechanisms and also detail the implications for operations in such areas as product performance, distribution methods, product pricing and staff training.

THE IMPORTANCE OF IDENTITY STRUCTURE

One of the ways in which an organization communicates is through the way in which it is structured. Small organizations tend not to have to confront this issue. However, a large complex organization may have a whole range of divisions, subsidiaries and products which need to be presented in such a way that they are understandable and supportive of the company's strategy. As organizations grow they rarely pay much attention to this issue. The consequence is that there is often confusion and contradiction in the company's branding policy.

Essentially there are three broad types of branding policy (with variations in between), which are defined by the extent products and companies are associated with a parent.

The Unitary Structure

This prevails where an organization adopts one name throughout its structure. It could be applied to such companies as Sony, BMW and Yamaha where the company name is applied to the divisions and products of the company. This type of structure exists either because a company is new, operates within a tightly defined product area or has a name which has considerable goodwill and elasticity associated with it. Although there are exceptions, most companies in this category tend to have grown organically rather than through acquisition.

The advantage of this structural type is that each product or service that is introduced has the endorsement of an existing reputation. This helps achieve economies of communication, as a consistent message is created by the sum of all brand communications. This structure also helps to create a clearer sense of direction within the company, as the corporate name does not have to fight with subsidiary brands for allegiance and visibility. However, there are some attendant negatives. First, because the company name is directly associated with any new product launches, this may inhibit decision making. Second, the degree of uniformity may inhibit managerial innovation, especially within subsidiary organizations.

The Branded Structure

This is the opposite of the unitary structure. Here a parent company will have a series of seemingly unrelated subsidiaries or brands. This is typical of fast moving consumer goods (fmcg) companies and conglomerates. Companies such as Unilever traditionally have not stressed the link between such products as Persil and its parent, although in recent years the name Lever has been added to packaging. The rationale for divorcing the corporate name from the product has been that it enables a company to put competing brands onto the market without the consumer being made aware of the fact. With the high failure rate in fmcg areas, it means product failures are not directly associated with the parent and there is no confusion between a powerful brand personality and its owner. However, there has been a notable trend away from the branded structure in recent years. Increasingly companies have recognised the importance of communicating the strength of their brand portfolio, not only to consumers, but also to financial audiences. Thus Cadbury Schweppes, Nestlé, and Allied Lyons have begun to stress the links between product/subsidiary and parent.

The Diversified Structure

This structure sits between the branded and the unitary. It exists where a company has developed from one core area of activity into new ones or has expanded geographically and has retained its original name for part of the business. An example was Wolff Olins' work for Midland Bank, where the Midland name was used with subsidiaries where it could be of value, but not with inherently strong brand names such as Thomas Cook. The benefit of this approach, if well managed, is that an organization has the flexibility to use its corporate name where it is appropriate and avoid making connections where it might be disadvantageous.

However, there are negatives with a diversified structure. The holding company with one set of audiences can all too easily get confused with a business unit's audiences. This was part of the rationale behind Woolworth plc's name change to Kingfisher. Secondly, a separate name can suggest to employees a separation from the corporate perspective. For example Grand

Metropolitan's drinks division, IDV, sees itself as very distinct from the rest of the group. This may be acceptable if this is the company's strategy, but in instances where the company wants to draw a subsidiary into line with corporate aims, a different name may become a symbol of resistance.

Resolving the Structure

Some companies have organizational structures which suit their strategic needs, but others grow haphazardly without any real logic. At some point these companies find that buyers cannot understand the organization or cross selling opportunities are missed or two divisions are competing with each other for business. Changing the branding structure will not necessarily solve these problems, but they are part of the process of change. Mostly organizations opt for more unitary type structures, sometimes choosing a diversified structure as an interim solution. This is becoming used in corporate banking where as markets have globalised and cross border investment has grown, national subsidiaries have gradually disappeared in favour of an international unitary structure. However the move from a branded to a unitary structure is not without its traumas, even if the pain is eased by an interim move. Employees who have worked with a business unit for many years may identify with it to the exclusion of the parent company – especially if the cultures are very different, as is the case say with a bank and a corporate broking subsidiary. Imposing a new name may symbolise a loss of autonomy and be deeply de-motivating. This does not mean the change should not be made if it makes sense strategically, but it does suggest the change will need to be carefully managed.

DESIGN, PR, ADVERTISING AND EMPLOYEE COMMUNICATIONS

As well as resolving the presentation of corporate structure, the communication of the identity needs to be managed. This will involve the presentation of the company through design, public relations, advertising and employee communications. The rationale behind drawing these communication mechanisms together is one of cohesion – of ensuring that the various messages sent out by the company support and endorse each other. There is little point in creating a logo, such as ICI's which features a strap line of 'World Class', if it is ignored by advertising and contradicted by the actions of employees. Therefore in addition to an identity consultancy making specific design recommendations, the implications of the programme for other communication areas needs to be identified. Of these, the most important and ignored is employee communications. It is employees who probably exert the strongest effect on external opinions through their day to day interaction with consumers, suppliers, buyers and shareholders. And it is employee attitudes and actions which determine the strength of the corporate identity. Yet within the context of corporate identity programmes, the focus is almost always on external rather than internal communications.

> Most corporate strategy statements never actually penetrate the ranks of management to touch the minds and imaginations of the employees doing the everyday work of a company. Yet they are the people facing customers and clients daily and for good or for ill, creating the true image and reputation of the business...If your employees don't know what the strategy of the business is, or can't translate it into workable terms, the strategy will simply grind into oblivion somewhere in the offices of senior management. (Drennan, 1988)

Most identity consultancies are ill equipped to take on the role of public relations advisor or advertising agency or indeed employee communications gurus. However, the research programme and the visual audit will uncover points about the quality of communications in these areas. The consultancy should report its findings and be prepared to work with the company's other advisors, but in my view should not get intimately involved with areas outside its specific competence. (For a more detailed discussion of the issues related to employee communications, see Chapter 5).

From the design perspective the corporate identity will have implications for a whole host of areas. In the case of a retailer or a bank it will have implications on how shops or branches are designed. This will include the design of the fascia, the configuration of space, product adjacencies, interior decoration, point of sale systems and furniture. In the instance of a manufacturing company it will include the design of the products, styling, branding and packaging. Companies such as Braun, AEG and Apple Computers excel in this area of making a corporate statement through all areas of design. One of the most famous perpetrators of cohesive design was the London Underground which in its heyday of the 1920s and 1930s, was using typography, advertising, station architecture and train design to present a consistent image. Referring to Frank Pick, who engineered the scheme, Stephen Bayley (1985) says:

> ...he institutionalised one of the most thorough corporate identity programmes in history by appointing the architect Charles Holden and the

typographer Edward Johnston to create uniformity in the company's appearance.

In some programmes, the issue of branding and the presentation of names and logos is not the main focus. With a bank, for example, the focus is often on the design and layout of branches; with the Metropolitan Police it was primarily concerned with changing internal attitudes. However, in most corporate identity programmes there is a concentration on visual identity and the presentation of the corporate brand. This involves four key elements: naming policies, graphics/style, slogans, language.

Names

Unless a corporate name inhibits the corporate strategy it should be left alone. Most company names have some positive attributes. If a company elects to change its name it will have to go through the process of re-building its reputation. However, there are instances when changes have to be made. Woolworth to Kingfisher has already been mentioned, as has Sperry Univac/Burroughs to Unisys. Other examples are the creation of Zeneca for ICI's drugs division, which was hived off from its parent and the creation of Signet to replace the Ratners Group, which became tarnished after its erstwhile chairman, Gerald Ratner called his company's products 'total crap.'

If a change does become necessary, then it makes sense for a company to look at an alteration of its name or the use of a name from its existing portfolio before embarking on the expensive and difficult process of finding and then registering a new name.

Graphics

Graphics includes typography, logo design, colours, layout, style and illustration. The interaction and manipulation of these elements will transmit a message dependent on their associations. Handwritten logos such as that used by Cadbury seem personalised because we associate them with signatures, faces such as that used by Quaker suggest tradition and figures (dependent on their style) can suggest a human scale and accessibility – consequently they are popular with organizations which might otherwise appear faceless: BT, Prudential. Sometimes humour is used, such as the round tree device used by Rowntree and the open mouth suggested by the 'O' in ENO (English National Opera). Whether these work or not depends on their relevance to the corporate culture. The ENO device works, because English National Opera is innovative and irreverent. It would be difficult to see it working for the ROH (Royal Opera House) which is more traditional and has a more conservative customer base.

If an organization decides to change its graphic presentation, there are two basic approaches. First, it can evolve its existing presentation. This would tend to suggest to audiences (if they indeed notice the change) that the company has not altered in any significant way. Perhaps the presentation of the company has become a bit dated and needs revitalising or perhaps discipline needs to be re-installed or perhaps one element of the branding needs to be stressed at the expense of another, (according to an analysis of identity programmes during 1993, this type of project accounted for one third of identity reviews). Companies such as Shell, BP, Texaco and ICI have changed their logos very little over the years, but each has periodically reviewed its visual presentation. Texaco in particular has undergone half a dozen changes over the last ninety years and has ended up with a logo that is most notable for its similarity to the one it had in 1903.

The second approach is a more fundamental change in visual style. If a company has changed its direction in a fundamental way and wants to signal this change and get people to re-appraise it, then this route is more appropriate. For example, when the American company AT&T lost its telecoms monopoly and had to change its strategy to compete effectively, it also radically changed its visual presentation. This helped signal its move from a national telephone company to a worldwide telecommunications group.

Whichever route is chosen, symbols, type and colour can be used to signify the links between the component parts of an organization or stress their diversity. A consistently applied logo, such as ICI's, stresses the power of the group and helps to unify activities. Courtaulds, Renault and others may have a consistent logo, but they stress the autonomy of their divisions, through the use of different colours. The group of palaces known as Historic Royal Palaces, (eg Hampton Court, The Tower of London) are linked through typography and style, but have their individuality defined by their own specific crests. A conglomerate such as Hanson, has a corporate logo which is applied to group activities, but is not used by operating companies.

In all cases the graphic system has to be sufficiently versatile to be used in a wide variety of sizes and formats. It will have to work in colour and black and white. It will have to work on newsprint as well as on high quality paper stock. It will need to work with a company's technology. It may have to work in other countries and it may need to appear in conjunction with other logos.

Slogans and Language

Although the longevity of identity programmes is questionable, the visual representation of an organization is intended for the long term. However, the corporate identity may need to include the verbal as well as the visual. Sometimes, verbal expressions of corporate direction can be sustained over time, but more often the perspective is shorter. Nonetheless, such mechanisms as slogans can be valuable in signalling to external and internal audiences the essence of what an organization is. Famously cohesive was Avis' 'We Try Harder.' ICI's 'World Class' said something about quality and the global focus of the company's business (the identity scheme was implemented in 70 countries). Less well known, but notable for its consistency, is the 'Working Together' slogan of the GMB (The General, Municipal, Boilermakers and Allied Trades Union).

The verbal aspect of identity programmes is also important in the tone and style of language used to described an organization and its component parts. Within the venture capital company 3i, which prides itself on the creative use of money, the word 'institution' is taboo. Arcane or inappropriate language can all too easily contradict the visual and thereby create confusion.

MANAGING AND EVALUATING

Once consultant and client have agreed the design concepts, the thorny issue of implementation has to be addressed. The literature on corporate identity largely overlooks this, yet in a large and complex multinational company, implementation will be expensive, time consuming and emotionally fraught. Companies and brands can lose their names, re-structuring of divisions and procedures may occur, and confusion amongst both external and internal audiences may become the norm during the period of transition. It is quite likely that the identity programme will be operating within the context of an overall programme of change or indeed the identity programme may have been the catalyst for further change. Overall then the phase of implementation will be unsettling for everyone. And it is the phase when identity programmes can easily go awry.

Most identities that falter do so at implementation. Difficulties abound. The client has usually to choose between cost and delay. Prescriptions rarely fit all eventualities. What is pure fights with what is practical. Technologies change. A cohesive result is ruled out when outlying units misunderstand, resist or do things their own way. With major programmes, a further identity exercise usually follows within a few years. (McAlhone, 1993)

Large programmes are indeed logistically complex and the client will have to choose between implementing the programme all at once or over time. The former has undoubted impact but is costly. The latter is less expensive, but has the potential to create confusion. Whichever route is chosen, the prerequisite of a successful programme is the support and endorsement of senior management. The Chief Executive and the Board need to show their commitment to the programme. This is vital both in the first instance and to the management of the programme over time. Some writers suggest that the identity needs to be policed by management. However, policing suggests a degree of rigidity which is inappropriate to the changing circumstances a company will face over a five or ten year period. The one certainty about the business environment is change and an identity needs to be sufficiently flexible to cope with it.

Most consultants will provide an organization with an identity or style manual, which will specify how the visual presentation of the company should be controlled. Whilst this is a useful method of control it again suggests rigidity and encourages the identity programme to be seen in purely visual terms. The programmes that seem to be most effective are those where identity schemes are part of a total and cohesive process of change that affects everything the company does. Not only does it mean operations and communications are working together, but it tends to encourage the involvement of employees. Whatever the scope of the programme, involvement should be a core objective. This can be achieved by including as many people as possible in the research programme, discussing findings, developing solutions together and conducting workshops/seminars with various levels of employees.

When it comes to judging the effectiveness of a programme, the process is fraught with difficulty. Corporate identities tend to have a long term perspective and isolating the effectiveness of individual elements is problematic. Also, so much of the programme is concerned with effective implementation, that poor management in this area can undermine what otherwise might be a well founded and creative solution. Nonetheless given the expense of identity programmes, companies should take the time to evaluate what they have done. At its most subjective level, research by consultant and client into the cohesion of the visual presentation can be undertaken on a regular basis. More objectively the awareness and attitudes of employees, shareholders, suppliers, buyers and consumers can be tracked over time, using a pre-programme benchmark. What is more difficult to achieve is any direct correlation between an identity programme and sales performance or share price movements.

Probably the true measure of effectiveness is that the identity programme lasts the distance. If it was designed with a ten year perspective in mind, did it make it? Most do not. Organizations and markets change, companies cease to exist and sometimes the programme was poorly conceived or implemented. None of this means that organizations should ignore the issue of 'identity', but it does suggest that both consultants and clients have to be realistic about what they are trying to achieve.

Bibliography

S. Bayley (ed.), *The Conran Directory of Design*, Octopus.
D. Bernstein, *Company Image and Reality*, Holt, Rinehart & Winston.
D. Drennan, 'Down the organization', *Management Today*, June 1988.
M. Hancock, 'The Soul of a Company', *Design*, January 1992.
N. Ind, *The Corporate Image*, revised edn, Kogan Page.
N. Jenkins, *The Business of Image*, Kogan Page.
C. Lorenz, *The Design Dimension*, Blackwell.
B. McAlhone, 'The living and the dead', *Design*, November 1993.
W. Olins, *Corporate Identity*, Thames & Hudson.
M. Porter, *Competitive Advantage*, The Free Press.
M. Porter, *Competitive Strategy*, The Free Press.

15 Corporate Culture

Colin J. Coulson-Thomas

Corporate culture can facilitate or inhibit internal and external communication to such an extent that it often becomes a strategic issue in its own right. 'Culture change' programmes are becoming more widespread as 'corporate transformation', and specifically the creation of flatter and more flexible 'network organizations', has become a pre-occupation of a growing number of CEOs and their boardroom colleages.

While there is some consensus concerning the nature of the responsive organizations that are sought, great difficulty is being experienced in making it happen. Many culture change programmes are little more than words on paper. Slogans abound, but attitudes, values and behaviour, or hearts and minds remain untouched.

So what is to be done? This chapter examines the new organizations and cultures that represent the vision and an emerging requirement for cross-cultural communication. It also considers the barriers being encountered, and assesses the priorities.

The chapter draws upon both practical involvement in major change programmes, and the results of an extensive programme of surveys which have been undertaken by the author, and which deal specifically with the achievement of corporate transformation (Coulson-Thomas, 1992).

WHAT IS CULTURE?

Culture consists of the assumptions, beliefs, norms and values that consciously and unconsciously influence, shape or determine attitudes, expectations and behaviours, and what is acceptable and tolerated. In essence, it is 'the way we do things around here'. Culture influences perceptions and priorities.

Culture has many determinants. For example, a national culture can be shaped by landscape and climate; historical experience, traditions, customs and values; and passed on through education and the process of socialization. It finds expression in the built environment and the economic and social infrastructure; language and the media; habits, behaviour, consumption, lifestyle and the work ethic; leisure pursuits and the arts.

248

Some cultures are self-contained, while others are more open to external influences.

Companies too can have their cultures, although some are stronger than others. Certain corporate cultures are so distinctive that they have a significant impact upon both image and reputation, for example 'the Hewlett-Packard way'.

One way of better understanding a particular corporate culture is to ask people how they would describe the organization if it were a person. The qualities and attributes that come quickly to mind are often extremely revealing.

There are many elements of, and determinants of, corporate culture. For example:

- A mission statement, values, concerns and business ethics.
- The form of organization, location or pattern of authority, criteria for assessment, the extent of empowerment, methods of control and terms of employment.
- The approach to decision making, communication practice, importance of network relationships, sharing of information, emphasis on teamwork, focus on quality, degree of specialization, and speed of action.
- Tolerance of diversity, extent of mutual trust, commitment to learning and development, openness to outsiders, and sensitivity to values and feelings.

Those seeking to change corporate attitudes and behaviour need to understand what determines and sustains culture in a particular context. What are its impacts or consequences and its dynamics?

Attitudes and behaviour influence, and can reinforce, each other. Hence one may need to act directly to change both by a combination of measures, for example by re-engineering processes and changing the conduct of meetings, or by defining role model conduct and linking role model behaviour to reward and remuneration practice.

HOW APPROPRIATE IS THE CULTURE?

Whether or not a particular corporate culture needs to be changed will depend upon how appropriate it is thought to be. The culture of an organization should reflect and match its situation and context. It is particularly important that corporate culture is compatible with that of customers.

The culture of an organization can create 'insiders' and 'outsiders'. Stereotypes can result from crude generalizations about cultural and other differences. Those from a particular national culture could feel excluded from the 'inner group', or even alienated from a corporate culture.

The culture of an international organization may need to accommodate, and indeed encourage, considerable diversity. Those from different cultural backgrounds may have quite distinct attitudes towards time, status, formality, communications, meetings, etc. Even business priorities and timescales can vary across cultures.

Compatibility of corporate cultures can be a key factor in determining whether or not arrangements, alliances and joint ventures will succeed. The following examples appear in the book *Creating the Global Company* (1992)

- The logic of marketplace requirements and relative technical capability might suggest Apple and IBM should form a joint company to develop new systems software. The challenge for those managing the relationship is the extent to which the relatively open, free and flexible approach of Apple can be reconciled with the relatively greater emphasis IBM has put upon hierarchy, structure and operating according to standard procedures.
- Strategically it made sense for Sony to acquire Columbia Pictures from Coca-Cola in 1990, in order to link the past and future output of Californian creativity at producing 'software' with Japan's traditional 'hardware' manufacturing strengths. However the 'ad-hocracy' and flair of the film-making culture is so different from the discipline and sustained incrementalism of manufacturing as to put great strain on the management of Columbia under Japanese ownership. The acquisition was followed by some expensive termination payments.
- As a combination of both 'hardware' and 'software' has increasingly become the electronic product so Matsushita Electric of Japan also bought a US entertainments company in 1990. Matsushita acquired MCA, and again a degree of 'culture clash' occurred.
- When the Japanese computer manufacturer Fujitsu acquired the UK company ICL in 1990 an attempt was made to put a 'management ring fence' around ICL in order to preserve its cultural identity and standing as a European company. It was agreed that ICL would operate as an autonomous entity, raising its own finance in Europe and seeking continued participation in European collaborative programmes. To preserve their complementary qualities Fujitsu and ICL agreed to treat each other as trading partners.

● Nestlé, following its acquisition of Rowntree in 1988, took action to preserve Rowntree's autonomy and standing in the English city of York. Certain headquarters functions were transferred from Switzerland to the UK.

CHANGING ORGANIZATIONS

Many boards have come to the conclusion that, in a more turbulent and demanding business environment, their organizations and cultures are not appropriate. The survey, *The Flat Organization: Philosophy and Practice* (Coulson-Thomas and Coe, 1991), reveals the extent of change activity that is occurring. Approaching nine out of ten of the participating organizations are becoming slimmer and flatter, while in some eight out of ten of them more work is being undertaken in teams, and a more responsive network organization is being created (see Figure 1).

However, while there is a strong desire to change there is little satisfaction at the top with what has been achieved to date. A gap has emerged between aspiration and action.

Layers of management are being taken out of organizations with little thought as to the consequences. Many companies are unable to identify the critical management and business processes that add most value for their customers. Few are equipping their people to cope, or to use those tools and techniques which can be employed to re-engineer processes and transform managerial productivity. In almost all cases, fundamental changes are taking longer to achieve than was first imagined.

Creating a slimmer and flatter organization	88%
More work is being undertaken in teams	79%
Creating a more responsive network organisation	78%
Functions are becoming more inter-dependent	71%
Procedures and permanency are giving way to flexibility and temporary arrangements	67%
Organizations becoming more inter-dependent	55%

Figure 15.1 What respondents organizations are doing to better respond to challenges and opportunities within the business environment
Source: C. Coulson-Thomas and T. Coe, *The Flat Organization* (BIM, 1991).

THE NETWORK ORGANIZATION

Before we examine why corporate transformation is proving so difficult, let us consider another question: What is the network form of organization and culture that almost one in eight organizations (Figure 1) are moving towards? Its distinguishing characteristics are:

1. Electronic links along supply chains forward to customers, backwards to suppliers, and sideways to business partners; which results in,
2. A more blurred or less clear cut boundary between the organization and the external world;
3. The importance attached to the management of relationships between organizations, harnessing human talent, supporting technology, facilitating processes, and the integration of learning and working; and
4. Work undertaken by a community of people organized into multi-functional, multi-location and multi-national project groups, task forces and teams; that are,
5. Coordinated by a core group that focuses upon refining the vision and mission of the network and ensuring it is able to learn and adapt in order to maintain responsiveness and flexibility.

To the network organization the business environment is rich in potential people and other resources that can be tapped on an ad hoc basis, or by means of more permanent arrangements and ventures. Lewis Galoob Toys of the US retains a small core team who co-ordinate a network of sub-contracted activities. These range from design, manufacturing and distribution to account collection.

The network form of organization is shown diagrammatically in Figure 15.2. (Coulson-Thomas and Brown, 1989, 1990).

THE INTERNATIONAL NETWORK

By its nature, in that it might embrace a number of companies, the network is negotiated, and capable of organic expansion abroad. A Euro-network or sub-network could be established in response to the emergence of a Single Market. As it becomes international more work within the network is undertaken by multi-national teams. This can give rise to another cultural issue of strategic importance, namely cross-cultural communication.

In many cases the cooperation and involvement of external parties within an international network will stem from the fact that the vision of

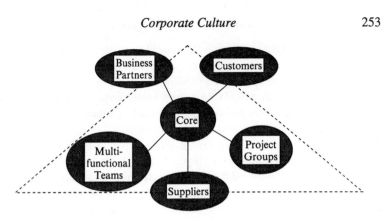

Figure 15.2   The international network organization

the network has 'turned them on'. A desire to contribute to the achievement of the vision may be a more significant motivator of participation than the prospect of financial rewards. We will return to the importance of vision in a moment.

The truly global network is by its nature decentralized. Its purpose is to respond to customer opportunities and access relevant resources where-ever these might be. Information technology provides a variety of means of securing access to relevant skills.

Many opportunities and resources are more likely to be found in some locations rather than others. Rarely however will they be concentrated at a single point. The Ford global network links designers in the US and engineers in Belgium with its manufacturing plant in Spain. All can work together, and with colleagues throughout the world, by means of an international corporate network.

Within the international network business units with particular needs can form direct linkages with other units and groups that may be able to help them. In the bureaucratic organization such units may have been tucked under a layer of management that was not sympathetic to their requirements, or a part of the organization into which they did not really fit. In the network organization there is greater freedom and opportunity to seek out relation-ships based upon mutual interests and needs.

THE NETWORK CULTURE

By and large people work for and within the network because they share its values and empathize with its mission. Many will consider themselves to have joined a community of knowledge workers with a common purpose. Members of the core team are seeking participants, colleagues and partners rather than employees.

Culture (along with vision) holds the network organization together. Without them the network can fragment, or dissolve into its constituent elements. To hold an international community together, an international network may need to have a corporate culture that is distinct from any particular national culture.

The features that distinguish the organic network organization from the more traditional bureaucratic organization have been identified below (see Figure 15.3). The network has a porous skin rather than a hard shell. In theory, it is open, flexible and receptive, puts more emphasis upon

Bureaucratic Organization	**Network Organization**
Managers	Leader & facilitators
Decision makers	Counsellors & mentors
Departmental specialism & values	Shared vision & mission
Rivalry	Interdependence
Rules & procedures	Processes
Jobs & organization charts	Roles & responsibilities
Hierarchy	Project teams
Status	Contribution
Homogenous	Diverse
Privilege	Democracy
Committees	Taskforces & teams
Vertical Communication	Horizontal & all-channel communication
Central direction	Individual initiative
Control	Empowerment & support
Narrow specialism	General awareness
Strong head office	Effective customer interface
Competition, office politics	Co-operation, mutual trust
Factions	Common interests
Continuity	Change
Loyalty	Participation
Generalization & standardization	Responsive to individual, customers & employees
Automate	Support
Centralization	Decentralization & delegation
Closed & secretive	Open & transparent
Suspicion & monitoring	Trust & encouragement
Hoarding expertise	Sharing exprience
Sophistication	Simplification
Inflexible & fixed	Responsive & dynamic
Teaching & talking	Learning & listening

Figure 15.3. Perceived attributes of bureaucratic and network organization.
Source: C. Coulson-Thomas, *Transforming the Company* (Kogan Page, 1992)

establishing and maintaining relationships, and ideas are judged by their quality rather than their source. Ideally, deficiences should be tackled rather than concealed, and the emphasis should be upon cooperation as well as competition.

IMPLICATIONS FOR MANAGERS

Many managers face a 'culture change'. In the network organization senior managers act as counsellors, facilitators and guides. They need to become more intuitive and sensitive, aware of when they are adding value rather than conscious of their status. Their advice and participation will be sought to the extent that they are able to add value, rather than because of their position in a management hierarchy.

Managers within network organizations need to listen rather than talk. Relationships and outputs are important rather than activity for its own sake. The transition may not come so easily to those who have experienced a more authoritarian framework.

VISION AND MISSION

In order to turn the rhetoric of the network organization into reality, where should one begin? Participants in *The Flat Organization* survey identified the determination of a distinct and compelling vision as the starting point. In creating a new philosophy of management to cope with changing organizations and cultures every respondent assessing it believes clear vision and mission to be important. About three quarters of them consider it 'very important' (Figure 15.4).

Sir John Harvey-Jones considers it essential that a vision be 'collective' and 'owned by all': 'It should present an attractive and clear view of the future which can be shared. It must motivate, be ambitious, and should stretch people to achieve more than they might ever have thought possible' (Coulson-Thomas and Coe, 1991).

When transitioning away from the bureaucratic form of organization there is a danger that control can be lost. People may work harder at the 'wrong things'. The more a vision and mission are shared, the greater the likelihood that those to whom discretion is delegated or devolved will be moving in compatible directions.

The Flat Organization survey goes on to reveal the relatively common phenomenon of a gap between vision and reality: 'While clear vision and

Clear vision and mission	74%
Customer focus	66%
Harnessing human potential	66%
Attitudes, values & behaviour	52%
Personal integrity & ethics	40%
Individual learning & development	29%
Processes for ongoing adaptation & change	29%
Turbulence & uncertainty	19%
Organizational learning	14%
Management techniques	5%
Others	3%

Figure 15.4 Factors for creating a new philosophy of management in order of 'very important' replies
Source: C. Coulson-Thomas and T. Coe, *The Flat Organisation* (BIM, 1991).

mission are thought to be essential, in many companies both are regarded as just 'words on paper', and they do not act as a guide to action.'

Another survey, identifies both 'clear vision and strategy' and 'top management commitment' as the most important requirements for the successful management of change. 86% of the respondents ranked these as 'very important' (Figure 15.5).

Clear vision & strategy	86%
Top management commitment	86%
Sharing the vision	71%
Employee involvement & commitment	65%
Communicating the purpose of change	65%
An effective communications network	54%
Communicating the expected results of change	44%
Understanding the contributions required to the achievement of change	42%
Communicating the timing of change	38%
Linking a company's systems strategy with its management of change	38%
Project management of change	27%
Ongoing management education and development programmes	23%
One off management education and development programmes	8%

Figure 15.5 Change Requirements in order of 'very important' replies
Source: C. Coulson-Thomas and S. Coulson-Thomas , *Communicating for Change*, (Adaptation, 1991).

Without a shared vision and strategy, effort may be devoted to the wrong priorities. People need to 'know where they are heading' in order to establish their own roles and contribution. Many visions of network organizations are neither compelling, nor shared. They tend to be vague, and the intermediate milestones are missing. The network consists of much ad hoc activity, but there are also repetitive management and business processes to be identified or created. However, many people lack the approaches and methodologies to 're-engineer' their organization, ie. model and build the network. This is a serious deficiency as changing a process can act directly upon behaviour.

VISION AND RE-ENGINEERING

The growth of interest in process and organizational re-engineering is of great significance to those intent upon changing organizations and cultures. Re-engineering is all about the vision led transformation of processes, or even of total organizations.

A re-engineering methodology should provide a framework for both modelling and building a new organization. Indeed re-engineering is distinguished from simplification or process improvement by its emphasis upon radical or 'framebreaking' change.

However, the author's experience of working with organizations is that many approaches to re-engineering are mechanical and proceedural rather than creative (*Business Process Re-engineering: Myth and Reality*, 1994):

- Overall goals and strategy are generally not clear or shared, while very often the resource and capability required for implementation have not been assembled. Many re-engineering initiatives are doomed from the start as other complementary change elements are not in place.
- The focus is invariably on the organization and its processes, rather than on what represents value for the customer, while the people aspects are downplayed because these are perceived as difficult or intangible.
- Excessive amounts of time are devoted to documenting and understanding what is rather than thinking imaginatively about what ought to be. In some cases, the day of action is postponed almost indefinitely while complex process models are developed.

Pioneers of re-engineering are finding that process owners can squabble and have boundary problems just like heads of functions. Also, many companies are not as open as they could be about the real motivation behind re-engineering initiatives. Often it is all about downsizing and head-count reduction in order to reduce the cost base rather than value to customers.

CREATING THE INTERNATIONAL NETWORK

To date few processes and process re-engineering exercises have been 'international'. This is because many multinational companies operate through relatively self-contained national operating companies.

There are other problem areas. The multinational company may operate in many countries, but it tends to regard one as the home base and so many of its attitudes and values will reflect those of this country of origin – hence it is possible to speak of the US or Japanese multinational. Nationals of the home country are likely to dominate the ranks of senior management, but, equally, profit opportunities may be sought in national markets and the company's senior staff may be concerned with national competitiveness.

The company that is referred to as transnational or pan-global tends to operate with an international perspective and to be free of attitudes associated with a particular home country, so the company might be quoted on several stock exchanges around the world. Its management team may be drawn from various nationalities, profit opportunities may be sought on a global basis and the company's senior staff may be concerned with the company's own global competitiveness vis-à-vis other global players.

The following means have been identified of moving from the traditional multinational to an international network form of organization:

- Encourage international networking and cross-border all channel communication.
- Create opportunities for informal international contact.
- Recruit to secure most relevant skills on an international basis.
- Replace national procedures with international project groups, task forces and teams.
- Strengthen functional, business and sector units, and customer account groups, at the expense of national geographic units.
- Involve international participation in planning and issue monitoring and management exercises.
- Create mutual respect for, and build understanding of, cultural differences and variety.

- Encourage shared and joint use of resources and facilities on a regional or international basis.
- Build interfaces between national IT networks, and develop a global computing and telecommunications network.
- Encourage organic growth and the shift of power and resources away from historic centres of bureaucratic influence and strength, and to areas of greatest customer opportunity.

THE PRIMACY OF THE CUSTOMER

At this point a word of caution is needed. Because some markets are becoming global, it does not follow that all are. Honda came unstuck with its vision of the global car. For a period, the lure of the economies of scale of global production blinded the company to the realities of local market differences and a growing desire for customization.

The needs of customers should determine a company's 'international' responses. For example, as MNCs increasingly demand European and international solutions to regional or global problems, so their suppliers are having to establish European and international project groups, teams and taskforces in order to respond.

Internationalization should not be sought for its own sake, but only in so far as it results in more satisfactory long term relationships with customers. Hoechst has recognized the need for diversity by allowing each element of the business to organize in a way that is most appropriate in terms of its own situation and circumstances.

The Opportunity

The extent to which organizations and cultures can be transformed is clear:

We have an unprecedented opportunity to transform the capacity of companies to harness the talents of people and deliver value to customers. Managerial productivity could be increased by a factor of ten or more. This is not wild speculation, but a tantalizing prospect.

All the individual elements, from attitudes to processes, that are necessary to achieve the transition have been identified. These are already in place in leading edge companies. Their use has been demonstrated and documented. (C. Coulson-Thomas, *Transforming the Company*, Kogan Page 1992)

The global network form of organization offers the prospect of being able to overcome the barriers of nationality, distance, and time in order to access relevant resources and capabilities, and bring together groups and teams composed of people with complementary abilities in order to address the needs of individual customers wherever they may be. It can reconcile the desire for a global unity of purpose in terms of vision, values and goals, and the need for diversity in response to local market conditions. Responsibilities and empowerment can be moved around the network as customer needs and market conditions change.

However, for too many companies the failure to question, anticipate and think things through' means that frustration is being snatched from the jaws of success:

> Corporate transformation is taking longer to achieve than was first thought. Momentum is being lost, and attitudes and behaviour are proving stubbornly resistant to change.
>
> In many organizations a wide gulf has emerged between expectation and achievement. There is disappointment where there should be elation. Why is this? Why has so much aspiration, intention and vision had such apparently limited impact upon reality?
>
> Desperate for results, many companies are becoming victims of peddlers of hype and simplistic solutions. Well thought out programmes, even a variety of distinct initiatives that in themselves are worthy, may not be enough. Their introduction, along with changes of structure, may fail to influence attitudes and behaviour. (C. Coulson-Thomas, *Transforming the Company*, Kogan Page, 1992)

THE REALITY

More progress has been made in shaping the intended structure of the network organization, than in changing corporate culture. Insufficient progress has been made in building the attitudes and values, and in encouraging and rewarding the behaviour, that will allow the full potential of the network organization to be achieved. People are not being empowered, equipped and motivated to do what is necessary to turn aspiration into achievement.

Few companies have identified and manage the cross-functional and inter-organizational processes that deliver customer value and satisfaction. Expenditure on training and information technology is too often devoted to supporting departmental activities, rather than these key processes and the achievement of business objectives.

Some companies are reluctant to recognize the reality of non-achievement. They seek refuge in a world of appearances, rhetoric and collective self-deception. Gaps between aspiration and achievement should be assumed rather than treated as an unwelcome surprise. Barriers and obstacles should be actively identified and tackled.

In the 'real world', changing the corporate culture often proves elusive:

- Many directors are not competent, and many boards are ineffective. Visions and strategies are too often 'words on paper'. Arenas of conflict exist. Customers are treated as targets rather than as colleagues.
- Most quality programmes fail to transform attitudes and behaviour. The blather and hype of communications emphasize the gulf between words and actions, and spread disappointment and despair. Many managers feel betrayed and conned.
- Standard approaches drive out diversity, while 'development' often destroys the desire to learn. Information technology sets existing organizations in concrete. People 'go automatic', rather than challenge.
- In very few organizations are significant changes of attitude and behaviour occuring. In most they are unlikely to occur while crucial change elements are not in place.
- In many cases managerial productivity is actually falling as managers struggle to cope with extra responsibilities, and little is done to equip them to work in new ways.
- A few organizations have developed new approaches and techniques which are resulting in substantial improvements in management performance. However, most companies cling to traditional approaches which have been shown to be wanting.

Simple and superficial change, such as shifting priorities or those involving the use of words, can and some times do occur overnight. However, fundamental changes of attitudes, values, approach and perspective usually take much longer to achieve. Sustained commitment is required.

Moving from Intention to Action

The desire for change is genuine enough. Companies such as BP, BT, General Electric and IBM are seeking to bring about a fundamental transformation of corporate organization and culture.

We have seen that boards are seeking to create more flexible, responsive, and team based organizations. Networks of relationships, embracing customers, suppliers and business partners, are sought that can access and tap relevant resources and people, irrespective of function, distance and time in order to deliver values for individual customers.

TOP MANAGEMENT COMMITMENT

We have seen already that in one survey, *The Flat Organization*, 'clear vision and mission' and 'top management commitment' emerged as the number one change requirements. The extent to which top management are committed to the implementation of a shared long term vision as opposed to 'short term survival' was a major issue for participants in that survey.

The need for top management commitment emerged even more starkly in a further survey: *Quality: The Next Steps*. The main 'quality barrier', by a large margin, in terms of 'very significant' replies is 'top management commitment'. Over nine out of ten respondents consider 'top management commitment' to be a barrier to the successful implementation of a quality process (Figure 15.6).

Top management commitment begins in the boardroom. The effective board is composed of a united team of competent directors who share and can communicate a common vision. The first step in formulating and communicating vision and strategy is for the chairman to ask the following questions:

Top management commitment	92%
Too narrow an understanding of quality	38%
Horizontal boundaries between functions and specialisms	31%
Vested interests	29%
Organizational politics	28%
Cynicism	28%
Organizational structure	27%
Customer expectations	26%
Speed of corporate action	24%
Too general an approach	18%
Loss of momentum	17%
Boredom	15%
Gap between management expectation and process achievement	15%
Vendors'/Suppliers' capabilities	15%
Subsidiary/parent relationships	9%
Cost	6%

Figure 15.6 Quality barriers ranked in order of 'very significant' replies
Source: C. Coulson-Thomas and S. Coulson-Thomas, *Quality: The Next Steps* (ODI, 1991).

- Do the members of the board share a common, clear and compelling vision? If a fundamental change of corporate organization and culture is to occur there must be an agreed vision of a better future.
- Are the directors also committed to a common and realistic strategy for the achievement of the vision?
- How effective are members of the board at communicating with customers, employees and business partners? A clear and compelling vision has to be communicated and understood if it is to be shared, and if it is to motivate.

Overall, many boards need to devote more effort to ensuring that the people of an organization are motivated, empowered and equipped to implement the strategies, including those for corporate transformation, which emerge from the boardroom.

COMMUNICATION SKILLS

To communicate something as intangible as the vision of a new corporate culture requires communication skills of a high order. How do boards and management teams match up?

Those interviewed in *The Flat Organization* survey identified the lack of communication skills as a major cause of the gulf of distrust that has grown up in many companies between the board and management. Those at the top of many organizations appear unable to communicate their commitment to a shared vision. They lack policy deployment tools and techniques. All too often their companies' staff perceive a wide gulf between words and deeds, especially in the area of culture change.

The *Communicating for Change* survey reveals that in most companies the traditional channels of, and approaches to, communication do little to share an understanding of corporate vision, values, priorities, mission and goals. People do not appreciate how they can contribute to the vital few programmes that lead to culture change, satisfied customers and market-place success. Many communications vehicles are regarded as gloss, and are viewed with cynicism and distrust.

Participants in *The Flat Organization* survey were asked to assess 15 management qualities in order of importance. When these are ranked in order of 'very important' replies, the 'ability to communicate' appears at the top of the list. Two thirds of the respondents consider this to be 'very important' (Figure 15.7).

Ability to communicate	67%
Flexibility	55%
Adaptability	52%
Ability to handle uncertainty & surprise	47%
Understanding of business environment	45%
Broad perspective on the organization's goals	43%
Ability to assume greater responsibility	38%
Ability to contribute to teams	38%
A balanced perspective	29%
Commitment to on-going learning	26%
Awareness of ethics & values	24%
Tolerance of ambiguity	14%
Specialist expertise	12%
Multi-skills	10%
Mobility	5%

Figure 15.7   Management qualities in order of 'very important' replies
Source: C. Coulson-Thomas and T. Coe, *The Flat Organization Report* (BIM, 1991).

Participants in the *Communicating for Change* survey were asked to rank a number of 'barriers' to internal and external communication in order of significance. Their responses (internal communication) in order of 'very significant' replies are summarized in Figure 15.8).

Both in terms of 'significant', and when adding 'very significant' and 'significant' together, the top barrier to internal communication was felt by

Communication skills	33%
Top management commitment	27%
Employee attitudes	19%
Lack of two-way communication	19%
Organization structure	13%
Ability to access people when needed	10%
Management processes	8%
Speed of communication	8%
Organizational politics	8%
Cost of communication	6%
Communications technology	2%

Figure 15.8   Barriers to effective internal communication ranked in order of 'very significant' replies
Source: C. Coulson-Thomas and S. Coulson-Thomas, *Communicating for Change* (Adaptation Ltd, 1991).

respondents to be that of 'communication skills'. Not a single respondent considered 'communication skills' to be 'insignificant' as a communication barrier.

The 'skills problem' as identified by interviewees in both of these surveys is one of commitment, and of attitudes and approaches to communication, rather than 'technical' communication skills. In fact culture has to change in many organizations if communication is to be significantly improved. The least significant 'barriers' to effective internal communication are 'communications technology' and the 'cost of communication'.

Those who were interviewed believe that:

- Many managers do not have the competence to effectively use the full potential or capability of communications technology. They have not been equipped with the tools and techniques that are transforming management performance in benchmark companies.
- Many managers do not understand how they might best contribute to corporate goals. Their employers do not use policy deployment type approaches that can turn board aspiration into management action.
- Many managers do not know whether or not their activities form part of management and business processes that contribute significantly to customer satisfaction. Much management resource, even in slimmed down companies, is devoted to tasks and proceedures that add little if any value for customers.

Most survey participants believe the communication skills of their managers could be greatly improved, but they are not finding this easy to achieve. Interviewees are aware of many courses on the market concerning traditional communication techniques, but few if any of these are thought to have much impact upon deep rooted attitudes and approaches to communication.

What is needed are culture change; policy deployment type approaches that can be used to share vision, values and goals; and techniques that enable the key business processes the add value for customers to be identified and improved. We will return to the latter in a moment.

CROSS-CULTURAL COMMUNICATION

For those intent upon increasing international communication, another cultural issue emerges, namely that of cross-cultural communication. To communicate effectively across cultural barriers there are a number of factors to bear in mind:

- It is necessary to understand conventions concerning greetings, interruptions, listening, giving tips, treatment of staff, etc.; and to be aware of and observe local sources of respect and status.
- There are also pitfalls to avoid. For example, do not infringe upon personal space, and avoid gestures, value laden judgements or comments which may cause offence. Another common mistake is to interpret nodding or the word 'yes' to mean agreement, when its usage is merely an indication that a point made has been understood.
- To build cross-cultural relationships, it is necessary to accept that differences of values and opinions can exist. Knowledge and what is regarded as right or best is often relative to the context. Those who persist is thinking in absolute terms may find it very difficult to 'settle in' or achieve a rapport.
- Remember that cultural and other sources of diversity can be a source of creativity within groups. Such diversity should not just be tolerated, it should be actively encouraged.
- To establish and build a relationship, it is necessary to understand the perspectives of the other parties involved. Expectations regarding outcomes and timescales may have to be adjusted to suit the local circumstances. On occasion considerable patience may be needed, along with the self-control to avoid emotional reactions to frustrations and disappointments.

An effective communicator is always ready to listen and learn, and has a high degree of self-awareness. In particular, one should avoid over-estimating linguistic ability. Many problems in communication result from a failure to recognize limitations. Success will also require the ability to understand how local, regional and global perspectives may differ and build relationships based upon mutual respect, reciprocity and trust at each of these levels.

International Managers

Some managers are more sensitive to cross-cultural communication issues than others. Cultural awareness needs to be taken into account when international task forces and teams are brought together. Some people may need to be specifically equipped for cross-cultural communication and multi-cultural team working.

The globalization of the marketplace has given rise to a growing requirement for the internationalization of management. The demand for international managers currently exceeds the supply. According to one headhunter: 'they are much talked about, but rarely met'.

It is easier to spell out what international managers are not, than describe what they are. A knowledge of airport timetables, 'having languages', or being able to order meals in foreign restaurants, do not of themselves make you an international manager. Mobile managers, foreign language courses, and heavy expenditure upon airline flights could actually be an indicator of a lack of internationalization. Perhaps too little discretion is given to locally recruited managers.

In essence, being an international manager is a question of international attitude, awareness, perspective, responsibilities, understanding and vision. People who are spread around the globe, or are criss-crossing it in aeroplanes may appear worldly and jet lagged, but they may not necessarily have an international perspective. Ford takes the view that an international perspective should precede the assumption of international responsibilities, rather than be left to arise as a consequence of them.

Working abroad does necessarily give people an international perspective. Expatriate managers are often among the most bigoted people on earth. National cultures vary so much that experience of just one or two can merely confirm prejudices, and result in stereo-typing and over-generalization.

Qualities for Effective International Operation

Those building an international corporate culture should aim to accommodate cultural diversity and encourage an international awareness. Success as an international manager demands the empathy, openness, scepticism and tolerance of the diplomat, rather than simple models, blinkered certainties, and hyped up panaceas.

The international manager strives to be free of the mis-perceptions and misunderstandings that can result from viewing events, people, situations and requirements through the distorting lens of a single national culture or narrow corporate culture. To do this requires a relatively high degree of awareness and sensitivity to others. Self-centred and intolerant people who practice self-deception do not make good international managers.

Let us consider some other qualities which have been identified:

● An international manager must cope with surprises and shocks. In the international business environment wars, disorders, revolutions, disasters, and economic and diplomatic crises are not exceptions but common features.

- A tolerance for ambiguity, contradictions, paradoxes and contending forces is required. Sensitive and intuitive antennae are needed to monitor and manage international issues.
- Flexibility is also required. A company may need to respond differently at local, national, regional and international levels. Cross border links, relationships and processes may need to be established to meet the needs of customers who wish to purchase at the local, regional or international level.

The importance of travel to international managers has been much exaggerated. The key requirement is the capacity to quickly access and harness relevant skill, regardless of function, location and nationality, in order to deliver value to individual customers. Today, people can communicate by telephone, fax, and electronic mail; and work together by telephone, video and computer conferencing. International managers know how to communicate across barriers of distance, culture and time.

Companies that know the qualities of their managers are able to put together teams of those with complementary qualities. Increasingly, companies are sharing a common vision and values with all members of the management team irrespective of function, location and nationality. Equipping people with a common set of techniques and tools can facilitate the coming together of cross-functional, multi-location and multi-national groups and teams, but this benefit should not be obtained at the cost of wiping out the diversity that can be so beneficial.

THE RISKS OF RADICAL CHANGE

Transforming or internationalizing a corporate culture, along with the associated changes of organization, process and technology can amount to a revolution. Hence, the growing interest in re-engineering approaches and methodologies for the achievement of radical change. It is possible to re-engineer both individual processes and a total organization.

Many people face a dilemma:

- There are bread and butter, and relatively low risk, approaches to simplification than can generate considerable short-term benefits, but will they be enough if radical change is required in order to survive?

- Full-scale re-engineering has the potential to transform an organization, but the risks of failure and of doing great harm are correspondingly greater.
- The timescale to achieve fundamental change may extend beyond the lifetime of the change requirement.

Whether or not re-engineering is required will depend upon how much change is required to build a world class capability that delivers value and benchmark levels of satisfaction to customers, employees and business partners; differentiate in the marketplace; or achieve business goals and objectives.

Much of what is being referred to as re-engineering is actually incremental rather than radical change. Many boards are genuinely worried about turning their worlds upside down. In view of the risks involved, the halfhearted should look elsewhere.

IDENTIFYING THE CHANGE REQUIREMENT

The review that is required to transform a corporate culture and organization is a holistic one. It involves:

- Monitoring and understanding economic, political, social and technological developments in the international business environment.
- Determining a customer focused vision, mission, goals, objectives and strategy in the context of the opportunities and challenges in the external business environment.
- Securing and developing appropriate people, creating a flexible and responsive organization, building supporting and facilitating technology, and arranging adequate finance.
- Applying management and business processes that allow these resources to work effectively together, and with the resources of other organizations, in the generation and delivery of value to customers and the achievement of business results.

A re-engineering review will typically pass through modelling, analysis, design and implementation planning phases and be tailored to the corporate situation and context. It will involve the assessment of internal and external requirements; the use of benchmarking, environmental scanning, modelling, visioning, design and planning tools; and the analysis of the interaction of people, work processes, information and technology.

Of particular importance are the key processes for organizational learning. These are shown in Figure 15.9.

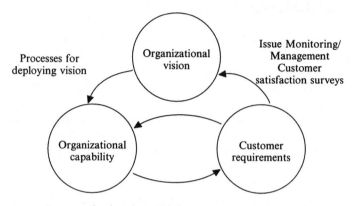

Processes for focusing on delivery of value to customers
Processes for harnessing talents of groups and teams to add value for customers
Processes for continuous learning and improvement

Figure 15.9   Organizational learning
Source: Transforming the Company, 1992.

CHANGE REQUIREMENTS

The surveys we have examined suggest there is some consensus concerning what is important, and what needs to be done to bridge the gap between expectation and achievement that is found in many companies:

- A compelling vision is essential for both differentiation and transformation. Clear vision and strategy, and top management commitment are of crucial importance in the management of cultural and organizational change. If either is lacking, a change or transformation programme is likely to be built upon foundations of sand. The vision and the commitment need to be sustained. This requires an effective board composed of competent directors.
- The vision must be shared, the purpose of change communicated, and employee involvement and commitment secured. The ability to communicate is an essential management quality. Successful communication and sharing of a vision requires integrity and a relationship of trust.

- More effort needs to be devoted to equipping people to cope with change, and to identifying and re-engineering the critical business processes that do most to add value for customers. New facilitating processes, supporting technology and competencies in such areas as project management are also required.
- Corporate cultures do need to change. For example, many managers are tired of the ritual and cosmetics of communication, and feel betrayed when the words of the copywriters are not matched by deeds. Changes of attitude, approach and perspective are required.

Effective communication occurs when there is mutual understanding between the elements of the network organization, vision, values and goals are shared, individuals understand their contributions, and people are equipped to do those things that lead directly to satisfied customers.

The contribution Business Process Re-engineering (BPR) can make is to ensure that people work on, and apply technology to, those tasks and activities which deliver value to customers and contribute to the achievement of corporate objectives.

Processes provide the vehicle for corporate communications within and between organizations. Figure 15.10 illustrates how various corporate activities and processes feed into the communications process.

COBRA

We have seen that the use of methodologies for re-engineering or transforming organizations and their associated cultures is spreading. What is the experience of their use?

The European Commission has commissioned Adaptation Ltd to undertake a pan-European study of business process re-engineering (BPR) experience and practice, and of the implications for new patterns of work and corporate organizations and cultures. The project, 'Constraints and Opportunities in Business Restructuring Analysis' (COBRA), is the largest study ever undertaken of BPR across Europe and is resulting in reports on current practice and future prospects, case studies and methodologies. Members of the COBRA team advise the Governments of five EU Member States on BPR and related issues.

Next Steps

Corporate leadership is about setting and communicating a vision and strategies for organizational and cultural change. The keys to corporate

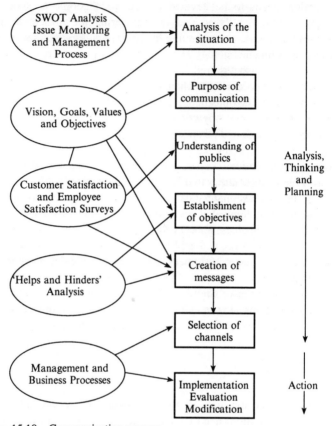

Figure 15.10   Communication process
Source: Transforming the Company, 1992

transformation are vision and communication, top management commitment and a focus upon the support of cross-functional and interorganizational processes.

A first step is to identify or acknowledge the existence of a gap between aspiration and achievement. Some companies are reluctant to recognize the reality of non-achievement. They seek refuge in a world of appearances, rhetoric and collective self-deception.

Gaps between aspiration and achievement should be assumed rather than treated as an unwelcome surprise. If they do not exist, it is likely that aspirations are too modest.

The experience summarized in *Transforming the Company'* and a recent survey sponsored by Lotus Development, 'Harnessing the Potential of

Groups (Coulson-Thomas, 1993), both suggest that many companies would benefit from an objective and first-principles review of their approaches to organizational and cultural change. Areas to examine include the extent to which there is:

- A distinctive and compelling vision;
- Clear and measurable objectives;
- Top management commitment;
- Role model behaviour;
- Focus on the customer and key processes;
- Employee involvement;
- Quality as an enabler rather than a bureaucratic constraint;
- A practical and comprehensive toolkit;
- A holistic and comprehensive approach; and
- Obstacles and barriers are identified and tackled.

Success is dependent upon the effective management of cultural change. It is ultimately all about feelings, attitudes, values, behaviours, commitments, and personal qualitities such as being open-minded. Techniques, methodologies and supporting IT are only elements of what needs to be done.

MAKING IT HAPPEN

Significant progress towards the network organization can be achieved, but a combination of elements need to be assembled to make it happen in the situation and circumstances of a particular context. No two contexts are likely to be the same, and the key elements needed can vary greatly between them.

In general, people appear too wedded to what is. The existing organization is used as a point of departure when it may be quite inappropriate compared with alternative models that are available. The innovative culture is one that provides an environment that is conducive of innovation and encourages the spread of innovations to other units (Figure 15.11).

Those who go to the essence of what needs to be done to generate value and build relevant capability, and who keep it simple, tend to be the most successful. No amount of technique can save people from a lack of purpose, direction, shared vision and focus.

The good news is that organizations and cultures can be transformed where a more holistic approach is adopted. The experience of benchmark

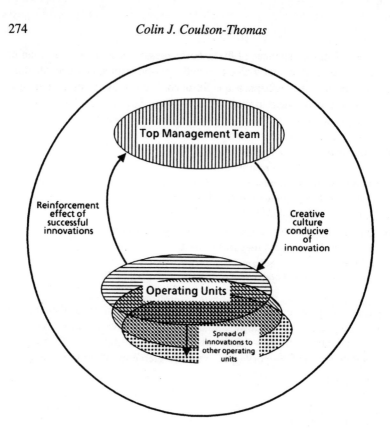

Figure 15.11   The innovative culture
Source: *Transforming the Company*, Kogan Page, 1992.

companies is that certain combinations and applications of change
elements do work, and can bear fruit when they are correctly applied.

Let us conclude with some key messages from *Transforming the
Company*:

> Single solutions should not be sought to a challenge as fundamental as
> transforming a company. A combination of change elements need to be
> in place to 'make it happen' in the unique context of a particular com-
> pany. When they are, the results can be dramatic.

The successful implementation of a transformation programme
depends critically upon the relevance of the selection, combination and

Above all, every piece of the transformation jigsaw puzzle must be in place. People need to be able to see that all the change elements that are required to make it happen are lined up. They must come to the conclusion: this is going to work. This is when they become believers and committed converts. This is when transformation occurs.

Bibliography

C. Coulson-Thomas, *Transforming the Company: bridging the Gap between management myth and corporate reality*, Kogan Page.

C. Coulson-Thomas, *Creating the Global Company: successful internationalization*, McGraw-Hill.

C. Coulson-Thomas, *Creating Excellence in the Boardroom*, McGraw-Hill.

C. Coulson-Thomas, *Developing Directors: Building an effective boardroom team*, McGraw-Hill.

C. Coulson-Thomas, 'Harnessing the potential of groups', an Adaptation Ltd survey for Lotus Development, Lotus.

C. Coulson-Thomas, Business Process Re-engineering: Myth and Reality, Kogan Page.

C. Coulson-Thomas and R. Brown, *The Responsive Organization*, BIM.

C. Coulson-Thomas and R. Brown, *Beyond Quality*, BIM.

C. Coulson-Thomas and T. Coe, *The Flat Organization*: Philosophy and Practice, BIM.

C. Coulson-Thomas and S. Coulson-Thomas, 'Quality: the next steps', an Adaptation Ltd survey for ODI International, ODI.

C. Coulson-Thomas and S. Coulson Thomas, *Communicating for Change – An Adaptation Ltd Survey for Granada Business Services,* London.

16 Strategic Crisis Management

Michael Bland[1]

INTRODUCTION

Just a few years ago crisis management was a virtually unknown term. Now it is a PR flavour of the month. Much of this new-found popularity resulted from a wave of highly publicized catastrophes in the late 1980s – Bhopal, Zeebrugge, King's Cross, Piper Alpha, Lockerbie and the Exxon Valdez – followed by a number of public relations firms cashing in on corporate fear ('what if it happened to *you*?...') and adding "crisis management" to their stable of skills.[2]

It is still a new science and much of the practice relates only to media handling and copycat manuals. But in fact, crisis management at a strategic level is uniquely absorbing and challenging for the serious professional. Some of the challenges that present themselves, for example, are:

- *It's a Grey Area*   In most other fields of PR, so long as you have sufficient experience and take a sound strategic approach you can have a fair idea of whether or not you've got it right. Crisis is different. No matter how much you research, plan and organize you will still often end up flying by the seat of your pants. And you often have to make crucial decisions based more on gut feel than those dictated by the strategy or plan. Yet, paradoxically, the sounder the strategy the better the chances of success.
- *Management Attitudes*   If you think it's hard to get bolt-headed managements to communicate effectively in PR terms, you should try it when there's a crisis! At least they can be taught over time to communicate with, for example, the media, politicians and employees if persuaded that there's a commercial advantage in it. But getting them to do so when the factory has just blown up is a whole new ball game. In real life it can be a very different matter to get the chief executive to go out there and face the cameras when he has never done so, when he has got to the top through a lack of the very human sympathies that he now

276

needs to display, when his understanding of crisis psychology is absolute zero, and when the lawyers are telling him: 'Don't say anything – it could cost us millions'.

- *Driving Force*   Allied to this, successful crisis management is more about *attitudes* than *procedures*. The temptation is to create written plans (the infamous crisis manual) to cover every eventuality and to dictate precisely who should do what. But elaborate plans simply don't work in real life. Some of the best handled crises involve a minimum of planning and a maximum of the people at the top instinctively saying and doing the right things.
- *Strategic Structure*   So, if elaborate plans and manuals don't work... what does? The strategic challenge is to devise a workable structure which is prescriptive enough for management to understand – yet flexible enough to operate in practice. It isn't easy.

From the experience of several years of devising crisis programmes and handling actual crises the (sequential) approach which seems to work best is:

- *Theoretical Training*.   This gets management *thinking* about crisis and the psychologies involved. They can agree on a common definition of crisis and be presented with the many questions that will form the skeleton of the crises plan. syndicate exercises and media role plays help with team building and 'hands on' practice.
- *Brainstorming*.   The now crisis-aware management can thrash out the many different crisis which could hit them – and how they would respond. Here a 'planning by question' approach works well. By asking themselves a set of questions the team can develop a logical plan (this approach is described later).
- *Planning*.   Any written plans are now drawn up – usually in the form of a crisis manual.
- *Media Training*.   Any media spokespeople *must* be trained in crisis interview techniques.
- *Simulations*.   Crisis simulations are a useful way of assessing the team's strengths and weaknesses, and keeping them crisis-aware.
- *Audits*.   A 'crisis auditor' should drop in on individual team members unannounced and check their top-of-the-head knowledge of crisis procedures. He/she should also check that changeable data in the manual (e.g. team members, telephone numbers, etc.) is kept up to date.

LEARNING FROM CRISES

Much can be learned about modern crisis handling by examining other well publicized crises and asking ourselves:

– What happened?
– Why did that crisis get the amount and type of publicity that it did?
– How did the management handle it? What seemed good and bad about their response?

Each crisis has its own 'personality' and lessons to teach us. Go back in your mind through some of the well-publicized crises – Aberfan, Thalidomide, Tylenol, Zeebrugge, Guinness, Salmonella, BSE and a host of oil spills – and see what you can learn from them.

And don't just examine old crises. Whenever a company or product has a rough time in public, analyse as it goes along and see what you can learn about good and bad crisis management.

Some Lessons

While each crisis is different, there are often some common features for it to have occurred and been seen as a crisis:

● Someone is to blame. If lightning strikes your head office and it burns down, it's an accident and people sympathize. but if it burns down because the lightning conductor isn't in working order – or if people die because your evacuation procedure is inadequate – you have a crisis. In almost every case, human error or malice is in there at the start of it.
● Something is at stake (e.g. profit, reputation, survival)
● Someone finds out.

And it is when an incident gets into, or is in danger or getting into, the public domain that it really starts to take off as a crisis. Also, in most cases (except major political and financial scandals) the publicity is much bigger if:

– It concerns the person in the street
– It is geographically close to home

When we study crises we can see how times have changed – and how professional we must be to cope. The days are long gone when management could bury their heads in the sand, put up a barricade of lawyers and 'no comments', and wait for it to blow over.

Here are some characteristics of modern crisis management:

- *It's A Moving Picture.* Years ago there was more respect for those in charge; less questioning; fewer challenges. So it was much easier to stifle the adverse effects of a crisis. Then there was Aberfan. And Thalidomide. And Watergate.

  Gradually the crisis 'audiences' such as the media, employees, customers, regulatory bodies and the general public were not prepared to settle for inaction and a refusal to say sorry. They wanted and expected more or there would be hell to pay. And in many cases there *was* hell to pay. Quite right too.

  And it's changing all the time. The way a crisis was successfully handled ten years ago may no longer be appropriate today. We must keep learning.

  For example, there is now a relatively new breed of specialist disaster lawyers in Britain – lawyers who use adverse publicity to force companies into paying higher compensation than the minimum required by law. Are they a good thing or a bad thing? How do they operate? What influence could they have on *your* crisis? You need to keep up to date.

- *Perception is Reality.* In PR terms the real crisis is not what has actually happened; it is what people *think* has happened. And your most vital messages are not what you *think* you should say; your most vital messages are what people *expect* you to say. Look at some of the examples: Perrier, Opren, Exxon Valdez, Salmonella in eggs. A serious analysis shows that the damage in each case, while serious, was not as great as the public perception and that the 'culprits' had some good arguments on their side.

  For example, there is more benzene in a single cup of non freeze-dried decaffeinated coffee than in a whole bottle of contaminated Perrier. The public were in no danger. But once they started to *think* they were in danger...

  Simply communicating your good arguments is not enough. For example, the most vivid public impression of the Valdez spillage was the black, oily carcasses of thousands of birds. Later the Chairman of Exxon was to say: 'There were 30 million birds that went through the sound last summer and only 30,000 carcasses have been recovered. Just look at how many ducks are killed in the Mississippi Delta in one hunting day in December!' (*Time Magazine*). Technically, he had a point.

But it was hardly the most sensitive message to put out if you wanted to win people over to your side.

- *We Operate In A Goldfish Bowl.* There have been many social, media, consumer and educational changes in recent years. People are brought up believing they have a 'right to know'. The world is full of consumer groups, pressure groups, investigative journalists – and corporations are much more accountable for their actions. It's also fair to say that we are entering an age of greater corporate responsibility – towards safety, the environment, customers, employees etc.

- *Global Village.* For international companies the media make the world a very small place. For example, when Lucozade had a recall of dangerous bottles in Europe, consumers in Singapore rushed to return their (perfectly safe) bottles!

- *Heads Must Roll.* Increasingly every incident must have a culprit in the public mind. Something that might have been seen as no more than a tragic accident a decade ago will now be the subject of endless investigations, law suits and publicity until the 'villain' has been exposed and punished.

- *Management is Getting Better.* Some senior managements are setting excellent examples from which we can all learn. In a number of recent crises the top person has been available immediately and has shown concern, competence and the all-important human face.

    Some have even learned the valuable psychology of the 'constructive Mea Culpa'. That's when you admit to your faults as a way of convincing your audience of your honesty. Only then will they start listening to your other arguments.

    For example, compare the Exxon approach with that of Shell Chairman, Bob Reid who immediately apologized in public when his company polluted the Mersey. He came over as a credible person and then communicated some other vital messages about the importance of oil, how hard the industry works to control pollution, what they were going to do about it, and so on.

    'Ah', you say. 'But what about the legal aspects? It you say sorry you can be sued for millions'. True... sometimes. A good excuse for inaction... usually.

- *Crises into Opportunity.* Johnson and Johnson's handling of the Tylenol poisonings is held up in standard texts as the classic example of coming out of a crisis better than when it started. And there have been many since.

Yes, a crisis gives you a great deal of unwanted publicity. But it's publicity that you would not otherwise have had. And there's almost no such thing as bad publicity. The attention of the world on you, your company, your product can often be a potential promotional *opportunity*.

Three other factors can play a significant role at a time of crisis:

1. How well known/perceived you are: The bigger the name the bigger the coverage.
2. Luck of the draw: Saddam Hussein removed Salmonella and BSE at a stroke! In other words, how much coverage you get will depend on what else is going on in the news at the time. If it's a quiet news day you've got a problem.
3. Flavour of the month: Remember police car crashes? And child abductions? And pit bulls? At the time of these public scares there were actually no more police car crashes, child abductions and dog attacks than at any other time in recent history. But once the media are on to a vogue theme they will make a meal of it.

PREPARING FOR A CRISIS

You cannot prepare for all eventualities by developing elaborate lists and detailed responses. Remember: the bigger and fatter your crisis manual the less people will remember what's in it (that's if they read it at all), the less flexible they will be to cope with the unexpected – and the more complacent they will feel ('It's all in the manual so we don't have to worry').

But one thing is for sure: *some* crisis preparation is essential. While many companies over-prepare in terms of trying to plan for every contingency, most under-prepare by doing nothing and hoping it won't happen.

Remember, too, that successful crisis management is more about attitudes than about procedures. So proper strategic crisis preparation is not just about creating lists and plans. The whole of senior management must be involved from the outset in a continuing process.

The best way to approach crisis preparation is to ask yourselves a series of key questions. In developing the answers relevant to your company you are developing a workable crisis plan.

These are the questions:

What crises could hit us?

Most crises can be better anticipated by:

- *Awareness*
  Meet every few months for a crisis management session and look at what crises have been in the news; could they have happened here? If so, how would we have coped?
  And take a good look at all that is happening in your company that might provide vital 'cracks and warning signs' of a possible crisis. Note how much of the coverage is often devoted to how the warning signs were ignored. The time to spot them is now.

Look at:

- *Risk Exposure*
  In what ways might you be exposed to the risk of a crisis: chemicals, machinery, health, environment, sabotage etc? Do you use a firm of specialist risk consultants? If not, why not?

- *Underlying Causes*
  There are often underlying causes which lead to a crisis happening. Some examples:
    Low morale
    Customer complaints
    Poor housekeeping
    Staff quality
    Panic cost cutting
    Rushed output
    Rumour and gossip
    Corporate arrogance
    Rapid change
    Complex structures
    etc.

Are there any signs of these since your last meeting?
  The next question to ask is: if a crisis were to hit us now:

Who are the audiences?

List all the possible audiences with whom you may have to deal. In a real crisis you will probably have to communicate with all or most of them.

The main criteria for identifying an audience in the planning stages are:

- Who would be affected by the crisis?
- Who could affect us?
- Who else needs to know?

Most importantly, the time to list your potential audiences is *now*, not when you're immersed in a panic. If you wait till the crisis hits before you start thinking: 'Now who do I need to tell' you will quite certainly forget some vital groups of people who need to know. And by developing this list you will also see how inadequate is the approach to crisis management that thinks it's all about handling the media. Some typical audiences to consider:

Media

National – press: general and specialist
          – TV
          – radio
Local   – press: general and industrial
          – TV
          – radio
Trade and/or professional media

Official

Government – relevant department(s)
           – MPs (especially local)
           – MEPs
Authorities – regulatory bodies
           – local councils

Support

Police
Fire
Hospital
Ambulance
Remember that the support services have their own PR teams, who are often very professional – and who may also have a vested interest in deflecting unfavourable publicity.

Corporate

Employees
Group: head office; parent company, etc.

Trade unions
Lawyers
Insurers
Shareholders, investing institutions and City

Business

Competitors
Suppliers
Trade and professional associations

Other

Relatives
Local community
Environmental and pressure groups

'The general public' is also an audience, but it can usually only be reached via your communications with other target audiences (e.g. media).

Having established who you need to communicate with in a crisis, the next question is:

How do we communicate with them?

Do you have channels of communication in place to be able to inform those audiences immediately and effectively? Do *they* know how to contact *you*?
Some examples:

- Names and 24 hour telephone numbers for key press, MP, authorities, etc.
- Office and home addresses
- Telephone
- Correspondence
- Fax
- Mobile radio/telephone
- Press statements
- Press conferences
- Briefing meetings
- PR consultants

Do you know how to set up and man a telephone hot line for concerned relatives, consumers and others?

In particular, identify (and test if possible) your reporting structures and systems with staff, management, authorities, press, etc.

Now that we know who we must talk with and how we get to them, next:

What are the messages?

Obviously, the information you put out will depend on the nature and stage of the crisis at the time. Nevertheless, having identified in advance the types of crises, audiences and communication methods, it is possible to anticipate a number of 'core' messages, such as:

● *Human face.*   The best of all is when you can say 'Sorry' but clearly the legal position has to be considered. If it's obvious that your company is at fault and you are going to be clobbered anyway, then the chief executive should seriously consider over-riding the lawyers. One of his duties is to protect the *asset of goodwill*, which may be worth far more than is at stake in a legal battle over compensation.

Clearly, in many cases you can't actually apologize. But can you express 'regret?'. Again, the lawyers will tend to say 'No' because their concern is with playing it as safe as possible. As can be seen from a number of cases from Thalidomide to Lockerbie and the Valdez, 'playing it safe' can seriously damage your company's reputation. Would 'regret' *really* cost you millions? And what will a seriously damaged reputation cost? Be prepared to challenge the lawyers' and insurers' advice.

And in all cases you can certainly show sympathy, concern, compassion. One of the most important things that people want to hear from the faceless corporation in a crisis is 'We care'. So *tell* them you care.

● *Reassurance.*   People out there are worried and frightened. Could it happen again? Will there be long term damage? Is it under control? Do they know what they're doing? Remember to reassure them. And think about how to reassure them *convincingly* (e.g. via an independent expert). If possible, try to tell them that everything possible will be done to prevent it happening again and, if necessary, to make amends (e.g. a clean-up campaign).

● *We are doing something about it.*   Try to *demonstrate* that you are taking action.

Think, too of the other types of message that might be needed, such as:

● Demonstration of the company's excellent track record.
● Announcement of a thorough investigation (preferably independent).

It is useful to think of these messages and list them beforehand because:

- It will take up valuable time if you start thinking of them when handling an actual crisis. And it is easy to forget some messages in the heat of the moment. It's amazing how often senior management have cared deeply about what has happened but have not said so – not because of legal considerations but because they have been so wrapped up in the crisis that they have simply forgotten.
- Messages such as sympathy and concern will need sorting out with lawyers and insurers beforehand. *Their* priority in a crisis is to clam up. *Yours* is to express sympathy and give information.

This is also the time to prepare:

Background briefs for the media and other audiences. When the press descend on you they have to fill their pages with information about what your company does, how many people it employs, what its products are used for, how they are made – and so on. If you can provide these off the shelf you will (a) help to fill their pages with *your* information, not someone else's (b) ensure that at least they get that part of it right, and (c) make them feel better disposed towards you because you are being helpful.

Again, you simply won't have time to collate all these details while actually handling the crisis. The time to prepare your background briefs is *now*.

In preparing these briefs you will almost certainly encounter the 'Why should we tell them?' reaction – especially about items such as financial figures, hazardous chemicals etc. The answer is simple: the press will fill their pages with these details whether you like it or not; you are simply choosing whether they use your version or someone else's.

Who will form the crisis team?

The crisis communications team, who will do virtually nothing else during a major crisis, is not necessarily the top management team, though some (e.g. chief executive) may be identified as part-time members. Other top people (e.g. chairman) may be identified as 'audiences' rather than team members.

The key players in a crisis team include:

- Team leader
- Spokespersons
- 'Gatekeeper'

- Secretary/admin
- Media 'Minder'
- As required, executives with skills in public relations, legal matters, human resources, production, security, technical, safety, media and other relevant disciplines
- Group/HQ

The 'gatekeeper' is the single, central co-ordinating source who has tabs on all aspects of the crisis and filters all questions and information coming in – and is responsible for allocating information, briefs, requests for interviews etc out to the team. The centralising and control of information is vital.

The 'minder' is responsible for the physical aspects of handling the press, eg arranging briefings, providing them with facilities (especially access to telephones), marshalling them for press conferences, keeping them at bay etc.

Increasingly, organizations are also recognising the value of having *stress counselling* expertise available. In a serious crisis both the crisis team members and the affected audiences can suffer severe stress, which in turn will adversely influence behaviour. Much of this damage can be reduced by stress counselling – and in the case of the crisis team it should take place *before* the event as well as during and after it.

List and brief reserve team members in case any key people are sick or on holiday.

In a really big crisis – especially an international one – you may need the services of a specialist PR company and/or a telephone answering firm. Have you identified and briefed them?

The make-up of the crisis team will vary according to your own organisation and the nature and size of the crisis. But it is essential to develop some sort of team *now* – and to brief them and list their contact numbers in the manual.

The crisis PR team may also need to be completely separate from the team handling the physical crisis itself.

The most important considerations for selecting the crisis team members are:

- An executive(s) who has full power and authority, and who understands the human and media sides of the issue. He or she must be able to:
  - Ask for information and get it – in full – at once
  - Issue instructions and get a response
  - Be powerful enough to override the instructions of the lawyers if necessary – or to have instant access to someone who can.

- It is essential for the spokespeople to be sympathetic, articulate and trained/skilled in handling tough media interviews. There should be a leading spokesperson who does most of the work – especially on television – in a crisis. Ideally, this should be the chief executive but another senior spokesperson should be considered – especially if he/she is a better performer. Other spokespeople should be trained and available for general and local media interviews and handling the flood of press telephone calls and other enquiries.

Spokespeople must also be given space, to be allowed to get it wrong occasionally. If they are worrying about every word and looking over their shoulders the whole time they cannot come over as sympathetic or as speaking with authority. Besides, even if they get every word right the media will still get it wrong. They must be given the confidence and backing of senior management, who in turn must be educated in the realities of media PR. That management education is itself a challenge for any professional.

- The right temperaments: handling a crisis may involve nights of lost sleep and intolerable pressure from outside audiences.

- Back-up: some team members may be in the crisis room for days. Who will run your organisation in the meantime?
  And always consider how important it is for *everyone* who deals with the public, relatives, staff etc to be sympathetic and understanding. In a serious crisis, especially one involving human suffering, all your employees who answer telephones and meet the public are part of the company's PR. They must be well briefed–and trained if possible – in being human, concerned, understanding and patient.

What Resources and Facilities will be Needed?

The smoothness and efficiency of the operation will be strongly affected – for better or worse – by the ready availability of the right facilities.

For most companies it is impractical to set up a dedicated facility on the scale of the major airlines and oil companies. But the more that is in place or quickly available at the time, the greater the chances of responding quickly and keeping control. Compile your own checklist and purchase/ identify as much as you realistically can within your own company. Some examples:

- Venue: conference room? nearby hotel? Consider an alternative off-site venue in cases where a site might be inaccessible because of fire, pollution etc.

- Dedicated facilities (eg telephone hotline)
- Controlled entry
- Adequate room and furniture for the crisis team and others
- Whiteboard/flip charts (and Pentels that work)
- A number of telephones, including at least one with an ex-directory outgoing line
- Hotline facility
- Mobile communicators and cellphones
- Fax
- TV and radio monitoring equipment – and tapes
- TV/radio "studio" facilities – to rehearse interviews
- Stationery
- Access to mass mailing
- A means of logging all actions
- Services (press/broadcast monitoring: printing, distribution etc)
- If feasible, a means of recording telephone conversations
- Refreshments
- Nearby or on-site sleeping facilities
- A separate and nearby venue for hosting the press
- Telephones for the press.

Ideally, the crisis room should be away from the scene of the action so that the crisis PR team does not get embroiled in the physical handing of the crisis.

The Crisis Manual

Try not to produce a manual in isolation. Stand-alone instruction books seldom work. Your crisis manual should ideally be a document which supports the meetings, brainstorming, crisis awareness training and simulations. Prepare it as a *working tool* not a *prescriptive document.*

Every organization will have different requirements. The following is an example of the contents of a typical manual:

- *Introduction* Brief description of what is expected of team members in a crisis; corporate philosophy; how to use the manual.
- *Procedures* Brief summary of company's crisis procedures.
- *Crisis team* Names; titles; *brief* descriptions of their responsibilities; day and 24 hour phone numbers of team and services (legal, PR etc); details of stand-ins if on holiday or ill.

- *Audiences*   List of audiences and how to contact them; addresses and telephone numbers. Emergency numbers for eg regulatory bodies, employee communications, lawyers, MPs etc.
- *Messages*   Reminder list of the types of message to communicate in a crisis.
- *Resources*   Location of crisis room etc. What resources there are, where they are kept and how to use them. Instructions (in the manual and/or crisis room on how to operate fax and communicators, how to activate the freephone helpline etc.
- *Media*   Reminder checklists on handling media and preparing for and succeeding with interviews.
- *Background Briefs*   Copies of the briefing notes on company, products, processes etc. Useful technical data.
- *Useful Addresses and Numbers*   eg press monitoring service; caterers.
- *Other*   Any other useful and important information, eg list of frequencies of radio programmes for tuning in and recording in a hurry.

Does It Work?

Now that you have a crisis procedure in place, check its viability and efficiency:

- Check the control and chain of command: who gives instructions to whom? Who must authorise decisions and statements? How does a PRO obtain vital data? How is that data distilled – and distributed? To whom?

- Establish an emergency call-out procedure for assembling the crisis team in a hurry. If possible, test it occasionally.

- Crisis simulation exercises can be useful for spotting weaknesses and honing responses. But be warned: different things tend to go wrong each time, so don't place *too* much reliance on the results of a single exercise. And successful simulations, like fat manuals, can breed dangerous complacency.

- Crisis audits (see introduction).

Bridge Building

The better people know and understand you – both personally and as an organization – the less inclined they are to want to damage you when things go wrong.

It is well worth developing a pre-emptive communications programme with MPs, authorities, key journalists, the local community, support services PR departments etc.

And attitude research among key audiences *now* can provide a useful benchmark when you conduct tracking research during and after the crisis

HANDLING THE CRISIS

The strategic elements of crisis *handling* are:

- Planning and analysis of the actions to take
- Strategic assessment during the crisis itself.

The recommended actions at a time of crisis are:

Holding Action

Try to do something to seize the initiative and 'freeze the action' as far as possible. Examples:

- Stop production
- Close plant
- Product recall
- Announce immediate, independent investigation.

Decide, approve and immediately issue a *holding statement* containing some or all of the messages in the checklist. Promise to keep the media (and other audiences) thoroughly informed as soon as more details are known – with a time if possible.

The purpose of the holding action and holding statement is to buy time and get the initiative in your court – and to establish you as the authoritative source of information.

Assemble the Crisis Team

And isolate them. Brief the spokespeople at once – and get in some quick interview/studio practice if possible.

Assess the Situation

The temptation to get on with handling the crisis while trying to formulate a strategy as you go along is almost irresistible.

Phones ring frantically. People appear from all over the place with urgent messages and requests for information. Two members of the crisis team can't be found. The media are on the line demanding to speak to someone immediately. And the boss wants to see you right now.

This is your most vulnerable moment. If you cave in to the immediate demands you may make a crucially wrong strategic decision. You may say something that you wish you hadn't. And you will certainly forget things.

It is absolutely essential for a core group of the crisis team and top management to sit down as quickly as possible, isolated from the crisis and the phones, and take a cool, strategic look at the situation. In an ideal world this would take a good couple of hours. Even if you only take out a few minutes it will be better than nothing.

Here are some of the key items to assess:

● *What is the crisis?* What precisely has happened? Do we all have the same understanding of the situation?

● *Is there a more fundamental problem?* Could this be the tip of an iceberg? Could this incident call into question the reputation of the whole company; the group; the industry? Does it call our safety standards into question? Could this become a broader issue? And so on.

● *Is there more to come?* Are there likely to be more of these explosions; product tamperings; bent sales executives etc?

● *What is the worst case?* Think how bad it could get at worst. And be ready for it just in case.

● *What are the audiences likely to make of it?* Step outside the crisis and imagine what it's like looking in from the outside – for the worried local community; the staff who are only just learning what's happened; the opportunist politician; the official; the other audiences – especially the media? What would you make of it if you were they?

● *What are the likely time scales?*
  1. How long before the various media – daily, weekly, trade, TV, radio – start going to bed with the story? Is our holding statement all they will have to publish or do we have a little time to develop a more detailed brief for them? And by when do we need to have established communication with the employees; the regulatory bodies; group headquarters; the insurers?

2. How long is the crisis likely to run – the initial burst and then all the follow-ups; litigation; clean-up campaign; dealing with pressure groups etc?

- *What is actually at stake?* If the worst comes to the worst, what will we actually lose? How loyal are our suppliers, our customers, our shareholders – and will they stay with us in bad times? How long are people's memories? Are we panicking unnecessarily? (But don't let a positive answer to this question be an excuse for inaction).

- *Can we involve any allies?* Would our messages come better and more credibly, for example, from our trade association? An independent research department? If the MP praised us last month for being a good member of the community is he prepared to say it again now? The Health and Safety Executive gave us a clean bill of health recently and they owe us one...can we persuade them to put their heads above the parapet on our behalf?

- *Who else is (culpably) involved?* Another party to the accident? Slack regulatory bodies? Suppliers? An extortionist? Vandals? This could affect your strategy. It *might* be that if you're the first – and loudest – to speak you are automatically seen as the culprit. Or you may have an opportunity to focus your anger – and that of the public – on some other 'culprit'.

- *Can the spotlight be transferred?* As mentioned above, there might be other potential culprits. If so, is there a way that the finger might be pointed at them without you being seen as the finger-pointer? A leaked report? An independent third party allocating blame? A tip-off to a trusted journalist? Are there other stories you can use as red meat for the baying pack of press hounds: the heroism of the crew, for example, or how your safety people ensure your products are safe.

- *Can the crisis be contained?* In a broad sense: how can our actions now put a lid as quickly as possible on the speculation and publicity – and stop the crisis running out of control?
  In a narrow sense: can the crisis be identified with a single plant, a subsidiary or a product? If you only refer to, say, the geographical name of the plant and give all spokespeople a title relating only to the subsidiary, you can sometimes keep the name of the parent company and/or its other products out of the picture – or at least reduce the damage.

- *What is the broad strategic approach* Agree on the broad strategy, eg: high or low profile? Do we accept responsibility? Do we major on the investigation or some other theme? etc.

Identify the Audiences

Go through the audience checklists and ask yourselves:

- Who is affected by this crisis?
- Who can affect us?
- Who needs to know?
- Who else should be informed?

Decide on the Messages

In addition to the holding statement, what do you want/need to tell (and keep telling) your audience(s)? Use the prepared check list for guidance.

Where appropriate, remember to tell them of the *good* you do. Oil, chemicals, foodstuffs may play a vital role in maintaining the quality of life – and even saving it. But the public perception of your product may be only of the dirty, smelly, nasty disadvantages.

This is not a time for boasting – but an occasional reminder won't go amiss. *You* know how important and responsible your organisation is... do *they* know?

Having held the initial meeting, decided the above actions and got the holding statement under way, you should as quickly as possible:

Prepare and Effect a Plan

You now have a strategic approach and the crisis team is busy getting things under control. If you have time, try to develop a more detailed plan dealing with what you need to do, who does it, where and when etc. Review and update the plan constantly.

Brief Relevant People

Thoroughly brief everyone involved (including security, switchboard, reception etc) – and keep briefing them.

And try to expose the remote decision makers – such as big bosses and lawyers – to reality. Cold, corporate attitudes and decisions can change dramatically for the better when the person making the decision personally sees the victims and grieving relatives, and is subjected to intense grilling by persuasive journalists.

Centralise Information

Try to ensure that all information comes into – and goes out from – a single source throughout.

Understand Your Audiences

Probably the biggest single failing of a company at a time of crisis (and most other times) is a lack of empathy. Managers communicate in a vacuum, pouring out messages that *they* regard as important and satisfactory. But it is what is *received* that matters, not what is *communicated.* It is people's *perceptions* that will influence the situation, not the *facts.*

When communicating with hostile or frightened audiences you have a tremendous attitude barrier to overcome. And attitude barriers are strengthened, not weakened, by counter arguments, statistics and defensive messages (test it on yourself next time you have a domestic row – or you complain in a restaurant and the waiter argues back!). You can only hope to get through to an audience when you see the situation from their side.

Give Information

Information is your most valuable tool (and defence weapon). Give the audiences a regular flow of as much information as you can possibly release. Act, don't react.

At a time of crisis your audiences have a huge demand for information... and that huge demand is going to be supplied by *someone*. There is nothing you can do to stop it. The pages of the newspapers *will* be filled; MPs *will* make statements; employees *will* talk about it in the pubs; concerned relatives and residents *will* talk among themselves; action groups *will* be formed.

If you simply sit there, saying the occasional 'no-comment' and congratulating yourselves because you have protected your legal/compensation case by not putting a foot wrong (ie not saying anything)... then the vast information vacuum will be filled by your enemies – the pressure groups, the company mole, the rent-a-month MP and by rumour and speculation.

Again, think of the human *psychology* involved. People are like children: if they think you're holding something back, even if you actually aren't they will stop at nothing to find out what it is. But the more you tell them the quicker they lose interest. For example, when the book *Spycatcher* was banned in Britain people paid many times the cover price for illicit copies smuggled in from Australia. Once the ban was lifted and the book went on public sale... nobody bought it!

Remember too, that if they discover something for themselves that you should have told them, then your credibility will be blown for the rest of the crisis.

So aim, as quickly as possible, to establish yourselves as the single authoritative source of information on the crisis/issue. That way, you will fill the lion's share of the information gap with *your* side of things. This is where your prepared background briefs come in useful.

The faster you start to *fill* the information gap, the sooner you will start to *close* it. Remember the saying: 'A lie can be half way round the world before the truth has got its boots on.'

Some tips for dealing with the media:

- Be as outgoing, honest, human and communicative as possible.
- *Never* speculate.
- Choose your ground; avoid 'doorstep' interviews. If doorstepped and the cameras are rolling, tell them you are prepared to give an interview – but not at this moment (give a reason if possible) and arrange a time and place for an interview in more controlled circumstances.
- Don't *read* company statements. By all means memorise an agreed statement so you don't slip up – but reading aloud to the cameras and public takes away the all-important human concern and credibility that comes from a 'spontaneous' response.
- Avoid press conferences if you can. Sometimes they are unavoidable but you will have better control if you can deal with the press one at a time. Once they get together the pack mentality comes into play. And the less bright ones pick up the nasty questions from the smarter ones. If you must hold a press conference ensure that the top person is capable of handling a barrage of hostile questions and, very importantly, keeping his/her cool. Use a 'moderator' to field and allocate questions and to keep control – and a remote microphone for journalists' questions; that way they can ask only one question at a time.
- The press pool: in a big crisis where it is impossible for you to cater for all the media at once (eg showing them round the damaged factory) they will often agree to a 'pool', whereby single reporters and crews from the three main media – press, radio, television – will cover the story and then share their reportage with the rest.

● Try to keep tabs on them. Where are they staying, for example? Consider putting them all up somewhere so that you have them all together and can issue statements and information in a controlled fashion.

And when you issue information to the media remember to keep your own *staff* (and other relevant audiences) fully informed.

Resist Combat

Easier said than done! It is often hard to be polite to an irate public figure 'demanding to know' or to resist throwing a brick at a press photographer climbing a drainpipe to get photographs. But you must always be polite and dignified.

Try, too, to understand the pressure that the hacks are under. If the other papers get a photo or a quote and they don't, they needn't bother returning to their jobs.

Give Reassurance

Remember that audiences need reassurance that everything is under control and they are not in danger.

It is also a good policy *after* the event for the 'men in white coats' (ie independent experts) to give a public 'all clear' if appropriate.

Be Flexible

A crisis can twist and turn. So can the requirements of your audiences – especially the press. You may have to adapt the plan and re-brief people several times.

Think Long Term

It can be tempting to try to protect some short term interest – and pay for it later. But it is often best to be prepared to take a short term loss to protect your long term reputation.

As soon as you can draw breath from the immediate panic, start thinking as early as possible about the longer term plan. Good communications and intelligent handling of a re-opening or re-launch can turn crisis into opportunity.

WHAT HAVE WE LEARNED?

When it is over, examine:

- What you have learned from it.
- Will the publicity return, and when? eg:

  - Anniversary
  - Legal battle (especially if specialist disaster lawyers are involved)
  - Aggrieved victims
  - Inquest
  - Report

Be well prepared in advance for these stages. If the media have 'good' (ie unpleasant) photos and footage of the original incident they will seize every opportunity to re-fill the pages and TV screens with them.

Notes

1. This chapter has been adapted and digested from *The Crisis Checklist* by kind permission of the Public Relations Consultants Association.
2. There is often a semantic debate about the differences between 'crisis management' and 'issues management'. Put as simply as possible, the strategic PR management of an issue will broadly involve the same considerations and techniques as those required for a crisis. The biggest differences are the time scale and the sense of panic.

Bibliography

K. Aneletta, *Greed and Glory on Wall Street: the fall of the House of Lehman*, Penguin.

D. ten Berge, *The First 24 Hours: a comprehensive guide to successful crisis management*, Blackwell.

A. Chevalier and G. Hirsch, *Le Risk Management: pour une meilleure maitrise des risques de l'entreprise*, Entreprise Moderne d'Edition.

S. Homewood, *Zeebrugge: a hero's story*, Bloomsbury.

G. C. Meyers with J. Holusha, *When it Hits the Fan: managing the nine crises of business*, Hutchinson.

M. Regester, *Crisis Management: how to turn a crisis into an opportunity*, Hutchinson.

S. Slatter, *Corporate Recovery: a guide to turnaround management*, Penguin.

Index